Integrative Paradigms of Psychotherapy

Related Titles of Interest

The Rorschach Technique: Content, Interpretation, and
  Application
Edward Aronow, Marvin Reznikoff, and Kevin Moreland
ISBN: 0-205-14912-X

Hypnosis: The Application of Ideomotor Techniques
David B. Cheek
ISBN: 0-205-15595-2

Managed Mental Health Care: A Guide for Practitioners,
  Employers, and Hospital Administrators
Thomas R. Giles
ISBN: 0-205-14838-7

Cognitive Therapy of Borderline Personality Disorder
Mary Anne Layden, Cory F. Newman, Arthur Freeman, and Susan
  Byers Morse
ISBN: 0-205-14807-7

Handbook of Sexual Dysfunctions: Assessment and Treatment
William O'Donohue and James H. Geer
ISBN: 0-205-14787-9

Treating Adolescent Substance Abuse: Understanding the
  Fundamental Elements
George R. Ross
ISBN: 0-205-15255-4

Social Skills for Mental Health: A Structured Learning
  Approach
Robert P. Sprafkin, N. Jane Gershaw, and Arnold P. Goldstein
ISBN: 0-205-14841-7

Integrative Paradigms of Psychotherapy

Ted L. Orcutt

Jan R. Prell

Psychotherapists and Consultants
San Diego, California

Allyn and Bacon
Boston • London • Toronto • Sydney • Tokyo • Singapore

Library of Congress Cataloging-in-Publication Data

Orcutt, Ted L.
    Integrative paradigms of psychotherapy / Ted L. Orcutt, Jan R.
Prell.
        p.   cm.
    Includes bibliographical references and index.
    ISBN 0-205-14823-9
    1. Psychotherapy—Philosophy.   2. Psychotherapists—Attitudes.
I. Prell, Jan R. (Jan Robert) II. Title.
    [DNLM: 1. Psychotherapy.   WM 420 064i 1994]
RC437.5.072   1994
616.89'14--dc20
DNLM/DLC
for Library of Congress   93-24551
                                                              CIP

Printed in the United States of America
10 9 8 7 6 5 4 3 2 1   98 97 96 95 94

About the Authors

TED L. ORCUTT, Ph.D., is a clinical psychologist integrating transpersonal and cognitive psychotherapy in private practice and consultation. He completed his clinical internship at U.S. Naval Hospital and Saint Elizabeth's Hospital, Washington, D.C., as a Lieutenant in the U.S. Navy. Since 1981 he has been a consultant in group psychotherapy to the Psychiatry Department, U.S. Naval Hospital, San Diego. Formerly, Dr. Orcutt was Director of Psychological Services, Rancho Bernardo Pain Rehabilitation Center; Academic Dean, Professional School of Psychological Studies; and on the faculties of Dominican College, Eastern Virginia Medical School, Kutztown University, and United States International University.

JAN R. PRELL, Ph.D., is a marriage, family, and child counselor integrating clinical hypnosis with cognitive psychotherapy in private practice and consultation to industry. He completed his internship at New Alternative Home Based Services, San Diego, California. He completed post-graduate training in hypnotherapy at the Institute of Hypnotechnology and in entelechial therapy at the Spear Clinic, both in San Diego County. Dr. Prell is a registered and certified Master Hypnotherapist, a member of the National Commission of Certified Hypnotists, the American Association of Professional Hypnotherapists, and the American Association of Marriage and Family Therapy.

*To our clients, colleagues, families, and friends
who have helped us redefine our personal identities
and clarify our systems of psychotherapy.
It is with their support and comments that we are more effective in
implementing the reduction of pain, the expansion of self-fulfillment,
and the enrichment of interpersonal relationships.*

Contents

Preface

Few books written by experienced psychotherapists offer practical guidelines to both novice and seasoned psychotherapists. Many highly qualified psychotherapists, too numerous to mention, strive to fill this void. Significant contributions notwithstanding, the orientations of many of these psychotherapists are toward promoting personalized methodologies of psychotherapy.

This book presents inclusive and exploratory paradigms that allow psychotherapists to examine and discover the parameters of their present psychotherapeutic orientation. These paradigms provide an organized method for each psychotherapist to redefine his or her current orientation, as well as a direction for modification based on knowledgeable intent. We have no intention of promoting a new model or technique for implementing psychotherapy. Also, as with alternative orientations directed toward the psychotherapeutic integration of familiar models, our intent is not to offer suggested procedures of integrating diverse models for specific diagnoses. Indeed, it is essential to consider the paradigms presented here before attempting to integrate existing models. Our intention is to *reawaken* psychotherapists to clarify and *redefine* their psychotherapeutic orientation and to provide new inclusive paradigms that will allow each psychotherapist to *reevaluate* his or her psychotherapeutic orientation so it is decisive, inclusive, and flexible enough within known boundaries to be increasingly effective for healing. Following is a descriptive map of an exploratory adventure into the world of integrative paradigms of psychotherapy.

Chapter 1 challenges those conventional assumptions of psychotherapeutic training that are based exclusively on a *treatment-of-choice* orientation. We believe these psychological assumptions misrepresent the relationships among diagnosis, etiology, client input, and, especially, treatment. We believe that to support these conventional assumptions, without reservation, severely limits our optimistic view of the human capacity for change.

Chapter 2 focuses on disengaging the developmental beliefs of both psychotherapists and clients. Its purpose is to offer a process by which psychotherapists can further clarify the boundaries between personal and therapeutic views of the world. Appendix B provides scripts to disengage personal beliefs, clarify personal needs and motivation, and help with possible treatment.

Chapter 3 examines four perceptual attitudes through which all psychotherapists view the etiology of conflict or harmony in their clients. It provides an understanding of why psychotherapists from different training backgrounds often disagree about diagnosis, etiology, and treatment.

Chapter 4 provides three theoretical structures for psychotherapists to identify basic therapeutic beliefs and values. It offers an overview for examining the advantages and limitations of psychotherapeutic preferences. This chapter also provides the rationales and goals by which professional psychotherapists justify how they make sense of their therapeutic world.

Chapter 5 focuses on methodologies and the detailed implementation of practice. Its goal is to clarify function so that it is congruent with perceptual attitudes and theoretical structures. It details three methodologies by the linguistic specifications that psychotherapists use with their clients. Additionally, this chapter offers a new analysis of the variant levels of catharsis.

Chapter 6 focuses on the dynamics of interpersonal relationships. Its orientation is to provide an inclusive framework by which psychotherapists can understand their relationship to their clients as well as their clients' underlying relational dynamics.

Chapter 7 cautions us about mistaken, implied, or intentional imposition of ostensibly "healthful" values in the psychotherapeutic relationship. It focuses on the professional presentation of representational roles and authoritative policies to clients including techniques of implied observations.

Seldom, in clinical practice, do psychotherapists receive lengthy follow-up reports on their previous clients. Indeed, this is why the profession of psychotherapy still refers to the combined centuries of training and experience as *practice*. Therefore, collectively, psychotherapists need to remind themselves that most of their known effectiveness exists in the moment. The psychotherapeutic profession exists for the purpose of healing and making a *declared* difference in clients' lives as well as their own. With this intention, we offer an opportunity for enhancing psychotherapeutic effectiveness, integrity, and personal satisfaction.

Ted L. Orcutt
Jan R. Prell

Acknowledgments

We would like to express our gratitude for the invaluable editorial and conceptual assistance provided by Jeff Hecker, University of Maine at Orono, Orono, Maine; Lynne A. Kellner, University of Massachusetts at Amherst, Amherst, Massachusetts; Melissa Klotz, MKO Art Designs, San Diego, California; Sally Moore-Pollock, Hutchinson & Associates, Kansas City, Missouri; Marilyn Rash, Ocean Publication Services, Magnolia, Massachusetts; Jill Walters, University of North Texas, Denton, Texas; and Susan Ward, Eating Disorder Clinic of San Diego, San Diego, California.

1

Defining
Psychotherapeutic
Orientation

Psychotherapy is like a tapestry. The intertwining fibers and complex designs represent interpretations of the fulfillment, comedy, and tragedy of human life. The woven fibers are the structures of diverse developmental beliefs, perceptual attitudes, theoretical structures, and models. The intricate designs are the functions of disparate methodologies, techniques, strategies, and wary boundaries of authoritative imposition. Some structures and functions of our global profession are similar and mutually compatible; others are contradictory and incompatible. For example, the theoretical structures of the models of psychoanalysis and Gestalt therapy are mutually compatible, while their functional applications are exclusively contradictory. Additionally, the models of Gestalt therapy and psychodrama share a compatible functional application. However, their respective theoretical structures postulate contradictory views of human development, harmony, and conflict.

Complicating the diversity of psychotherapeutic orientations are the developmental beliefs and personal values of the psychotherapist. These include sexual, racial, social, religious, and political persuasions. Personal concerns also include opinions about diet, exercise, education, morality, intimacy, family, abortion, crime, punishment, drugs (licit and illicit), and war.

In ancient history and in primitive cultures throughout the world, members of societies sought relief from emotional suffering and mental conflict by seeking the counsel the chief, the shaman, or elders of the tribe (Kiev, 1964). These wise medicine and holy men or women usually identified physical, emotional, and mental problems with spiritual and religious understandings of the universe (Cox, 1973). Even to this day, the practice continues in these tribal cultures, including those of an estimated two hundred Native American nations in the United States.[1]

Separate from the time-honored cultural traditions in all countries, and within the contemporary world, there are far greater options for seeking emotional and mental healing services from various professionals. This is at once both a blessing and a curse. The physical, mental, and spiritual domains have been separated, mingled, blended, and recombined so many times that it is extremely difficult to ascertain the differences among professional authorities except as dictated or assumed by the largest membership or monetary majority.

Clinical training and apprenticeship programs in the Western world represent a variety of psychotherapeutic roles in modern society. Each role is sponsored by professions that have separate credentialing and licensing associations or boards that vary among the many states within North and South America as well as internationally.

Of these, there are twelve counseling professions in the United States alone, and each is licensed for independent practice by some authority. They are: psychiatry, psychology, social work, marriage and family therapy, hypnotism, psychodrama, religious counseling, psychiatric nursing, drug abuse counseling, educational/vocational counseling, probation rehabilitation, and shamanism.

All of these specializations are highly respected by scientific or social convention within their own organizations. Diverse models such as bioenergetics and shamanism, that are more somatically or spiritually oriented, are highly respected by elite minorities of homeopathic and spiritual leaders. Physicians (nonpsychiatrically trained), physical therapists, acupuncturists, chiropractors, veterinarians, attorneys, bartenders, hair stylists, astrologers, psychics, and fortune-tellers also perform psychotherapeutic functions and justify their advice or practice within the limits of a designated profession.

Regardless of professional identity, psychotherapists around the world vary because of their different developmental focuses on history, present circumstances, and future intentions. They view the etiology of human harmony and conflict through perceptual attitudes that extend from intrapsychic dynamics to universal lessons. Psychotherapists justify their orientation by theoretical assumptions and goals that range from reparative models to those that encourage personal development and transpersonal quests. Psychotherapeutic methodologies differ in their distinct emphasis on behaviors, thoughts, or feelings.

Some psychotherapeutic orientations stipulate procedural formulas and precise rules; others require creative flexibility and a repertoire of imaginative tricks and magical techniques. Psychotherapists view relationships and the underlying relationship dynamics of their clients in different ways. They also hold different beliefs and values about the intentional imposition of their authority. Some professionals assume complete responsibility for treating their clients; others demand their clients assume full responsibility for healing and wellness. Indeed, it is no wonder that psychotherapists, reflecting a myriad of orientations, often appear to represent entirely different professions (Gross, 1978).

Psychotherapeutic Limitations of Effectiveness

Historically, within the field of psychotherapy, there has been a move from model adherence to eclectic models and more recently to differential therapeutics. As a result of this historical development and a host of individually adopted psychotherapeutic orientations, psychotherapists have limited their effectiveness and continue to create unnecessary limitations in two major ways, which are described in detail later. These limitations are unnecessary because psychotherapists can easily clarify, define, and modify their orientations. With increased effectiveness, the nucleus of any orientation becomes more internally consistent and yet open to incorporating embellishments from alternative theories and methods.

Without clarification and definition, the effectiveness of psychotherapy suffers. This is a result of either a neglect of the nucleus or a neglect of expansive skills from potentially compatible systems. Observation indicates that there are two global limitations impeding optimal effectiveness in psychotherapeutic practice and are referred to here as Limitation I and Limitation II.

Limitation I

Limitation I results from a random and incompatibly inclusive orientation. It favors breadth of percept, concept, and method, at the expense of depth. It is exemplified through practice with an impulsively conceived or implemented orientation that is jumbled.

Psychotherapists who randomly conceive their psychotherapeutic orientations justify their understanding and diagnostic evaluation from diverse theoretical structures and models, not knowing that many theoretical structures and models are contradictory. Unaware of differences, their mistaken working assumption is that highly respected or equally valid theories, when randomly combined, will yield effective results.

Methodologies are also assumed by the same manner as orientations. Psychotherapists randomly implement their methodologies by arbitrarily borrowing and using techniques from a variety of models, many of which are oppositional. They use a vague combination of methods to justify their implementation. When the smoke settles, the process translates to "whatever works now." Random adoption of theoretical structures and methodologies is not to be confused with a well-defined eclecticism (Norcross, 1986).[2]

Obvious examples of Limitation I include those psychotherapists who randomly mix a conglomeration of disparate existential and humanistic models. Psychotherapists well-trained in multiple models use any number and mixture of these models within one session, and they arbitrarily shift modalities over several sessions. They vary the mixture according to personal mood and later try to justify it by the client's circumstances of the moment.

Such psychotherapists follow no predetermined plan or strategy. Observation of their sessions revealed they employed different theoretical structures, methodologies, perceptual attitudes, and techniques every time. Occasionally, when the psychotherapy is successful there is a shift of acknowledgment and awareness in the client. However, even in these instances psychotherapy often is either inconsequential or a failure. The evidence for this was determined in subsequent sessions by the lack of clients' lasting change.

When an orientation is average to unsuccessful, the therapeutic process is confusing and ineffective. The difficulty with a random and incompatibly inclusive process is that there are no predetermined criteria by which to test or duplicate success and effectiveness, or failure and ineffectiveness.

As a way to enhance psychotherapeutic satisfaction or client wellness, this process is unreliable. Accommodation is to modify mental processes to make room for a new concept or idea; to adapt one's mind; to alter the larger for the smaller fit. In attempting to *accommodate* the unique needs of individual clients, psychotherapists employing random and incompatibly inclusive orientations often confuse the client and disregard the larger context of personality development. Although psychotherapists are eager to motivate clients and heal in the moment, randomly conceived or implemented orientations are ineffective in attaining lasting results.

Limitation II

Limitation II is a rigid and conclusively exclusive orientation. It favors depth of percept, concept, and method, each at the expense of breadth. It is exemplified by a predetermined perceptual, conceptual, and implemented orientation that is systematic and self-reinforcing.

Psychotherapists who limit their effectiveness by rigid adherence and devotion to a conclusively exclusive orientation justify their conceptualization and implementation by the defined theoretical components of the orientation itself. They do this regardless of evidence that equally comprehensive and impressive models of psychotherapy contradict one another in both theoretical understanding and implementation. The mistaken working assumption is that comprehensive understanding and reliability yield effective results.

Although such orientations are meticulously organized, they preclude other possible expedient and effective healing practices. When psychotherapists interpret all events of human experience through an exclusively predetermined belief system, they restrict possibilities of understanding to the limitations of that belief system. Separately, when psychotherapists follow a predesignated implementation that is identical for diverse client circumstances, they preclude unique avenues of healing for disparate clients. Optimal possibilities for clients' healing and wellness are restricted to the statistically average data from which the orientation originated.

Observed examples include orthodox psychoanalysts and scientifically dogmatic behaviorists who disregard or negate unusual client experiences that do not accommodate their orientation. Specifically, the models of orthodox psychoanalysis and scientific behaviorism only *assimilate* spiritual and psychic experiences. To assimilate is to alter and thoroughly comprehend; to make similar; to alter the smaller to fit into the greater.

Circumscribed within its own theoretical constructs, psychoanalysis presumes and appraises such stated experiences as a regression, wish fulfillment, defense mechanism, illusion, or delusion. A valid experience of growth development of socially enhancing proportions can easily be relegated to disease or illness. This occurs because the model does not provide a structure that is malleable enough to positively integrate experiences outside its domain of understanding. Even the creative experience is defined in terms of the defense mechanism of sublimation as a "regression in service of the ego" (Kris, 1964). Such interpretations reduce even creativity—a hallmark for the evolution of the human species—to a developmentally negative motivation. This restrictive interpretation reduces the entire creative process to mere expression of neurotic behavior.

Similarly, but with more neutrality, the model of behaviorism takes the position that creative and mystical experiences are unworthy of scientific investigation because of a lack of public verifiability. Science depends on measurable variables. Profoundly creative, ecstatic, and mystical experiences are seldom replicable in the laboratory. Because science follows replication as a measure of evaluation, it excludes those dimensions of human experience that, under usual circumstances, are private and rarely easy to replicate. Behavioral science, however, is absolutely valuable for excluding many private experiences, which include the pathological as well as the mystical.

Behavioral science is a conventionally accepted and therefore extremely valuable methodological gauge of truth. Here again, however, a valid creative or mystical experience easily can be dismissed as unworthy of support or affirmation. As a model, behaviorism does not support an intelligible reconstruction of difficulties encountered in creative or mystical experiences.

Psychotherapists who fall in the Limitation II category always follow a predetermined recipe. Every one of their sessions appears to follow a programmed routine without consideration for the client. These psychotherapists do not take advantage of alternative models or techniques in the best interest of meeting the needs of the client. When the model of orthodox psychoanalysis is implemented rigidly, standard interpretations of the client's developmental fixations, resistance, transference, and defense mechanisms are followed. When the model of behaviorism is implemented rigidly, positive and negative reinforcement schedules and sequential patterns of learning are followed with little consideration for emotional and spiritual concerns. More often than not, success depends on the client successfully following the recipe.

Similar to random and over-inclusive orientations, effectiveness is determined by a shift in awareness or behavior of the client. However, with rigid and overinclusive orientations, there is never a failure. There are no incompatible ingredients because the same orientation is made repeatedly. When the orientation is average to unsuccessful, it is the client's deficiency. When the implementation is successful, it is a combination of affirming the accuracy of the orientation, reinforcing the successful adherence to predefined implementation, and confirming the importance of motivating the client.

Rigid and conclusively exclusive orientations always have predetermined criteria by which to evaluate or replicate success and effectiveness or failure and ineffectiveness. However, as exclusively credible as the orientations may seem at first, such biases can create a travesty of inaccurate representations of reality according to alternative systems that claim to represent the same reality. These simplified observations merely serve to illustrate that psychotherapists who rigidly require all experiences of their clients to conform to their state-dependent orientation may inadvertently limit clients' growth toward wellness.

Additionally, observations show that rigidly following any psychotherapeutic orientation limits effectiveness. When psychotherapists dismiss compatible elements from alternative structures and methodologies, they exclude assimilation of more inclusive concepts and potentially effective methodologies. Such alternative concepts, strategies, and techniques often increase effectiveness and client wellness when integrated with a predefined and flexible orientation.

Summary of Limitations I and II

All psychotherapeutic orientations and models have advantages and disadvantages. Professional orientations are learned at graduate or medical schools or during internships or residencies. However, academic faculty and staff traditionally orient themselves toward research and practice. They rarely offer individualized structure to help clarify personal perceptions, or the defined parameters of a personal psychotherapeutic orientation. Partially, this is because personal psychotherapy and a personal psychotherapeutic orientation are seen as subordinate to the dispensing of clinical information.

After completing academic requirements, internships, residencies, and apprenticeships, psychotherapists begin practice. Often, as a result of direct contact with clients, novice therapists change their perceptions, beliefs, theories, and methods of practice. Practicing psychotherapists need to be cautious about rating the effectiveness of their psychotherapeutic orientation by the number of clients. A more accurate way to evaluate the effectiveness of an orientation is to base it on client healing. However, regardless of whether psychotherapists judge the effectiveness of their orientation on number of clients or client healing, they modify their orientations, as compared to academicians, by exposure to the clinical world of client experiences. Sometimes even, academic and practical psychotherapists speak different professional jargon (see Figure 1–1).

It might seem helpful to have a universal answer. However, any ubiquitous solution would only homogenize the dilemma and decrease effectiveness through an imagined conformity. Academicians and clinicians alike want to believe that universal answers legitimize the profession by making it appear as if the psychotherapeutic profession is based on science in both theory and methodology. However, the question would remain as to which theory and methodology. At best, a universal theory or method for psychotherapeutic effectiveness is a utopian delusion. At worst, it is an economic exploitation disguised in altruistic clothing.

FIGURE 1–1.   Professional Jargon Varies.

Strange as it may seem, psychotherapists have much in common with other professionals including electricians, carpenters, and mechanics. Psychotherapists are similar to professional athletes and animal trainers who apply their skills based on established and tested principles of success and mastery. As with other service-oriented professions, psychotherapy is both a science and an art. More specifically, it is a subjective skill based on objective rules and precedents.

Psychotherapists express their identities by personal and professional orientations based on preferred views of reality and intervention. All professional services are, inherently, personally biased. They assume a subjective element specific to the person performing the service. For this reason alone, a utopian psychotherapeutic orientation is not only a fragment of fantasy but a barrier to the inevitability of taking responsibility for personally defining professional effectiveness.

Regardless of preferred orientations, most psychotherapists strive to increase professional effectiveness. The most rewarding way to increase effectiveness is for psychotherapists to define their psychotherapeutic orientation in advance. The definition needs to be flexible enough to include compatible strategies that compliment client circumstances. This requires that psychotherapists take the responsibility to clarify beliefs, adjust perceptual attitudes, refine theoretical structures and methodologies, and establish their boundaries of imposition. Additionally, it means that the orientation be adaptable enough to include unique client circumstances. However, before an examination of these principles, it is helpful to review the essential assumptions of current psychotherapeutic training and practice.

Examining Psychotherapeutic Assumptions

Traditionally, graduate students, interns, and residents learn psychotherapy with a *treatment-of-choice* objective. The treatment of choice is, by definition, the most helpful intervention for the client; the objective presumes that accurate interpretation of symptoms and client conflict explains the cause and determines intervention goals and methodology. There are seven assumptions inherent in this medically adopted and commonly accepted orientation. The treatment-of-choice objective assumes that:

1. Psychotherapists commonly agree on diagnoses, including symptoms and etiology;
2. Diagnoses determine specifically agreed on psychotherapeutic goals and a methodology required of the orientation;
3. Psychotherapists receive standard training, have the same beliefs, and equally can perform the same skills;

4. Some psychotherapists typically can select among a diversity of orientations based on client circumstance; assuming they can improvise methods of diverse orientations with equal skill or effectiveness;

5. Some psychotherapists naturally develop a personally effective orientation;

6. Values are ubiquitous subsuming, personal values of understanding and intervention for professionally generic and presumed values of health; and

7. Preferred treatment is determined by the psychotherapist with little or no input or preference from the client.

We believe these assumptions represent the usual training and practice of psychotherapy. To both the public and the professional, they are false impressions that may compromise or impede healing. Examining these misleading assumptions precedes integrating a personally defined psychotherapeutic orientation. After examination and redefinition, psychotherapists can increase curative effectiveness and their professional and personal satisfaction.

The Assumption of Diagnostic Agreement

The treatment of choice objective requires that psychotherapists interview a client and then make a clinical evaluation. Sometimes, an evaluation includes psychological testing to compliment interview data. The goal of this comprehensive evaluation is to determine an accurate diagnosis; the ostensible purpose of diagnosis is to determine a treatment of choice. This sequence is a reasonable way to determine a problem and repair something when it is broken. Deductive reasoning presumes that the professional interpretations made will determine methodologies to use with clients. This sequence of reasoning is similar to services performed in mechanical and industrial trades such as repairing cars, televisions, plumbing, and electrical breakdowns.

Psychotherapy, as commonly practiced in the Western world, began within the field of Western medicine, which started embracing psychoanalysis in the late nineteenth century. The medical model of psychotherapeutic treatment of choice resulted from initially treating severely disturbed populations, primarily in France, Germany, and England. The assumption remains in the Western world, and its scientifically influenced members in other countries. The justification remains that definable and accurate diagnoses determine interventions and medications.[3] The current assumption is that diagnoses are qualitative and specifically identifiable as separate.

With the historically recent development of the *Diagnostic and Statistical Manual of Mental Disorders* (currently *DSM-III-R* and soon to be released *DSM IV*), psychotherapists assume they usually can agree. This assumption is shared to a lesser degree by the World Health Organization in developing a similar classification of mental disorders—Section V of the Ninth Revision of the International Classification of Diseases (ICD-9).[4]

A review of patients' charts in hospital settings frequently reflects multiple diagnoses for either especially brief or extended periods. This is cause for neither alarm nor celebration. Diagnoses are often incompatible, reflecting a trial-and-error sequence of psychotherapy and medication. After a treatment proves effective, bipolar disorders are routinely and properly diagnosed. Phobias, as differentiated from anxiety and panic disorders, are often properly diagnosed after behavioral therapy proves effective. Diagnoses, when these examples occur, are similar to establishing a correct hypothesis after reviewing the results of research. The following example illustrates that common diagnoses are not as frequent as expected.

Seventeen psychiatrists and clinical psychologists were called in for a spontaneous conference and evaluation of a client. This was a standard procedure of the psychiatric training program of a local major hospital. The client was a thirty-two-year-old Japanese male.[5] Having received excellent evaluations and several awards for superior performance for the last ten years, he was an outstanding employee of a major corporation. He was admitted because he asked permission to commit ritualistic suicide after being ten minutes late for work. He was interviewed for one hour with all seventeen psychotherapists present. Each psychotherapist took the opportunity to ask questions. The following *DSM III-R* Axis I diagnoses were given at the end of the evaluation. The parentheses indicate the number of votes for each diagnosis.

(4)   *295.70 Schizoaffective Disorder*
(3)   *297.10 Delusional Disorder, Unspecified Type*
(3)   *295.40 Schizophreniform Disorder*
(2)   *296.44 Bipolar Disorder, Manic with Psychotic Features*
(2)   *298.80 Brief Reactive Psychosis*
(2)   *301.22 Schizotypical Personality Disorder*
(1)   *301.83 Borderline Personality Disorder with Psychotic Features*

As another separate example, the staff of a private psychiatric clinic evaluated a client brought in by her sister, who was seven years older. The client was a twenty-nine-year-old, attractive female, born and raised in southern Texas. The wife of a wealthy cattle rancher, twenty years her senior, she was a homemaker and a successfully influential fund-raiser for various charities in a large community. Following a benefit at which she was the honorary master of ceremonies, she was admitted to the clinic after taking an overdose of amphetamines.

In the initial interview, she admitted to the stress of not being a good enough stepmother to her husband's three teenagers from his previous marriage. She claimed she feared an impending divorce. This fear was the result of accidentally discovering her husband's recent infidelity from the gossip of a close female friend. The following morning, while appreciative of her emergency treatment the night before, she was uncooperative about further treatment. She asked to speak to her husband fearing that the clinic might not agree to her discharge.

She was interviewed for forty-five minutes by fifteen of the twenty clinical staff present. Each psychotherapist had the opportunity to ask questions. The following Axis I and II diagnoses were given at the end of the evaluation. The parentheses indicate the number of votes for each diagnosis, first in Axis I and then in Axis II.

(3)	*Axis I:*	*300.40 Dysthymia*
(3)	*Axis I:*	*300.02 Generalized Anxiety Disorder*
(2)	*Axis I:*	*305.70 Amphetamine or Similarly Acting Sympathomimetic Intoxication*
(2)	*Axis I:*	*309.28 Adjustment Disorder with Mixed Emotional Features*
(1)	*Axis I:*	*305.70 Amphetamine or Similarly Acting Sympathomimetic Abuse*
(1)	*Axis I:*	*300.23 Social Phobia*
(1)	*Axis I:*	*300.23 Panic Disorder without Agoraphobia*
(1)	*Axis I:*	*309.24 Adjustment Disorder with Anxious Mood*
(1)	*Axis I:*	*309.00 Adjustment Disorder with Depressed Mood*
(4)	*Axis II:*	*301.60 Dependent Personality Disorder*
(4)	*Axis II:*	*No Diagnosis*
(3)	*Axis II:*	*301.50 Histrionic Personality Disorder*
(2)	*Axis II:*	*301.82 Avoidant Personality Disorder*
(2)	*Axis II:*	*301.40 Obsessive Compulsive Personality Disorder*

These two cases are not an exception, nor are they to be interpreted as the rule. However, experience indicates that commonly interpreted diagnoses are less frequent than those that are consistently agreeable. For many years, over half the inpatient populations in England had a diagnosis of bipolar disorder. In the United States during the same period, roughly the same percentage of patients had a diagnosis of schizophrenia (Freemesser, 1978). Comparatively, no evidence substantiates that citizens of England are genetically or environmentally prone to major mood disorders. Nor is it reasonable to assume that U. S. citizens favor predispositions toward thought disorders.

What becomes obvious is that psychotherapists diagnose differently. Aside from psychotic disorders, diagnostic agreement is even more difficult with minor mood disorders, personality disorders, and behavioral dysfunctions. This is similar to the mechanical world. Diagnosing the infrequent, minor, and intermittent noise in a car is more difficult than diagnosing a consistent and loud noise.

Diagnoses are correlations of data. Based on substantial research, they reflect statistical frequencies correlated on current symptomatology and predisposing circumstances. Although psychotherapists expect agreement, commonly definitive diagnoses are not automatic. Commonly agreed diagnoses are just not as obvious as the collective profession of psychotherapy advertises and, would otherwise like to believe. Nevertheless, the assumption of diagnostic agreement is the least problematic assumption within the treatment-of-choice objective.

The Assumption of Correlative Methodology

Let us assume all psychotherapists could agree on diagnostic evaluations. Suppose, via satellite, one thousand psychotherapists[6] agree on the diagnoses of fifty clients. Further, they agree on the cause and symptoms of the clients' problems. If one thousand mechanics agreed that a car needed a water pump, they would reach for the manual of that car's model and engine specifications. This manual would identify the specific replacement part that would duplicate the original specifications. Following this initial evaluation, the service department would replace the water pump.

A human being is an entirely different system from an automobile. The assumption of correlative methodology treats human beings as if they were as simple as cars. Specific procedures are based on symptoms and not the entirety of the human system. An automotive service department uses a manual that prescribes a mechanical procedure for replacing the faulty water pump. The manual also offers cost estimates for labor that the service department uses as a basis to pay employees as well as give the customer an estimate before performing the work.

The profession of psychotherapy does not have a service manual. Even the four volume *Treatments of Psychiatric Disorders* (APA, 1989)—hailed as "twenty-five years ahead of its time" by *The Atlantic Monthly* and "the most useful psychiatric book ever printed"—does not dictate correlative methodologies for specific diagnoses. Rather, it discusses a full range of treatment modalities applicable to each disorder. As the advertisement claims, "there is certainly no substitute for clinical judgment." As stated, the book "won't give you a prescription for treatment planning but it can help put your judgments in perspective." This qualification is accurate because more than four hundred expert contributors to this monumental compendium of scientific and academic literature know that clinical diagnoses cannot possibly determine specified treatments. The unfortunate circumstance is that many psychotherapists and the public still believe that accurate diagnoses actually determine specific methodologies for cure.

The logic of the treatment-of-choice objective implies a therapeutically obvious intervention and a universally accepted methodology. It assumes that once we determine a diagnosis, we can refer to a corresponding volume of correlative methodology. This imaginary volume would define specific goals and methodology; however, it is just that, imaginary.

Major classes of diagnoses, such as schizophrenia, bipolar disorders, endogenous depressions, and panic disorders, frequently indicate psycho-pharmacological intervention. As most of us know, *The Physicians' Desk Reference (PDR)* recommends medication for all medical practice, not only psychiatry. The *PDR* is similar to the parts catalogue in an automotive service department. It describes medication and indications for usage and recommends dosages and contraindications. However, the *PDR* recommends usage for symptom relief, not causal cure.

Medication treats symptoms of malfunction. In certain cases of endogenous depressions, and genetically predisposed cases of schizophrenia and bipolar disorders, medication is effective in arresting chemical causes of psychopathology. However, the use of medication in these cases arrests psychophysical and chemical imbalances. As a result, in many cases, human functioning can be restored or increased. While psychiatric medication alters and arrests psychophysical and chemical contributions to illness, it does not directly resolve social and psychological causes of assumed psychopathology. With major psychoses, personality disorders, and many behavioral disorders, if the current symptoms disappear, the patient is always *in remission* versus cured. This belief mirrors the Western medical interpretation of physical disorders. Acute diagnoses, such as allergies, mild forms of arthritis, urinary and gynecological infections, are curable without expectation of recurrence. However, even with acute diseases, physicians often expect predispositions that enhance recurrence.

Chronic diseases—such as diabetes; heart, kidney, and liver disease; and cancer—are *chronic* and therefore always in remission. These assumptions imply that diagnoses remain with the expectation that original symptoms will inevitably recur. Correlative methodology is relegated to remedial implications versus curative expectations. Thus, correlative methodology is based on the statistical expectation of results of treatment versus the result often specified by the disease or disorder itself.

Psychopharmacological intervention is not specific about medications even within classes of diagnoses. Five psychiatrists recently evaluated a thirty-seven-year-old male at an inpatient psychiatric unit. Jeremie K. was a Senior Chief in the United States Navy; he had seventeen years of service and an outstanding record. He was happily married with two children. He was admitted as a result of "unspecified stress" for the past six months, during which he complained of intermittent sleep patterns ranging from two to six hours a night. During his waking hours at night, he would get out of bed and make his time productive either by working on the house or on a career-related activity.

None of his reported activity was bizarre. He merely complained of preoccupied thoughts and exhaustion from a lack of sleep.

The Mental Status assessment revealed a cooperative Caucasian male. Affect and mood were agitated and anxious with no discernable precipitating circumstances. Ego functioning was well intact and with appropriate humor. The patient admitted to ruminations of important activity without motivation to pursue such events. There was no evidence of a thought disorder, delusions, hallucinations, or paranoid ideation. Cognitive testing was well within normal limits with an above average intelligence quotient. The patient denied suicidal or homicidal ideation as well as drug, spouse, or child abuse.

The five Axis I and II diagnoses were:

1. Axis I   300.02   Generalized Anxiety Disorder
   Axis II   V71.09   No Diagnosis on Axis II

2. Axis I   300.01   Panic Disorder without Agoraphobia
   Axis II   301.40   Obsessive Compulsive Personality

3. Axis I   300.30   Obsessive Compulsive Disorder
   Axis II   V71.09   No Diagnosis on Axis II

4. Axis I   309.24   Adjustment Disorder with Anxious Mood
   Axis II   301.40   Obsessive Compulsive Personality

5. Axis I   296.41   Bipolar Disorder, Manic
   Axis II   V71.09   No Diagnosis on Axis II

Suggested medication by the five psychiatrists included antianxiety medication (e.g., Valium or Librium), panic disorder medication (e.g., Xanax), bipolar disorder medication (e.g., Lithium), and various combinations of the above.

In another case, five psychiatrists agreed on a diagnosis of schizoaffective disorder. However, they recommended a wide range of medications often prescribed for variant classifications of disorders. The recommendations included: antipsychotic agents (e.g., Thorazine or Melaril), salt (e.g., Lithium), tricyclics (e.g., Elavil), MAO inhibitors (e.g., Parnate or Nardil), and selective serotonin re-uptake inhibitors (e.g., Prozac).

With less severe disorders, medication is less specifically defined and even more symptom oriented. Psychiatrists adjust kinds, brands, and dosages of medications by precedent. Even then, trial medication frequently confirms a diagnosis rather than the other way around. Again, this is like determining a hypothesis after conducting research. It is like figuring out a car needs a water pump after replacing several other parts that did not solve the original problem. The *PDR* parts manual, then, is for the relief of reported and observable symptoms. It is not for treating the etiology of conflict.

Professional psychotherapy offers a service. The dilemma is that the profession does not have a service manual. The profession, however, proceeds and represents itself as if it did. There is no indication of specific treatment for each of the diagnoses in the *DSM*, and there is no *treatment manual* for mental disorders. Diagnoses do not determine psychotherapeutic methodology. Neither do they determine developmental beliefs, perceptual attitudes, theoretical structures, nor boundaries of imposition. Because diagnoses do not define, each psychotherapist needs to establish these criteria in a way that does not rely on diagnostic symptomatology. That is, psychotherapists are professionally obligated to define their own service manuals. They are obligated to create their own perceptual, theoretical, and methodological parameters that correlate with a personal understanding of human conflict and suffering.

The Assumption of Standard Training, Beliefs, and Skills

Here again, let us assume that psychotherapists commonly agree on the diagnoses of clients. Second, let us fantasize that an imaginary correlative treatment manual exists. This hypothetical manual specifies a treatment methodology of choice for each diagnosis in the *DSM*. Another problem surfaces with the treatment-of-choice objective—the lack of an objective rule for training and practice.

If psychotherapists could agree on specific diagnoses and correlative methodologies, all psychotherapists would need training in all methodologies. However, methods and techniques require opposing beliefs and skills. Expecting psychotherapists to be trained in all methods is like assuming that all mechanics could repair all vehicles ranging from bicycles to jet planes. Even with the volumes of mechanical service manuals that exist, this would be an unrealistic expectation.

For example, suppose that several psychotherapists agree that a client has a simple phobia of flying. Suppose also that the imaginary treatment manual prescribes the specific methodology of *implosive behavior modification* or *systematic desensitization*—techniques designated and designed for extremely well-trained psychotherapists in the model of behaviorism. Comparatively few psychotherapists are proficient in these techniques or strategies.

Many psychotherapists use a neopsychoanalytic theory and modified psychodynamic method. This orientation assumes that lengthy focus on the mature development of internal dynamics will eventually resolve current symptoms. Many others use affective, cognitive, or family therapy models. It just doesn't make sense to expect that psychotherapists with different orientations could or would want to shift to a behavioral theory and method for a particular diagnosis. Not only is this expectation unreasonable; it is not an accurate reflection of psychotherapeutic practice.

In our mythical therapeutic kingdom, this phobic client would be referred to a behaviorist who specializes in implosive therapy or desensitization. According to the imaginary treatment manual, this would be a perfect match for both psychotherapist and client. Indeed, this might be an ideal way to practice psychotherapy, however, psychotherapists don't practice in a mythical kingdom. They practice with mythical ideas.

Observation of common practices reveals that psychotherapists actually treat a client's phobia of flying according to personal psychotherapeutic orientation; there is no standard training. The belief in a *standard* is a mythical idea. Various universities and medical, social, and psychological schools pride themselves on specializing in diverse theoretical and methodological orientations. Separate schools, however, reflect the beliefs of current faculty and staff. Each proposes variant and often incompatible beliefs about the etiology of and intervention in human conflict and suffering.

In reality, psychotherapists practice *orientation of choice* rather than treatment of choice as defined by diagnosis. However, even this obvious assertion often encourages claims of clinical blasphemy. Observation confirms that while this is cause for concern, it also initiates the opportunity to increase the effectiveness of the profession. Limitations of training and personal beliefs always will determine the quality and practice of psychotherapy, certainly more than any imagined standard interpretation of clients' problems.

The Assumption of Arbitrary Eclecticism

Many psychotherapists gain training in a variety of models. They want to increase skills to meet the diversity of clients' needs. Some of these psychotherapists identify their orientations as *eclectic*. An effective eclectic orientation is selecting "compatible features from diverse systems of metapsychology in an attempt to combine whatever is valid in any theory or doctrine into an integrated, harmonious whole" (Hinsie and Campbell, 1970). Eclecticism is integrated and systemic (Patterson, 1986). It is not a spontaneous delivery dependent on professional mood and circumstance. It is not an impromptu, randomly mixed, or casually implemented collection of techniques.

Justifying *arbitrary* methodology by an eclectic orientation is inaccurate and a convenient rationalization. Randomly implemented skills do not heal. Effective psychotherapy requires that psychotherapists select a primary orientation from a myriad of models. Personal beliefs and perceptual attitudes are not easily changed. Neither are the theoretical structures on which psychotherapists base their methodologies. Various methods and techniques may be abstracted from a variety of orientations. However, they are ineffective when randomly mixed or blended. They endure effectively only when they are part of a planned sequence that is specific and delineated.

Like other fields of expertise, psychotherapists become effective with the orientation they practice most often. Breadth of knowledge and diverse skills can be an essential adjunct. However, a multiplicity of skills is not a substitute for a well-defined and intentional methodology. Both psychotherapists and clients need consistency for healing.

Psychotherapists who identify themselves as psychoanalysts likely would be extremely poor at implementing behavior modification or Gestalt therapy. These theoretical structures are incompatible. Family therapy and systems models employ an entirely different perceptual attitude from cognitive models of psychotherapy. Practicing psychodrama requires an entirely different theoretical structure and methodology from the model of clinical hypnosis. These are just a few of the vast list of incompatible perceptual attitudes, theoretical structures, methodologies, and techniques. Effectiveness results from a deliberate and sequential orientation. It requires that the features included in an orientation be definitive, mutually compatible, and representative of personal beliefs.

The Assumption of Natural Development of Orientation

Unseasoned psychotherapists assume they will naturally gain a personal and effective methodology by developing skillful interviewing techniques and diagnostic acumen. It is not unusual for graduate students, interns, and residents to expect that the academic and apprenticeship rites of passage will ensure wisdom and success. This belief is similar to children assuming their parents will teach them all the necessary skills for survival and success by the time they leave home.

The difficulty with this assumption is that it is based on a treatment-of-choice objective. When this assumption is accepted as valid, the logical conclusion is that individual success is chiefly the result of an indisputable understanding of known scientific principles. Any personal application is merely expected to clear the slate and resolve any intrusive pathology. Clinical staffs usually do not make time to invite novice psychotherapists to personally define their orientations. Indeed, the opposite is true. Novice psychotherapists are not encouraged to follow their own course, specifically because of the treatment-of-choice objective. It usually is not until later in a career that psychotherapists discover the more demanding responsibility of defining their own orientations.

Some novice psychotherapists assume that by combining professional skills with a caring commitment to humanity, they will become effective in practice. This is like saying, with a love for automobiles and a sophisticated knowledge of all breakdowns, everyone has a good chance of becoming a master mechanic. It implies that anyone could repair everything from a door lock to the transmission on any make or model of car. As difficult as it is to be a master auto mechanic, the human factors in relationships complicate the natural acquisition of a psychotherapeutic orientation.

Diagnostic skills and a knowledge of psychopathology alone do not engender an effective psychotherapist. Altruistic love is not enough. This has been noted about the treatment of emotionally disturbed children (Bettelheim, 1950) and the compatibility of intimate relationships (Beck, 1988). Professional knowledge, in addition to a caring commitment, is essential. However, neither clinical knowledge nor personal or professional caring automatically generates professional effectiveness. Indeed, neither guarantees the development of an effective psychotherapeutic orientation.

Psychotherapists do not gravitate naturally toward an effective orientation. The blessing and curse of being a psychotherapist is that no singular correct theory or methodology exists. There is considerable freedom in beliefs about etiology, diagnosis, and intervention. Besides artists, few other trades or professions allow such personal beliefs and individual implementations. As a result of these authorized freedoms, psychotherapists are responsible for more than the legalities of state laws and the ethics of professional associations; they are responsible for specifically defining all facets of psychotherapeutic orientation.

The Assumption of Ubiquitous Values

The treatment-of-choice objective subsumes individual values of understanding and intervention for professionally generic and the presumed values of Western health. The ethics of all mental health professionals stipulate consideration and respect for the client's cultural, racial, religious, and sexual differences. However, the treatment-of-choice objective intrinsically assumes ubiquitous values—values that are assumed as important for everyone regardless of cultural, racial, religious, political, economic, and sexual preferences. At best, this difference of statement and practice is an apparent paradox. Mid-range, it is an incongruence. At worst, it is a lie. The problem with this assumption occurs when clients are interpreted and experienced in a "mono-valued sphere of being" (Pattison, 1966).

Research indicates that psychotherapists are not amoral (Pattison, 1969). However, psychotherapists, either willingly or unknowingly, often transfer the seemingly ubiquitous values of the profession to clients. The problem with the ubiquitous assumption is that it is extremely difficult to consider client differences when the profession is convinced of alternative persuasions. That is, while the psychotherapeutic profession commonly requires consideration of individual differences, it heralds itself as the authoritative consciousness of mental health and advising wisdom. This declaration occurs not only in Western culture, but with a beckoning call for multicultural and worldwide application.

As a conservative example, this is particularly evident with members of the Christian Science religion. Members do not believe in and abstain from conventional medical intervention, including physical and mental—any medical treatment, hospital visit, or use of medication. It is paradoxical that this religion claims it is both Christian and scientific, concepts that represent Western thinking. It also is interesting to note that this religious persuasion has sponsored and sustained one of the most well-respected and prestigious newspapers in the Western world—the *Christian Science Monitor*.

While the psychotherapeutic profession would like to honor the values of Christian Science members, it is compelled to persuade them otherwise by the ubiquitous values of the profession. Both the interpretation of disease and severity of psychopathology are determined by the psychotherapist and supported by the profession of membership. The more severe the disorder or disease, as interpreted by the presiding psychotherapist, the greater the likelihood of increasing persuasive measures or direct attempts to manipulate.

Psychotherapy is both a science and an art. It has a distinct Western European and North American heritage and flavor. Anthropologically, sociologically, politically, theologically, and philosophically, psychotherapy obviously is biased by its national origins. Of course, it is sometimes difficult to view this from within the belief structure and Western culture.

In the United States, the Native American nations do not routinely subscribe to conventional psychotherapeutic practice. Outside their industrialized centers of commerce, South America, Africa, the Middle East, and Asia follow alternative values of healing and mental health. Sometimes these alternative values are mixed with Western conventional science. Rarely, except in major urban cities, do they mirror conventional Western psychotherapy. This should not be a surprise since psychotherapists do not always resemble each other when they subscribe to many of the same cultural values, even within the United States. This assumption is not so much a cause for alarm as a reminder that psychotherapists need to take increasing responsibility for the personal and professional values they quite naturally transmit, and that generally reflect the profession with which they identify.[7]

The Assumption of Clinician Determination of Intervention

Interrelated with the above psychotherapeutic assumptions, the treatment-of-choice objective assumes that psychotherapists act with professional authority to determine diagnoses and appropriate intervention. Their beliefs and actions are sometimes irrespective and exclusive of client input or preferences. Of course, there are times when such authoritative ethics and legality demand intervention. During these times, professional authority supersedes consideration of client preference and is justifiable as prudent for the safety of the client or the protection of others.[8]

The problem with this assumption is not that psychotherapists implement authority when required by the pertinent ethical and legal statutes. Problems surface when psychotherapists implicitly make this assumption outside these explicit circumstances. Problems occur when psychotherapists, as designated mental health authorities, either willingly or unknowingly administer their power without determining the preferences of their clients.

Our observations are that this assumption is not usually a direct result of personality differences nor variant training programs. It is the result of psychotherapists who view themselves as the appointed, or rather anointed, mental health caretakers of society. Such views only serve the dominant power structure at the expense of diminished respect for personal credibility. When intervention excludes client input and preferences, it reinforces clinical treatment of interpreted disease rather than empowering clients to heal themselves with professional assistance.

Redefining with Direction

The treatment-of-choice objective does not adequately define nor direct psychotherapy. Defining all facets of psychotherapeutic orientations is an evolutionary process. Psychotherapists are responsible for choosing their psychotherapeutic orientation and clarifying the parameters of the one they practice. Before we confirm a decision or make a new one, we need to understand the process of disengaging developmental beliefs, which is similar to a shamanic purification process (Eliade, 1972).

As part of the training to become a shaman, apprentices are required to go on a *vision quest* or alternative initiation ceremony. The vision quest is a four-day event to explore a career as an authoritative physical and mental healer of the society. However, before any vision quest or final initiation, a purification process is necessary to prepare the body and the spirit.

Aged and seasoned shamans routinely undergo purification rites to purge their bodies of toxins. They also use such rites to cleanse spirits and remain focused on their designated function as healer. Purification rites are also used before healing especially difficult diseases and for intentional paranormal experiences. Using purification rites as a traditional metaphor, the diagram in Figure 1–2 is a visual map of increasingly complex principles and stages reflecting the authors' version of a purification rite designed for Western psychotherapists. Each section is a continuation of all the concepts in the previous sections. The entire area of the hexagon represents integrative paradigms of psychotherapy.

Individual psychotherapeutic orientations follow the exploration of personal beliefs. With progressive evaluation, psychotherapists can then review, clarify, and define a personal psychotherapeutic orientation. The intent of this process is an effective and satisfying practice. The treatment-of-choice objective is redefined as intervention of choice by the client and orientation of choice as predefined by the psychotherapist.

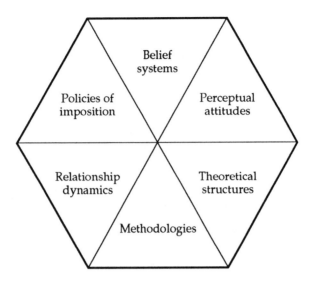

FIGURE 1–2. Integrative Paradigm of Psychotherapy

Notes

1. The largest or most well-known of these nations are the Apache, Cherokee, Chippewa, Choctaw, Dakota Sioux, Eskimo, Hopi, Iroquois, Navaho, Pueblo, and Zuni.
2. This issue is discussed later in this chapter under the subheading The Assumption of Arbitrary Eclecticism.
3. This is a secondary assumption discussed under the next subhead.
4. As the *DSM-III-R* makes clear, the ICD is a statistical classification, not a nomenclature or "catalogue of approved terms for describing and recording clinical and pathological observations" of diseases. Within its spectrum of focusing on physical diseases, only a small segment pertains to mental disorders. "Its principal use is in the classification of morbidity and mortality information for statistical purposes" and "as a nomenclature of diseases for indexing medical records" (*DSM-III-R*, 1987). For further information on this interesting document, please see *DSM-III-R* pp. 433–443.
5. This example is intended to illustrate that diagnostic agreement cannot be assumed within a treatment-of-choice objective. It also reflects cultural bias when diagnosing clients of different cultural backgrounds and is more specifically addressed later in this chapter under the subheading The Assumption of Ubiquitous Values.
6. This figure is less than one percent of the approximate number of licensed mental health practitioners in the United States.
7. Imposition of values and authority is a diferent matter and is discussed in chapter 7, Boundaries of Imposition.
8. A thorough explanation of boundaries of professional imposition is discussed in chapter 7, Boundaries of Imposition.

References

American Psychiatric Association. (1989). *Treatments of psychiatric disorders*. Washington, DC: American Psychiatric Press.

American Psychiatric Association. (1987). *Diagnostic and statistical manual of mental disorders* (3d ed. rev.) (*DSM-III-R*). Washington, DC: American Psychiatric Association.

Beck, A. (1988). *Love is never enough*. New York: Harper & Row.

Bettelheim, B. (1950). *Love is not enough*. Glencoe, IL: Freepress.

Cox, R. (Ed.). (1973). *Religious systems and psychotherapy*. Springfield, IL: Charles C. Thomas.

Eliade, M. (1972). *Shamanism*. Princeton, NJ: Princeton University Press.

Freemesser, G. (1978). Symposium on holistic healing. Presented at Naval Hospital, Portsmouth, VA, and sponsored in conjunction with the Committee on Medicine and Religion, Medical Society of Virginia.

Gross, M. (1978). *The psychological society*. New York: Random House.

Hinsie, L., & Campbell, R. (1970). *Psychiatric dictionary* (4th ed.). New York: Oxford University Press.

Kiev, A. (Ed.). (1964). *Magic, faith, and healing*. New York: The Free Press.

Kris, E. (1964). *Psychoanalytic explorations in art* (pp. 13–63, 310–312). New York: Shocken Books.

Norcross, J. (Ed.). (1986). *Handbook of eclectic psychotherapy*. New York: Brunner/Mazel.

Patterson, C. (1986). *Theories of counseling and psychotherapy* (4th ed.). New York: Harper & Row.

Pattison, E. (Ed.). (1968). *Clinical psychiatry and religion*. Boston: Little, Brown.

Pattison, E. (1966). Social and psychological aspects of religion in psychotherapy. *Journal of Nervous and Mental Disorders, 141*, 586–597.

Webster's New Collegiate Dictionary. (1973). Springfield, MA: G. & C. Merriam Co. (Used throughout this book as the source for word definitions.)

2

Disengaging
Developmental
Beliefs

The psychotherapeutic session is a state of reciprocal interest in commercial and social matters. These mutual concerns have a logical and an interpretive causal connection between the members. The psychotherapist and the client in a psychotherapeutic session are therefore in a relationship.[1] As would individuals involved in any relationship, both psychotherapists and clients inevitably contribute separate components to this professional relationship. The interaction of these separate components includes the dynamics of the relationship.[2] The pattern formed by the relationship dynamics is the dance of the relationship interaction. A psychotherapeutic session, and its implied or stated contract, encompasses and subsumes a unique healing function into this relationship. To achieve this psychotherapeutic function, psychotherapists must give special attention to understanding and controlling their careless introduction of personal components or dynamics into the psychotherapeutic dance.

Untold hundreds of thousands of academic, internship, and residency hours are spent on education and training to accomplish and instill appropriate psychotherapeutic boundaries. The vast majority of these boundaries limit the psychotherapist's personal beliefs and input and maximize the client's involvement in the psychotherapeutic session. Psychoanalysts have historically gone to this extreme by sitting behind the client and out of sight. This position is encouraged in an attempt to limit the therapist's responses and prevent contaminating involvement or transference.[3] Regardless of the techniques or the extent of the boundaries, psychotherapists inherently bring personal beliefs into the professional relationship.

Seasoned psychotherapists strive to control the expression of their known beliefs during sessions. As an example, Dr. Silverman, a psychotherapist, was in session with Athena L., a married woman who had just reported having an ongoing, sexually-involved extramarital affair. Dr. Silverman's belief system held fidelity and honesty as essential elements for a healthy marriage. He also had a strong negative emotional reaction when he heard about his client's affair.

- What should Dr. Silverman do with his emotional reaction?
- Should the psychotherapist's beliefs be imposed on the client?
- Would it be better to help Athena formulate or discover her own values and beliefs?

Beliefs formed by Athena likely would be more acceptable and functional for the world in which she lives. However, some psychotherapists might say that they need more information before they can answer these questions. Needing more information is the wrong answer. All the necessary information is given! Additional information would only be useful for *how* Dr. Silverman could help Athena decide, and *not* for whether he should apply his beliefs to the client's situation.

If Dr. Silverman were to become involved in "what the decision should be," then he would impose his belief system of "how or what he would do" if he were in Athena's situation. It is obvious that Dr. Silverman is not Athena. He was not in her situation. He has no way of knowing the multitude of details about how Athena got into her situation. Nor does he have her resources to solve the situation. Therefore, it can be only Athena's decision or constructive solution that will work for her. Eventually, only Athena's decision will elicit enough self-responsibility for implementation and commitment to completion.

It is for these reasons that psychotherapists must be ever vigilant for the many ways their beliefs influence the psychotherapeutic session. The example of Dr. Silverman presents an obvious belief. However, many less-conscious belief systems are inevitably present. These subconscious belief systems require special and careful investigation and consideration. Psychotherapists must investigate their belief systems with the same professional diligence they use for their clients and apply their skills to change their known and subconscious beliefs as appropriate. Only the technique used to investigate varies.

With a prior consideration of personal subconscious belief systems, psychotherapists can disengage their developmental beliefs and restrict them within appropriate boundaries during the psychotherapeutic session. In this way, they prevent themselves from contaminating the client's healing process. To accomplish this, psychotherapists must gain greater conscious insight into subconscious processes. Through looking at the development of belief systems they can apply this insight to their beliefs. They can discover how beliefs formed, and a means by which they may change them, if they so choose. This investigative process starts with how people, including psychotherapists, perceive themselves. It progresses to how they perceive the world, and then to what they believe about the world.

Self-perception

Self-perception is a separate focus and reference of orientation about who one is relative to all other entities in the universe. The separatist concept assumes a fundamental distinctness of each entity in the universe. This concept is a philosophical outgrowth of René Descartes' postulate, *Cogito, ergo sum* (I think, therefore I am) and provides an explanation for feeling separated from all that is not us. As a result of this separation of entities, relationships exist between them. Belief systems form when people consider themselves and their distinctness in relation to the universe. These belief systems become self-perception and are distinct personal reference points on which people base their judgments about all other events that occur in the world around them.

People relentlessly strive to establish their distinctness as individuals, separate from others in the human community and from their environment. This is observed when people express their opinions or strive to excel. Everyone wishes recognition for their achievements. However, the way people express themselves is wholly influenced by self-perception or belief systems. The catch is that self-perception and belief systems form by social feedback and from the way they relate to the world. The elements of the perception of self—feedback from their world and the beliefs about themselves in relationship to the world—comprise a feedback loop.

The development of self-perception requires people to make comparisons, evaluations, interpretations, judgments, and definitions from the sensory information they take in every second. Such categorizing is a cognitive process. It is a *thinking-about* process of inquiry. However, this process of self-definition for self-perception depends on how people experience themselves in relation to others and all other entities in their environment. This process evolves over the entire period of individual development. The unborn infant is one with its mother and the world—the fetus has not experienced a separation between itself and everything else. At the beginning of conception, there is only one entity, one consciousness. After birth, newborn infants have just experienced, so far in life, the greatest trauma of separation (Rank, 1929); this trauma starts the process of developing a conscious sense of differentiation.

Any sense of conscious differentiation initially arises from a sensory awareness in relationship to others. The infant's definition of self begins to emerge as it senses and learns that it is separate from others. The infant develops sensory ownership. This concept of sensory possessiveness is the essence from which the initial beliefs of self develop into self-perception. Children develop by learning from their experiences in the environment. Their conceptualization of their sensory possessiveness and self-perception determines the quality of their environmental experiences.

During the child's first years of development, parents and significant others create and control the infant's environment; it lives in the parents' world. The child has extremely little, if any, influence on the world's structure and interaction. This parental environment reinforces and molds the child's identity in alignment with parental expectations and roles; it happens subtly and insidiously. Learnings later become subconscious, yet fundamental in creating adult identity. These subconscious and fundamental learnings result from our early self-perception and become our *initial, fundamental beliefs*.

An example of this was observed in the interaction of a mother and her three-month-old daughter. The child was the first born, the pride and joy of the mother. She was showing her new child to a group of friends, including her older sister and mother. The older sister had three children of her own, ages seven, five, and three, and she considered herself very experienced at parenting. The grandmother had had four children all of whom were now adults and had their own homes and families.

The group of women were talking loudly, several at a time, smothering the new child with adoration. This continued for approximately ten minutes as they followed each others' news. The child became more and more agitated by the confusion and overload of sensory information as she was jostled about and talked to by one after another of the women. The child was trying to make sense out of the various faces, voices, and handling. She was trying to find some point of familiarity from the sets of sensory signals compared to those she normally received from her mother. Eventually, her comfort level was exceeded when the number of sensory mismatches overcame the number of matches. Her only choice was to resort to behavior that had worked. She started to cry, with the objective of attracting comfort from her mother.

In this few moments, the child learned she was separate from her mother. Although this event may not have been her first experience of separation, it was markedly a strong reinforcing experience; she learned that the incoming sensory information was not of her world as she knew it. She had no way of matching it to previously experienced stimuli. It was therefore separate from her, and she sensed the uncomfortableness of being alone. She had, by earlier experience, learned that crying would bring comfort and relief from her discomfort of separation, so she cried to bring her world back to the familiar.

Both the grandmother and sister tried to comfort the child to no avail. They inadvertently aggravated the situation by adding foreign stimuli to the child's situation. The escalated crying caused them to pass the child quickly back to the mother. They each quipped that this was a whining baby who would grow up to be a complaining and whining girl. The mother reacted out of her pride and attempted to quiet the child with the least amount of attention. Thereby, she prolonged the amount of time the child was uncomfortable and lengthened the period of crying.

From this experience the child learned that she had to cry louder and longer. As a result, the child fulfilled the prediction of a whiny child. The child subconsciously learned that separateness was, indeed, uncomfortable and should henceforth be avoided at all cost. If separateness did occur, she would quickly retreat to the safety of mother with the greatest amount of crying that would receive comforting. In essence, she became more dependent and started the belief that she had little self-esteem or self-reliance.

Subconscious fundamental beliefs, formed from self-perception, circumscribe the individual's psychological identity. The first perceptions of self are the initial building blocks that define and delineate fundamental belief development. The pattern of these initial, fundamental beliefs form belief systems. The combination of these belief systems constitutes personality.

By investigating our original childhood experiences and learnings, we can reevaluate self-perceptions and fundamental beliefs. We can discover the conclusions initially drawn from them. This is an invitation to further define and integrate psychotherapeutic orientation. As we logically redefine our psychological identity from the fundamental building blocks, global perceptions, and functions, we can develop a more life-enhancing self. The beginning of this journey is to bring into awareness how past decisions influenced the formation of our belief systems.

From this insight into belief system formation, we can bring about individual change and growth. We can create new and life-enhancing belief systems based on a more accurate adult view of the world and our experience. For, adult interpretations are generally more accurate than those of a child. However, when we build a new belief system on our adult interpretations, we must be cautious that these interpretations indeed are accurate. With new insight and accurate adult interpretations, we can develop a life-enhancing approach to relationships based on new belief systems.

Investigating belief formation permits us to decide how we relate to others, as opposed to defaulting to childhood experiences and beliefs from distorted family environments. However, before we investigate and attempt to change our beliefs, the first essential step is to understand how fundamental beliefs form. The next step in discovery is to dislodge old beliefs that may be limiting. Following discovery and dislodging, the third step is to construct new life-enhancing belief systems to replace *life-limiting*[4] beliefs.

Beliefs

Beliefs form as a personal way of understanding and relating two or more experiences. Stated in reverse order of its formation, the beliefs we hold are our way of explaining the connective patterns between and among perceptually separate experiences. Keep in mind that our earliest definition of self-perception dramatically influences how we perceive the separateness of experiences.

The very first beliefs formed are referred to here as initial fundamental beliefs. They are constructed, learned, or accepted during the first perceived experiences of satisfying our five fundamental areas of human desires, motivations, or drives—categorized as *basic needs*. As our basic needs are encountered or requested from the world around us, we form beliefs. The collective pattern of these beliefs is the foundation of individual personality. They reciprocally filter the experience of ourselves in relationship to the universe.

To get a better understanding of belief systems, we will begin with the most fundamental beliefs. These beliefs first form in response to the satisfaction of basic needs. In turn, to understand these fundamental beliefs, we will categorize the five basic areas of human needs.

Basic Needs

The subconscious or preconscious learnings for satisfying the five basic needs are the basic beliefs. Conversely, the five basic needs also prescribe the five areas around which fundamental beliefs form. From these five fundamental beliefs many *supporting beliefs* branch into complex belief systems later in the infant's growth and on into adulthood.[5] For now, we will start with the five basic needs or drives.

1. *The need to be safe and secure:* This is our need to believe or feel physically safe, without threat of harm, discomfort, or pain. The satisfaction of this need does not require that we actually are safe or without pain; nor does it require that we be in control of this need's satisfaction.

Our experiences with clients processing the need to be safe and secure indicate that the associated primal fear is of death when this need for security is not felt or knowingly satisfied. This is defined in the organismic sense of loss of life, to die (Kübler-Ross, 1969).

2. *The need to belong:* This is the need to believe or feel accepted by a significant person or become part of some larger significant social group, including the need to belong to a territory, idea, or social concept. Again, the satisfaction of this need does not require that we actually be accepted or respected by a significant other or group. Nor does it require that we somehow control this need's satisfaction only that we believe or feel that we belong (May, 1974; May, 1967).

Our experiences with clients processing the need to belong indicate that the associated primal fear is of abandonment when this need is not felt or knowingly satisfied. This also is defined in the organismic sense as lacking companionship and in the emotional sense as being lonesome or without emotional support.

3. *The need for love and sex:* This is the need to procreate and ensure the survival of the species. It includes physically expressed love, all the chemical stimuli associated with sexual attraction, and the affectionate touching of others—believing we are sexually attractive to someone else and sexual contact. Here again, the satisfaction of this need does not require that we have sexual contact, intercourse, or any of the other aspects of this need. Nor does it require that we somehow control this need's satisfaction. It only requires that we believe we are being satisfied.

Our experiences with clients processing the need for love and sex indicates that the associated primal fear is of impotency when this need is not satisfied. This is defined in the organismic sense as loss of the ability to participate or perform sexually, and in the emotional sense as being unable to enjoy loving with the goal of procreation.

4. *The need for autonomy:* This is the need to believe or feel separate from everything and everyone else. It is our need to believe that we *can* be self-determining and self-governing. The satisfaction of this belief does not imply that the person actually is autonomous, separate, or self-governing. Again, it only requires that we feel or believe we can be autonomous or have the option and ability to achieve autonomy.

Be aware that the need for autonomy is not in opposition to the need to belong. Both needs coexist and therefore must be satisfied simultaneously. As we will discuss later, any trading of one need satisfaction for another causes conflict and consequently indicates that life-limiting beliefs are being followed.

Our experiences with clients processing the need to be autonomous indicate that the associated primal fear of engulfment when this need is not felt or knowingly satisfied. This fear is defined in the emotional sense as feeling consumed, drowned, suffocated, and losing of self-identity and distinctness.

5. *The need for spirituality:* This is the need to believe or feel that we are in someway part of a greater purpose or power in life. We need to believe or feel that we are: (1) part of a higher power, (2) part of the plan of a higher power, or (3) part of a plan greater than our personal development and individualized growth in the universe. Whether we actually are spiritually connected or not does not affect the satisfaction of this need. We do not imply that people need a religion or that they must be religious, although most religions entail believing or feeling spiritual, thereby satisfying this need.

Our experiences with clients processing the need to have spirituality indicate that the associated primal fear is of meaninglessness when this need is not felt or knowingly satisfied. This fear is defined in the cognitive and emotional sense as emptiness, lack of purpose, lack of spiritual continuity, and lack of *logos* (Carlsen, 1988; Frankl, 1978, 1985; May, 1967).

The concept of basic needs has historically been supported in a number of psychotherapeutic models. Some of these inclusive models were formulated and presented by Abraham Maslow, Robert Dilts, Sigmund Freud, and Erich Fromm. For comparison only, a brief discussion of them follows.[6]

Basic needs are similar in content and yet developmentally different from Abraham Maslow's (1968) hierarchy of needs. The significant developmental differences are that basic needs are organismic and are fulfilled concurrently. Additionally, they occur during the child's same developmental time frame. Basic needs also differ from Maslow's hierarchy of needs in that: (1) all basic needs exist from the beginning of consciousness, and (2) all five basic needs are motivators for developing fundamental beliefs and supportive systems simultaneously long after the individual has forgotten the original needs.

The concept that belief systems form from basic needs is not singularly new. Although the authors have not found any one theorist's concept as comprehensive as belief system theory, many are incorporated in the concept. What follows is a brief summary of various theories encompassed by belief systems. In this discussion, our goal is to provide a frame of reference to explain belief systems, increased relevancy, and understanding.

During the early developmental stages, the theoretical concept of fundamental beliefs is similar to the behavioristic approach of Robert Dilts' (1990) *imprint systems*. Dilts uses the term *imprint* to identify these basic memory learnings. He names the first imprint biological intelligence and claims that these imprinted memories result from the way we manage our basic biological functions. This corresponds to our belief system formed from the basic need to be safe and secure.

Dilts' second imprint is the emotional imprint. It develops when the child's *emotional energy* emerges. This is similar to the basic need to belong and determines the methods by which we relate with other people to satisfy our emotional needs. Dilts defines it as our desire to be social and socially bond. Additional information about emotional imprinting can be found in *Somatic Reality* by Stanley Keleman (1982).

Dilts' third imprint is intellectual development. It includes being intelligent, developing common sense, and the behavioral management of our lives. Although not an exact match, the intellectual imprint is similar to our basic need for autonomy, which determines our striving to know intellectually that we are separate from others. People need to know that they are a separately functioning part of the whole for self-development and identity.

Dilts' fourth imprint is the social imprint. It governs our sexual relationship to others. This is similar to the basic need for love and sexual expression. Dilts defines it to include the drive for procreation and the need for acceptance by the social group to achieve sexual bonding.[7]

Dilts defines his last imprint as the *meta* imprint. This is similar to the basic need for spirituality. He defines this belief to include awareness of our relationship with the larger universe. Viktor Frankl (1978, 1985) refers to this as "meaning in life." He describes it as having a purpose to someone or something outside oneself.

Other similar theoretical models are those of Erich Fromm and Sigmund Freud. Although Fromm's (1947) social view of individual development is in disagreement with Freud's (1927) view that biological forces motivate human development, both fit comfortably within belief system theory. Fromm (1955) contends that forces of the society and culture motivate psychological development. These social forces form qualities of our personality like identity, belonging, and the meaning of life. Fromm focuses his developmental process on how society and culture influence our development into social beings with cultural values.

Fromm maintains that people have five needs for socialization:

1. *The need for rootedness*: This is feeling connected with nature and others.
2. *The need for a frame of orientation*: This is a stable point of reference in our world.
3. *The need for relatedness*: This includes love, caring, respect, and understanding from and of others.
4. *The need for identity*: This is the feeling of personal uniqueness.
5. *The need for transcendence*: This distinguishes us from the animal kingdom by demonstration of creativity.

Our basic needs are inclusive of Fromm's five needs for socialization. Specifically, our basic need of belonging includes Fromm's need for rootedness, frame of orientation, and relatedness. Included our basic need of autonomy is Fromm's need for identity and the need for self-transcendence.

Basic needs also include Freud's biological view of the human condition. Our basic needs of safety and security and love and sex encompass Freud's theory of biological forces. Basic needs encompass both Freud's and Fromm's motivational theories of human development as well as Dilts' developmental theories of learning.

Belief Theory

Developing children are automatically motivated to satisfy the five basic needs. Fundamental beliefs develop as a result of their immediate interaction with their parent-controlled environment. That is, very young children learn patterns of interaction that allow satisfaction of the basic needs within their immediate environment.

Self-identity and personal psychology are formatively like the singularity of a snowflake. The fundamental belief is similar to the initiating particle of dust at the core of each snowflake. All snowflakes are composed of countless individual water molecules; each with the same molecular structure. The water molecules of the snowflake crystallize or attach themselves according to the limited possibilities of the crystalline confines of a water molecule. However, it is the initiating grain of dust that creates a different crystalline base structure for each snowflake. The initial dust grain, with its unique pattern, determines the finished structure of the snowflake in spite of the limited bonding characteristics of the water molecule. That small variant dust grain produces infinite variations in snowflakes—no two are exactly the same. Each, however, is recognizable as a snowflake.

Like the initiating grain of dust in a snowflake, fundamental beliefs initiate the pattern of how people relate with the world. Fundamental beliefs establish the structural possibilities of the development of self-identity and the unique psychological structure and function of being human.

Fundamental beliefs begin developing during early, infant experiences. Once the initiating belief sets the direction for the fundamental belief, the developing child interprets ensuing events so they continue to support the fundamental beliefs. If the new event does not fit the fundamental belief, then the child subconsciously modifies the interpretation to match the fundamental belief. The modified interpretation is the result of the previously set belief system parameters. It is this modified interpretation that assimilates into the existing belief. The new finding supports the fundamental belief, never replaces it. As a result, fundamental beliefs change minimally even when new evidence could directly contradict them. The child develops perceptions by decisions from prior experiences. As long as the new decisions and perceptions match the child's world, the child continues to function well.

If a new event does not fit a preexisting belief, then people subconsciously bias their interpretation to match their current belief system. It is because of this biased interpretation or filtering that people assimilate new information. As discussed previously, assimilate means to alter and then take into the mind and thoroughly comprehend—to make similar or to alter the smaller to fit the greater by assimilation. Belief system processing does not accommodate information that is radically different. Accommodate means modifying or adapting the recipient's mental processes to make room for a new concept or idea or to adapt one's mind. People perceive information that they prejudicially interpret and then assimilate it into their existing belief system. Newly interpreted perceptions of experiences and experiments of the world routinely support a belief system and never replace it. As a result of this subconscious cognitive process, belief systems change minimally over time, even when new evidence would appear to the outside observer to directly contradict them.

Fundamental beliefs begin to develop during the first moments of experiencing the self. The perceptions of the developing child interpret events so they continue to support the original, initiating belief. This, in turn, leads the following experiences to be predisposed by the fundamental beliefs and thereby they become supporting beliefs. The child's environment is most influenced by parents at the earliest stages of development and while the infant is first perceiving self. Infants form their beliefs mainly on the feedback of parents or substitute authority figures.

This initiating experience and subsequent initial, fundamental belief begins the generalized direction for beliefs. For example, the first time baby Emmet gets hungry, he makes a fuss or noise that builds to crying. It is usually mother who comes to pick him up and feed him. According to behavioral conditioning, the baby associates crying with feeding and comfort—baby starts a fundamental belief that crying or fussiness and noise are effective behaviors to satisfy his need for safety and security. Emmet, over time and by trial and error feedback method, will begin to use this belief; he will reproduce the behavior the next time he becomes hungry or uncomfortable. After numerous times when his crying leads to feeding, refining the method of crying will begin to occur. Emmet will experiment with slight variations of his original belief and method of crying to acquire food. He will experiment until specific types of crying receive better results in differing situations than others; he assimilates new information into the existing belief.

As Emmet gets older, the fundamental belief will continue to be supported with minor modifications. Each new supporting belief will expand the application of the original belief system into greater and greater uses of the same belief. This occurs for two reasons. First, the parental environment is continually giving supportive feedback for this form of behavior and thereby reinforces the belief by satisfying the basic need. Second, any feedback from a source outside his immediate parental environment will be perceived by a predisposition to be supportive of the fundamental belief.[8]

Let us review the information in this example. Baby Emmet's basic need is safety and security; he needs nourishment and comfort. His fundamental belief is that making noise brings nourishment. He formed this belief with the first sequence of events where he made a noise and received nourishment. Every following experience assimilates more information and refinement into the fundamental belief. Each experience that noise brought nourishment supports, by interpretation, the original fundamental belief.

Fundamental and supportive belief systems are intertwined, interrelated, and interconnected and form simultaneously. Supporting belief systems are also interdependent. They interrelate and interconnect with each other in nested fashion to form the individual personality. This mixing by interrelatedness create multiple and complex belief systems that often create patterns of self-initiating beliefs and reciprocal stimulation for additional supportive belief development.

Belief development occurs when the child interprets responses from environmental interactions, forming a belief about how to satisfy personal needs. The growth of fundamental beliefs into a personality is much like the growth of a seedling into a tree. The five fundamental beliefs form the direction and the specialization of the seed's cells into roots, heart wood, the trunk, bark, or leaves (see Figure 2–1). The fundamental beliefs branch or grow, according to environmental restrictions, into many supporting beliefs as the child gains new experiences. Like the tree's branches that conform to the availability of light and water, while also being shaped by the wind and damages from insects, birds, and chewing animals, supporting beliefs grow under similar psychological conditions that become a complex interrelated series of beliefs.

Differing growing conditions cause the tree's branches to intermingle in varying ways, becoming the tree's branching structure that represents a unique characteristic for each tree. The leaf crown of the tree, formed by the underlying branches and canopy of leaves, is what is prominently seen as the individual characteristic of the tree. Like a tree's canopy, belief systems are a complex interrelationship of numerous beliefs. The belief systems form complex qualities such as attitude, self-esteem, worthiness, responsibility, respect, and confidence—some of what people regularly judge as the characteristics of an individual. These qualities mold, direct, and motivate the person. Often, they also can restrict the behavior and qualities of the individual and their relationship with the world.

Infants usually form their beliefs based on feedback from parents or substitute authority figures. Take, again, the example of Emmet. The first time baby Emmet got hungry, he became physically uncomfortable, irritable, and eventu-

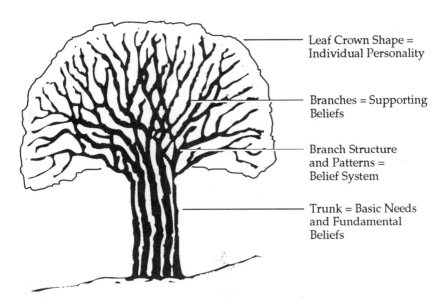

Leaf Crown Shape =
Individual Personality

Branches = Supporting
Beliefs

Branch Structure
and Patterns =
Belief System

Trunk = Basic Needs
and Fundamental
Beliefs

FIGURE 2–1   The Development Process of Beliefs Is Like the Growth of a Seed into a Tree.

ally cried. Mother picked him up, gave him some attention, and then fed him. Behaviorally, Emmet associated crying with feeding and comfort. He started the belief system that crying was an effective behavior to satisfy his need for nourishment and belonging. Slowly, by trial and feedback method, he began to use this belief and behavior each time he became hungry.

The belief system, at this early stage of Emmet's learning process, has imposed a parameter on how he interprets responses to his crying. At first there were various responses to Emmet's crying. Mother talked to him, checked his diaper, changed him, picked him up, held him close, or fed him. Since Emmet was crying because of his hunger, he interpreted all responses except that of being fed as unsupportive of the crying. The act of crying became goal focused, not because of the lack of feedback, but because of the belief system parameters. After several experiences, when crying led to feeding, refining the style of crying took place. The parameters became more restrictive. Baby Emmet experimented with variations of his original method of crying to get food until he perceived that certain styles received better results than others.

Emmet's fundamental need was safety and security; he needed nourishment and comfort. His fundamental belief was that making noise brings nourishment. He formed this belief with the first sequence of events when he made a noise and received nourishment. The result of each new experience assimilated more supportive information and refinement into the original belief. Each experience in which crying brought nourishment supported, by a parametered interpretation, the original belief.

To demonstrate assimilation, let us start baby Emmet all over. However, this time suppose baby Emmet does not know that crying elicits food. In this situation he will experiment with a variety of behaviors until he finds one that precedes being fed. By infant sequential logic this will be the behavior that *works*. If in this unique parental environment, when he is hungry, he only gets fed while he is quiet, then he associates quiet with feeding. He interprets that the way to get control of feeding is to behave quietly. This belief system continues to elicit results in a world where his parents follow the same rules. Beginning from this point in his belief development, refinement of being quiet to receive food continues within the parameters of his belief system and follows the same rules as Emmet's previous situation.

As a different example, suppose newborn baby Steve has not learned that crying can elicit food. Baby Steve will experiment with various overt and covert behaviors until he receives attention and is fed by his parent. By the reinforcement and satisfaction of his need he associates and knows which behavior works. Baby Steve's parents have taken a child psychology class and have learned that they can train their baby to be quiet. In this parental situation, Steve is only fed when he is quiet. This is similar to baby Emmet's parents discussed previously.

Steve's parents are very diligent about his training. When he is hungry, he is fed only while he also is quiet. In this environment, he associates quiet with feeding. He forms a belief that the only way to get food is to be quiet, an overt behavior of nonaction. This belief continues to elicit results in a world where his parents and others follow the same rules. Thus far in our example, this is conventional behaviorism, specifically operant conditioning (Bandura, 1969).

However, let us transpose baby Steve to a different situation. Mother and Father have decided that child psychology is too much work and have gone back to grandmother's advice. Mother now feeds him only when he cries and ignores him most of the time while he is quiet. For a while Steve continues to follow his original belief, which does not elicit control of his feeding in this new situation. He tries to get fed by following his belief system that dictates that he become quieter and quieter. He behaves as if the belief will continue to work for him as it has in the past. His belief has now become a life-limiting belief due to the change in his environment.

The belief was life-enhancing during the original situation in which it formed. However, now that the environmental situation has changed, the belief is limiting his satisfaction. Baby Steve tries to get fed by becoming quieter and quieter. He behaves as if the basic belief will continue to work for him as it did in the past. It achieves the opposite effect; he is ignored and becomes hungry.

Baby Steve initially learned that his only option to obtain food was to be quiet. To begin crying for food is not one of his options in his current belief system. He learned that the opposing quiet behavior fulfills his needs. It is his only way to control food. He will remain quiet longer and longer until mother, father, or another adult notices he is hungry and feeds him. When this occurs, it reinforces Steve's belief about being quiet to receive food. Additionally, he associates whatever other behaviors he may be doing at that particular moment of being fed to the attainment of food. The world reinforced his original fundamental belief with a slight modification. He interprets all other behaviors and events as supportive of his fundamental belief that being quiet leads to feeding plus the other slight modifications. The collection of these new beliefs comprise his belief system, or pattern of beliefs about how to satisfy his safety and security need.

Our observations are that, like baby Steve in the example, children continually use these newly formed fundamental beliefs to develop additional patterns that will maintain and assure satisfaction of their five basic needs. These larger patterns then grow and branch from the fundamental beliefs and become the complex belief systems of the child's personality.

People are not, under normal circumstances, consciously aware of their fundamental beliefs because they form at such an early age. In addition to being early learnings, people subconsciously insulate their fundamental beliefs with numerous additional beliefs they collect throughout life to form and support their basic beliefs. This layering of supporting beliefs makes the basic beliefs more remote and inaccessible.

Because they have to repeatedly prove to themselves that they work, people successfully follow their fundamental beliefs. This occurs because subconscious fundamental beliefs filter perceptions and interpretations of sensory information. Fundamental beliefs, then, are antiquated solutions for how to get basic needs satisfied. They are processes that continue to operate and function for their original purposes. This process occurs regardless of whether or not the childhood situation and conflict, which they were initially formed to resolve, is still present.

Fundamental beliefs are closely related to Harry Stack Sullivan's (1953) interpersonal theories of social psychology. Sullivan proposed that our personality is continually in development. Society's influence brings on changes in personal psychology throughout life.

Our model of fundamental beliefs contends that people can change their belief systems after the age of five. The personality is constantly in transition, or development, at all ages of life. In this way, the basic belief framework is similar to Sullivan's. However, this fundamental belief model contends that people complete the basic psychological groundwork by the age of five. After age five, people have varying and increasingly less flexibility for change. We have found that after the age of three and normally by the age of five, all fundamental beliefs are formed. By fundamental beliefs we mean all the foundational beliefs about how children must be to satisfy their basic needs. These fundamental beliefs predetermine the limits of flexibility in psychological development. They direct and confine the amount and type of change society's influence will have in the development of the individual personality.

Sullivan's theory maintains that society is a major shaping force in the development of the individual. On this point we agree. The way society responds to need requests determines, in part, the content of beliefs about need satisfaction. In total, this is how belief systems expand and assimilate additional developmental information that formulates the personality. Therefore, personality is the interrelationship of the self and society by belief system dynamics.

Sullivan proposed that the child is in the *protaxic mode* during the first year of development. He defined this as when a child is unable to distinguish events between time and place. After this, the child progresses into the *parataxic mode.* Sullivan claims this is when children differentiate experiences though they are without logical connection. These two modes are prone to logical misinterpretations of the experiences related. Any conclusion drawn from the child's experience of logical events during these modes of development is potentially incorrect. They are incorrect because of (1) the misunderstanding of the time and place differential, and (2) the misinterpretation about the separations of experienced events. These misinterpretations can lead to limiting or faulty beliefs and belief-system formation. This is especially important for beliefs in which time, space, and their differentials are essential for correct cause-and-effect associations to be made.

As the child begins to use language, according to Sullivan, he enters a new *syntaxic* mode. The syntaxic mode occurs when the child learns to use society's verbal symbols and begins to perceive logical relationships between and among experiences by use of symbols. Well before the syntaxic mode begins, fundamental beliefs are well formed. From our work with clients, we know that fundamental beliefs are formed and set in the subconscious long before the child's verbal and logical skills are learned. For this reason it is easy to begin our belief structural system on faulty or life-limiting basic beliefs. This faulting can happen anytime events are not presented in absolute cause-and-effect timing. They also can happen if the child's environment is not identical to the later adult environment. In actuality, it is more likely that one or the other is occurring at any moment. As the child develops into the verbal/logical syntaxic mode, an important developmental distortion can occur. The previously formed fundamental beliefs significantly influence the child's perceptions of the verbal symbols presented in developmental relationships.

During syntaxic mode development, verbal symbols align by their self-definition with fundamental beliefs. They are perceived and associated by pre-verbal, subconscious symbols of fundamental beliefs. This becomes a predisposition toward biased interpretations.[9] Verbal symbols thereby become meanings with which to relate previously interpreted nonverbal experiences.

Fundamental beliefs are a result of our earliest and most significant efforts to survive organismically, emotionally, and psychologically. As a result, they form at the time we first associate efforts to survive with our experiences of the world and satisfying basic needs. Reciprocally, fundamental beliefs shape developmental perceptions, reactions, and proactions relative to need satisfactions. Basic belief formation begins the second the child is born, if not before.[10] From that moment they influence the perceptions and interpretations of both self and others. By these perceptions and interpretations of the world, the child forms new belief systems. This reciprocal influencing process only allows later beliefs to support, by assimilation, the original belief.

During most of the application of beliefs, people remain consistent with society's and personal requirements. People get what they need, and the cost is what they expect. At other times, beliefs are life-limiting. They are limiting in that people don't get what they need or the trade-off is too costly. When a belief system is life-limiting, people only recognize the negative results of the conflict after the belief system has been followed. Or, they recognize the negative results after the fact. Any psychological conflict is always between a belief system formed from a limiting fundamental belief and current experiences of our world.[11]

Also, fundamental beliefs are similar to and incorporate object relations theory.[12] Object relations theory is a neo-analytic outgrowth of orthodox psychoanalysis. It formulates the principle that people have learned patterns of behavior and emotional reactions. It postulates that people associate their references of these patterns to objects they perceived when they were children. For example, object relations theory states that people have a specific set of emotional reactions when they meet someone who looks, behaves, or sounds similar to their father or mother. The emotions elicited by such meetings are similar to the emotions they initially experienced as a child with their father or mother.

We contend that fundamental beliefs are similar to object relations theory in that people learn responses associated with events or situations in childhood. However, fundamental beliefs are more inclusive. Belief systems can form around any set of events or set of previous beliefs initiated by an event. Therefore, the associating link is not always to an object. The associating link could be a self-determined internal feeling, or as in object relation theory, an outside object that initiates the belief.

Fundamental beliefs also are conceptually inclusive of early learning sets— a term used in cognitive theoretical models of psychotherapy. Early learning-set theory contends people establish sets of beliefs early in childhood from interactions with people in childhood. They establish patterns of learning during these early interactions and apply them to the rest of their life.

The major difference between learning-set theory and the fundamental belief model is that, under all normal circumstances, fundamental beliefs are unknowable by the conscious self. They subconsciously influence perceptions well before people have the opportunity to process them consciously and remain subconscious. Therefore, they are far more difficult to know than those beliefs referred to by the early learning-set theorists. Early learning sets are knowable—people can think about them and cognitively figure out how they formed. With a cognitive process, people can change them by conscious attending. By contrast, basic belief systems are not easily self-knowable. Under normal circumstances, they are not consciously changeable. When they are made conscious by several special processes,[13] they can be replaced by a modified cognitive process.

Fundamental beliefs also are theoretically inclusive of the behavioral theory of operant conditioning. Some basic belief systems are conditionings— programs that people learn as children. However, people perceive and form their fundamental beliefs with the reasoning and logic of an infant's intellect. From these fundamental beliefs, they interpret operant conditioning into belief systems that they process similarly over and over. Each new interpretation draws process references from previous beliefs. We call this *process reasoning*. Childhood reasoning forms beliefs about the relationship of events, however, it is based only on the sequential time of the events. That is, the child assumes that the second event is always caused by the first or preceding event.

By one significant principle, fundamental beliefs differ from behavioral theory. Behavioral theorems postulate that people randomly learn from cause/effect experiences. The difference from the fundamental beliefs is that during belief formation we subconsciously modify choices to match and support subconsciously selected belief systems. The current beliefs limit the range of choices we use to explain and learn from the cause/effect experiences. In this way, fundamental beliefs create a system of parameters, and these belief system parameters restrict the range and variation of responses. Thereby, they limit the learnings we receive from new environmental situations and experiences. Our belief systems, therefore, are a system of parentheses in which we limit options or abilities to satisfy our needs. This occurs because the context of our choices only can be within the realm of parameters established by the belief systems. The action on any of these choices is predetermined only to be permitted within the current belief systems.

Belief system parameters can be observed most easily in younger children where they are implemented in their simpler form. Before jumping to an example, a summary may be helpful to perceive the full impact of belief systems on environmental learning. Fundamental beliefs develop during very early, infant experiences. Once initiating beliefs set the direction, the developing child interprets ensuing events so they continue to support the fundamental beliefs. If the new event does not fit the fundamental beliefs, then the child subconsciously modifies the interpretation to match the fundamental beliefs. The modified interpretation is the result of the previously set belief system parameters.

It is this modified interpretation that assimilates into existing beliefs. If a new event does not fit into preexisting belief, people subconsciously bias their interpretation to match their current belief system. It is because of this biased interpretation, or filtering, that people assimilate new information. Belief systems processing does not accommodate information that is radically different. Newly interpreted perceptions of experiences and experiments of the world routinely support a belief system and never replace it. As a result of this subconscious cognitive process, belief systems change minimally over time, even when new evidence would appear to the outside observer to directly contradict them.

An example of associative causality was observed at a preschool. Three-year-old Muriko was enjoying her play with a small doll when it was suddenly snatched away by her playmate, Samantha. Muriko quickly looked around the room hoping to catch the attention of an adult who would come to her rescue. Her facial expression showed that she was on the verge of crying and ready to use crying just in case an adult was close by. However, no one saw what happened or was close enough for Muriko to get their attention. All the adults were occupied at too great a distance to come to her rescue. After a moment, she acted. She grabbed the doll from Samantha's hand and said, "That's mine." She firmly pushed Samantha away, pulled the doll close to her chest, turned around, and walked away.

In that brief interchange, Muriko attempted to rely on an older belief that an adult would rescue her. When that choice was not available, she acted on what she knew. She knew that the doll was hers. She took it back and protected it from being taken away again. The events were: (1) the doll was taken, (2) she acted to take it back and protect it. A belief system formed; when something is taken, she can act to retrieve it.

As in this example, most sequentially ordered events in a child's life also are logically correct and cause-and-effect ordered. It follows that belief systems formed from such connected events are logically correct and usually life-enhancing. However, there are many times when sequential events are not logically connected or in proper cause-and-effect relationship. Said another way, the second event is not always caused by the first or previous event. For example, at the same preschool as the previous example, the following interaction between three-year-old Jeffery and three-year-old Leana was observed.

Jeffery and Leana were at the finger-painting activity table with Ms. Goldberg, the assistant teacher, overseeing them and five other children. Jeffery and Leana were sharing a small plastic container of yellow paint. At the same moment, both children reached into the paint jar. Because of the container's small size their fingers stuck in it long enough to cause it to be moved to the side of the table. When past the edge of the table, the paint jar slipped off and fell to the floor. The only damage was the splattered paint on the floor and the colorful drippings on each child.

Nevertheless, this incident happened near the end of a very strenuous day for the assistant teacher. Additionally, it is known that Ms. Goldberg was having some distressing personal problems. The assistant overreacted on the assumption that Jeffery and Leana had been fighting over the fingerpaint and their conflict led to the accident. Her reaction on seeing the splattered paint was to scold both children with a loud and gruff voice. She then disciplined them by terminating their finger-painting activity and sent them to the restroom with another assistant to get cleaned.

The sequence of events as perceived from Jeffery's perspective was: (1) sharing the paint container with his friend, (2) paint splattering on the floor and them, and (3) being punished by Ms. Goldberg. Due only to the sequence of events, Jeffery concluded that sharing paint with a friend leads to spilled paint, which results in being punished. It would follow that he will take on a belief that sharing with friends will cause accidents that result in negative consequences.

The above example demonstrates that often beliefs form from sequential events that are logically incorrect with regard to their causal relationship. This single belief can then become life-limiting. Regardless of the actual logical relationship of the events or conditions, the child reasons according to the apparent sequence of concrete events. The child reasons that the first event causes the second event. If there is a third event, then it is caused by the second event. In this example, the second event is the spilled paint. By Jeffery's logic, the spilled paint caused the teacher to discipline them. This conclusion is valid. Adults argue that spilling paint is an unwanted behavior and this belief would benefit the child. That part of the sequence of events is acceptable. It also could be argued that actually the teacher is the cause of the discipline because of her mood. This certainly adds understanding to the disciplinary action. However, this does not affect the outcome processed by the child, for Jeffery was not aware of this factor.

The two events described are spilled paint and discipline. However, this is not an isolated set of events representing reality in Jeffery's experience. This is only one segment of the total set of experiences. When this segment is combined with the total set of events, an entirely different conclusion results. Jeffery's other component to the set of events is that the first event was sharing with a friend. Sharing with a friend led to the second event of the spilled paint. With this segment added, Jeffery's interpretation is that sharing paint with a friend leads to accidents. Jeffery's concluding belief is that sharing with friends is bad. This belief, with further substantiation, likely will lead to a life-limiting belief system as Jeffery grows older and relates to others in an adult environment.

Evidence of an incorrectly formed belief is when a child self-blames for a traumatic event that the child did not cause. Self-blame is apparent when a child performs a socially identified negative behavior before a trauma occurs, although it is logically unrelated. In this context, identified means that the child's behavior is consciously recognized by someone or something in the environment. This occurs either by the child (internally), such as hurt or pain, or by someone significant in the child's environment (externally), such as a parent saying what happened is bad or wrong. In actuality, the child's behavior may not be socially acceptable or logically related to the traumatic event.

Such behavior even can be a positive, socially acceptable behavior that later could be a life-enhancing adult behavior. However, in this child's environment, it is identified as a negative, socially unacceptable behavior. The child only experiences and interprets the sequential relationship of the events, experiencing a socially identified negative behavior followed by an identified negative traumatic event. Because the identified negative behavior is the child's, the child assumes responsibility for the ensuing negative event.

An example of this is the case of Marla S. Marla, a thirty-two-year-old mother, and her six-year-old son, Richie, were referred for psychotherapy by a school counselor. Richie's teacher had become concerned when his class participation suddenly dropped below his previous levels. He was sent to the counselor as a standard procedure in case of child abuse. After an evaluation by the school counselor and a joint meeting with the parents, child abuse was ruled out. However, Richie's lack of participation in the class continued. At this point psychotherapy was recommended and initiated.

After an initial evaluation, psychotherapy was started with Richie and Eugene, his younger brother, using play therapy. During game playing, Richie repeatedly protected Eugene. When questioned about protecting his younger brother, Richie was unable to answer directly; his only comment was that it was his job to protect Eugene. Marla was brought into the session with Richie while Eugene was left to play in the waiting area. An inquiry was made as to whether something had happened recently to Eugene. It turned out that four weeks previously Eugene had been in the hospital overnight for observation of a possible concussion as a result of falling off a swing at home. The accident had occurred while Richie was at school. The parents had been late getting home from the hospital and unable to explain to Richie what had happened to Eugene until the next morning.

The day before the accident the two brothers had been fighting over a toy. During the fight Richie wished Eugene would go away so he could have all the toys to himself. Marla had overheard the fight, reprimanded them both, and separated them. Without his parents' explanation of what had happened to Eugene, it was a long evening for Richie after the accident. It was enough time for Richie to form the self-blaming belief that, his wishing Eugene would go away had caused his accident and the absence. In the child's experience, the wish came true, and he blamed himself for his brother's accident that required the overnight hospital stay.

Therapy was concluded by having the mother talk to Richie. She showed him what had happened to Eugene and took him on a tour of the hospital to explain the reasons for Eugene's stay. After repeated explanations, Richie's self-blame began to diminish.

Another case example of a limiting belief, taken on because of sequential linking or associative causality, is that of five-year-old Johnny. Johnny blames himself for the divorce of his parents. A few days before his father left, Johnny attempted to protect his mother, during a fight with her husband, by telling his father to go away. During the argument, many of the father's accusations were made directly to Johnny. A short time after the fight, the husband left home. His leaving was followed by a competitive divorce. Johnny linked the sequence of these events and formed it into a belief that he had caused the divorce. He believed he was responsible for the separation from and subsequent loss of his father, resulting in Johnny's self-blaming. A belief began that caring about people causes bad things to happen to them. The idea of being responsible for tragedies lowered what little self-esteem he had accumulated. Self-blame results in decreased self-confidence, less willingness to test the world, and lowered self-esteem.

It is evident that the classical and operant conditioning principles of behaviorism are fully operational in child development, however, there is another factor. This factor is the predisposition caused by the previously operational belief systems. The subconscious process of predisposition overrides the conclusive learnings brought about by operant and classical conditioning.

Biased Interpretations

Consistently and subconsciously, people interpret their experiences to prove their belief systems are correct. They assign the uncomfortable results of life-limiting beliefs to people or events they claim are outside their control. The comfortable results of life-enhancing beliefs are usually disclaimed as luck, fate, or deservedness. Seldom are the results realized as the consequences of personal belief systems either constructed or designed. People rarely consider themselves responsible for the comfortable events and experiences of their lives. This is because fundamental beliefs and their related belief systems bias their interpretations and filter their perceptions.[14]

Adults' perceptions of reality are inaccurate because of the distortions initiated by the parental distortions of adults' childhood environment. We concur with the widely accepted belief in developmental psychology that children's beliefs and cognitions are qualitatively more accurate than those of adults. However, though children have more accurate perceptions, their perceptions often are confined within a parentally controlled environment, which is equally as often a very distorted representation of the child's future adult world. An analogy is that of a person who has 20/20 vision but looks through pockmarked and broken glasses and still proclaims what is seen is an accurate perception.

People interpret their sensory information and relationship interactions according to their previous experiences, observations, and belief systems. Subsequently, when they logically process prefiltered information, this information supports their basic beliefs. This subconscious process, or filtering of experiences, creates biased interpretations that act to shield existing belief systems from changing. Events appear or are interpreted as supporting experiences that in turn create supporting beliefs, reinforcing the original belief systems. Seemingly, they give the original beliefs validity by repeated confirmation, making them less accessible for evaluation or criticism through typical conscious awareness.

Instead of a life-enhancing belief system, the limited belief systems create new limited perceptions. Under normal circumstances, people are unaware of their life-limiting beliefs.[15] Long past childhood, when life-limiting beliefs initially are learned, limiting beliefs continue to provide ways to meet the original needs of childhood situations. Limiting beliefs often create situations of contradiction. They can create conflicts between other beliefs assigned to satisfy other needs or can sacrifice satisfaction of other basic needs. These contradictions result in the loss of physical and emotional freedoms and psychological or physical well-being. Usually, people only sense that something does not fit—*not fitting* shows up as symptoms.

For example, teenage client Elizabeth dresses in unusual clothes to demonstrate autonomy from her parents and other authority figures. She joins a peer group of similar unusual dressers to satisfy her need to belong. Her unusual dressing is with the conscious intent of rebellious counter-dependency[16] from her parents. She has learned that wearing unusual clothes satisfies a need to be separate from her parents. The peer group is an appropriate method to satisfy this need. However, the broader range of satisfying her need is blocked by the adult criticism and ostracization from the remainder of her world.

She *knows* she is wearing the right clothes to gain autonomy from her parents because her childhood world of her dysfunctional family created this belief. Her belief system reasons that the parent world equals the adult world she now lives in, however, they are different worlds. Herein is the error of her belief system. She will continue to follow her belief system and socially isolate herself in the accepting peer group because of this error. She will sacrifice her need to belong to the world outside the peer group and seek identification with an ever-decreasing peer group as it ages. Her life-limiting belief system is that she *knows* the way to satisfy her need for autonomy is to dress unusually. As she must increasingly adapt to an adult world, this life-limiting belief creates conflict between the basic needs of autonomy and belonging. However, the outwardly demonstrated symptoms are rejection and depression. The beliefs that were life-enhancing in the dysfunctional family are becoming life-limiting in her adult world.

Developmentally, people form their beliefs by feedback from parents or substitute authority figures. When their perception of the world is inaccurate, their feedback is equally inaccurate. They will either get their needs met ineffectively, or they will meet them by a greater sacrifice elsewhere. This often is referred to as *symptom substitution*. Either way, their basic needs are not fulfilled. They may experience some temporary satisfaction, but the long-term effect is life-limiting. Eventually, it will create sacrifices in other equally essential areas of need.

When dissatisfaction occurs, people begin to experience their fundamental beliefs as *costing too much*. They begin to complain that the world is unfair. Their only conscious awareness is that something is wrong with their world either internally or externally. They are unable to realize that their limiting beliefs currently create biased interpretations that support previously limiting beliefs. In some cases, adults will resort to self-blame; they tell themselves they are doing something wrong, while unaware of the source. They continue fruitlessly to blame themselves, others, and the world. Adults usually focus on the symptoms of their belief systems, regardless of whether they are positive or negative. They seldom realize that symptoms are the result of following childhood beliefs that were necessary at the time, but do not apply in adulthood.

When people follow limited beliefs, they perceive their needs as not met. For example, when adults follow a limiting belief that causes them to get attention inappropriately, they eventually experience loneliness from the lack of attention. This is much like the previous example of client Elizabeth. They will not be aware that their ineffective and inefficient actions are direct results of a limiting belief.

Fortunately, there are many methods by which people can access and modify their limiting beliefs and belief systems. Our experience suggests that the most effective methods increase awareness of people's subconscious belief systems by use of some form of trance-hypnosis or variant altered states of consciousness.[17]

As an interim summary, fundamental beliefs predispose or bias the infant to an interpretation of experiential feedback. This biased interpretation or predisposition directly influences the subsequent belief system formation. Preexisting belief systems create biased or modified interpretations of all following experiences as supportive. Subsequently, belief predisposition reinforces and strengthens the basic belief. This process only allows prefiltered information to be used for belief system formation. If the infant's world is an accurate representation of adult reality, which it often is not, then life-enhancing belief systems will form.

The example here illustrates the severity to which predispositional belief systems can influence development and create an adult with a personality disorder. The juvenile court system referred Alan K. for psychotherapy as part of a treatment plan required to reunite him with his wife and three children. Alan's pending case, based on a police report, alleged he had physically abused his wife as well as physically and emotionally abused his children. Pending the outcome of the first three psychotherapy sessions, the court allowed him two, one-hour supervised visitations with his children per week. According to the court restraining order, he was ordered to move out of the home and was restricted from contact with his wife.

According to the court report by the children's social worker, the wife claimed Alan often drank until he became unconscious and on occasion used cocaine in the form of "crack." However, no evidence of cocaine was found by the police at the time of their intervention. The police reported Alan as legally intoxicated, threatening them, and combative when arrested. He spent one day in detention. The charges for threatening the police and resisting arrest were later dropped.

The first psychotherapy session occurred the week following the arraignment. The court ordered Alan to seek individual psychotherapy, attend Alcoholics Anonymous (AA) meetings, and join a local group for abuse perpetrators. These conditions were required before he could gain reunification rights with his wife and children. During the first session, a psychosocial history and a brief synopsis of the preceding events were recorded. Alan was resistant and angry. An appointment for a Minnesota Multiphasic Personality Inventory (MMPI) and Social Skills Inventory (SSI) was scheduled for the following week.

The psychosocial evaluation reported a long family history of physical and emotional abuse, parental alcoholism, and a mother physically abused by his stepfather. Although Alan displayed many symptoms of illicit drug abuse, he claimed he did not use drugs on a regular basis. Significant indicators of the MMPI were prominent in the supplemental content scales. Highest scores were in Marital Distress, Addiction Potential and Admission, Dominance, Authority Problems, and Social Alienation. Significantly low scores were in Social Responsibility, Over-controlled Hostility, and Ego Strength. The SSI indicated low Social and Emotional Expressivity and low Social and Emotional Sensitivity.

During the second psychotherapy session, Alan demonstrated the same level of anger as at the first session though rigidly in control. He directed blame to nearly everyone with whom he had come in contact since the beginning of the reported abuse. He blamed the neighbors for not minding their own business and calling the police. He blamed the police for not letting him settle the disagreement with his wife and for overreacting to his threats to leave him alone. He blamed his wife for not being a good wife and mother, giving a long list of her behaviors—left dirty dishes and clothes, didn't dress herself up enough for him, talked back too much, didn't fix the foods he liked, seldom had enough beer in the refrigerator for him, and so on. He particularly blamed the social worker, lawyers, and judge for not understanding him and justified his actions by stating how hard he tried to make his marriage work.

Twenty minutes into this second session, Alan's pattern repeated enough times that externalization became clear—everything always happened to Alan. He did not experience the world as resulting from self-directed actions, and had no concept that he was a participant in how his world related to him. After making Alan aware of his pattern, the session's focus turned to his childhood. Again, Alan's predominant pattern emerged. When Alan was one year old, his father had left home. He later lived in a family with an abusive mother and stepfather. Abuse began with the earliest time he could remember misbehaving. He related experiencing a radically emphasized punishment for a minor misbehavior, which he could no longer remember.

Alan remembered several more instances of severe punishment without any memory of the precipating behavior. Either his behavior was not pointed out to him or the misbehavior was minor compared to the severity of the punishment. It became evident to Alan that he was raised in an environment where the parents overreacted whenever their expectations were unmet. Alan learned that a small amount of inappropriate behavior leads to a disproportionally large amount of punishment. After similar repetitive events, a belief system formed about his world.

Children growing up in a healthy environment learn to expect that when they do something worse than before, they receive a more severe punishment. However, in Alan's family, the parent delivered equally severe amounts of punishment every time. They consistently reacted with the same degree of overemphasis. Alan quickly learned that any degree of disapproved behavior elicited the same amount of punishment. Alan formed a belief system that trying to meet his parents' expectations didn't matter. Regardless of what he did, he received equal amounts of punishment.

As a child, Alan's problem in his environment was that he did not receive accurate feedback. He was denied the opportunity to evaluate expected behavior by the severity of the punishment. He lacked ways to interpret appropriate and inappropriate behavior. For example, he experienced the same amount of punishment for throwing his blocks as he did for punching his sister. Therefore, hitting his sister was no worse than throwing blocks when he was angry. As a child, he likely increased bad behavior because he believed he would get the same amount of punishment regardless of social expectations. As he grew up, he increasingly chose behaviors that benefitted him the most, for he knew from experience that he would receive the same consequences regardless of the severity of what he did.

As he grew into adulthood, he learned to modify the other factor in his belief system. He learned to reinterpret bad behavior. He judged his own behavior as acceptable. Or, he learned not to judge his behavior, but rather judge the person from whom he received the consequences. Both dysfunctional methods result from the initial, ineffective, parental feedback creating a life-limiting belief. Precisely these patterns have been found in every Antisocial Personality Disorder we have encountered while practicing as psychotherapists.

In summary, people judge the results of their experiences in the world by application of their previously instilled belief systems. In the above case example of Alan, as he began to relate to the larger adult world outside his parents' controlled environment, he judged his behavior and the feedback ineffectively and inefficiently. As an adult, Alan did not judge his own behavior by the amount and quality of feedback from his adult environment. Instead, he judged the person or object who delivered the feedback by the amount of punishment delivered. His belief system was that punishment equals the punishing object, rather than what he did to elicit it. He confused the act with the object. By his own belief system, punishment became outside his realm of control. For him it was an act of which he was a victim. Without being responsible for its cause, there was no way to stop, modify, or prevent it. His belief system led to feelings that he was not in control of his world and its consequences. To Alan, the world was indeed unjust.

The epilogue to the above case of Alan was that after ten months of weekly psychotherapy sessions, he was able to replace parts of his original belief system with life-enhancing beliefs. The new belief system allowed him to more accurately judge the impact of his actions and thereby control his behavior. His new-found self-responsibility led to increased self-esteem and self-confidence. After numerous "baby steps" of experimenting with this new belief system, he learned that he could effectively create a more fulfilling family and social environment for himself. He has not returned to his wife. However, he has shared custody of his children and maintains a workable agreement with his ex-wife for the children's future development. He has had several rewarding relationships. Finally, he claims that he now has the best job he has ever held.

It is possible to modify or replace life-limiting beliefs with life-enhancing beliefs. The disengagement process is:

- Discover the life-limiting beliefs by tracking the reason for the symptoms
- Reassess the accuracy of the interpretation of experiences
- Construct new life-enhancing beliefs from these more accurate interpretations

The life-enhancing goal is to satisfy basic needs in the most direct manner allowable within the adult environment without sacrificing any other needs. The first step is discovering the life-limiting beliefs. Appendix B contains scripts to help with this step. Second is to disengage personal biases and reassess the accuracy of the interpretation of experiences. Begin the process of disengagement and reassessment by examining the interpretations of experiences in terms of perceptual attitudes.

Notes

1. *Webster's New Collegiate Dictionary* defines *relationship* as the state or character of being related; showing or having established a logical or casual connection between; or to have meaningful social relation with, as in the state of being mutually or reciprocally interested (as in social or commercial matters).
2. See chapter 4 for a further explanation of relationship dynamics.
3. See chapter 7 for further explanation of the limits of psychotherapeutic involvement.
4. *Life-limiting* is defined here as a reduction of the possibilities of optimal organismic health, emotional, and psychological fulfillment.
5. Further discussion of how these complex systems develop can be found later in this chapter.
6. Only a cursory rendition of each model is provided. For a more in-depth discussion of their philosophies, please research their individual works.
7. Dilts then claims as aesthetic imprint, defined as the need to know the nature of beauty and pleasure. This positions as an overall belief on a level above our five basic needs. We classify these positions as a belief system.
8. Predispositioning will be discussed later in this chapter.
9. Predispositions and biased interpretations are discussed further later in this chapter.
10. We have absolutely no scientific evidence to support this claim. However, actual beliefs and experiences from our clients are that basic belief formation often occurs prenatally.
11. Although the question of congruency and incongruency in self-perception and beliefs are distinctly Rogerian concepts, this polarity is included in belief system

theory. However, the polarity is insignificant to the overall individual's experience of the environment and the beliefs formed of its perception.

12. Object relations theory developed from Freud's ideas of the interaction of object with subject, and five additional principle theorists. One was M. Klein's theory of ego and its relation to internal, whole, or part objects. Another was W. Fairbairn's theory of the object-seeking goals of early ego development. For more detail, refer to his article (Fairbairn, 1963).

13. See Appendix B for one method to accomplish investigation and belief modification.

14. See chapter 3 on perceptual attitudes.

15. See Appendix B for Scripts on how to discover and modify belief systems.

16. See chapter 6 for more about counter-dependency.

17. Appendix B summarizes a method we have found useful to change and investigate belief systems. It includes those that are life-limiting as well as those that are life-enhancing.

References

Bandura, A. (1969). *Principles of behavior modification*. New York: Holt, Rinehart, and Winston.

Carlsen, M. B. (1988). *Meaning-making therapeutic processes in adult development*. New York: W. W. Norton.

Dilts, R. (1990). *Changing belief systems with NLP*. Cupertino, CA: Meta.

Fairbairn, W. (1963). Synopsis of the object relations theory of the personality. *International Journal of Psychoanalysis, 44,* 224–225.

Frankl, V. (1978). *The unheard cry for meaning*. New York: Simon & Schuster.

Frankl, V. (1985). *Man's search for meaning*. New York: Washington Square Press.

Freud, S. (1927). *The ego and the id*. London: Hogarth Press.

Fromm, E. (1955). *The sane society*. New York: Rinehart.

Fromm, E. (1947). *Man for himself*. New York: Rinehart.

Keleman, S. (1982). *Somatic reality*. Berkeley: Center Press.

Kübler-Ross, E. (1969). *On death and dying*. New York: Collier.

Maslow, A. (1968). *Toward a psychology of being* (rev. ed.). New York: Van Nostrand Reinhold.

May, R. (1967). *Man's search for himself*. New York: Signet.

May, R. (1974). *Love and will*. New York: Dell.

Rank, O. (1929). *The trauma of birth*. New York: Harcourt Brace.

Sullivan, H. S. (1953). *Interpersonal theory of psychiatry*. New York: W. W. Norton.

3

Selecting
Perceptual
Attitudes

Psychotherapists perceive their clients with different attitudes. These perceptual attitudes reflect their worldview and do not always synchronize with that of their clients. Although this statement may sound obvious, observations show that the ramifications of this reality are more obscure and critical than psychotherapists generally acknowledge—each client calls forth a distinct perception and attitude from each psychotherapist. Even when psychotherapists nearly agree on a diagnosis, observation shows they often disagree on their perception of a client's experiences. Similarly obvious, and complicating the perceptual attitude of psychotherapists, clients embrace their own special circumstances and demand unique attention. This is like saying that different people react differently to different people.

Without disengaging personal belief systems, some psychotherapists may be skeptical or cautious of their perceptual attitudes. They may even be afraid that the perceptual attitude they implement in certain cases is influenced by a projective, if not pathological, contamination as a result of believed deficits in their own personalities. Such critically assumed deficits are also a reflection of personal and clinical perceptual attitudes. Like everyone else, it is easier for psychotherapists to acknowledge the etiological roots of their personal and clinical limitations and then justify them than to take the responsibility to expand possibilities.

Our observation is that an unusual phenomenon occurs in this special circumstance. These psychotherapists would prefer to acknowledge their

personal neurotic or personality disorder tendencies than to take the responsibility for expanding their psychotherapeutic effectiveness. By interpreting these
tendencies as personal deficits, they can avoid increased responsibility for
expanding beyond them in their clinical practice. Considering perceptual attitudes, psychotherapeutic effectiveness can be expanded by either choosing to
limit one's expertise with a predetermined perceptual attitude or by learning
and taking advantage of alternative perceptual attitudes.

Other psychotherapists are all too sure they have disengaged their personal
biases and beliefs and often mistakenly think they are clear about the perceptual
attitudes they implement. Of course, this attitude is a belief in itself and reflects
both their personal and clinical perceptual attitudes. Even assuming that most
psychotherapists disengage personal and limiting belief systems as well as
could be expected, perceptual attitudes in clinical practice frequently remain
unclear.

Disengaging beliefs as a person, and then additionally applying these
concepts as a psychotherapist, is similar to personal development and intimate
relationships. After attaining a level of assumed comfort as a single person,
people often then apply their self-development in an intimate relationship.
Including another person magnifies the results and either verifies or refutes the
originating personal hypotheses or doctrines.

Psychotherapeutic practice is a magnified testing ground for the expertise
that increases with practice. When psychotherapists believe they have disengaged and clarified their own beliefs, they have the intentional opportunity of
checking and then verifying their perceptual attitudes with their clients. Zen
masters and saints not withstanding, psychotherapy is, indeed, one of the
pinnacles of culturally endorsed professions. Mentors actually are paid by their
client-apprentices not only to enhance their art and science but to evolve their
self-development. Many not only take advantage of the hospitable invitation
but choose the career of psychotherapy for precisely this reason. Of course,
others may not use this privileged opportunity; they may choose to cultivate
professionally what we consider an exploitative advantage.

Some psychotherapists assume their variant perceptions and attitudes are
an outgrowth of model adherence. They sometimes believe that the perceptual
attitude they use is the only and absolutely correct one. When psychotherapists
act as if their personal perceptual attitudes were the only accurate way to
evaluate and heal patients, they close opportunities to alternative perceptions
that could enhance client health. In these instances, the individual psychotherapist's power of healing, and the client's ability to get well, is diminished by a
reductionistic perception and the virtuous attitude of the psychotherapist.

Other psychotherapists assume their variant perceptions and attitudes are
determined by their specific clients' diagnoses and conflicts. When psychotherapists believe that the special circumstances of their clients determine their
perceptual attitudes toward treatment, they allow outside circumstances to

determine rather than influence their treatment. Outside circumstances include treating an identifiable disease or conflict rather than the patient. In this scenario, the individual psychotherapist's power of healing and the client's ability to get well is diminished by the psychotherapist's obdurate perception and naive attitude.

Of course, a third possibility is a vague and undefinable combination of these two beliefs. Such unclear thinking of either perceptions or attitudes does not provide an adequate understanding of the perceptual attitudes with which psychotherapists already perceive the life-enhancement, conflicts, and needs of their clients. Nor does it offer alternative, self-determined ways of attending to their client's special circumstances. Our observation is that most psychotherapists do not feel, think, or believe they are adrift within either grouping above. Most psychotherapists would prefer to believe that the perceptual attitude they use is expansive—this is precisely the problem. It is also because of our particular concern that we address this issue and clarify known and alternative perceptual attitudes. These perceptual attitudes are applicable to people in general, and more importantly to psychotherapeutic practice in particular.

Perceptions

Perceptions, as we know, are the cognitive way in which all people process and interpret incoming information through the five organismic sensations—sight, sound, smell, touch, and taste. These sensations are interpreted as the respective perceptions of visual, auditory, olfactory, kinesthetic, and gustatory experience. There is a sixth sense, scientifically and commonly called *extrasensory perception*; it is unusual in that it is not identified or associated with an observable physical organ. Nonetheless, evidence of this sixth sense is well-documented and adequately substantiated (Targ and Harary, 1984; U.S. House of Representatives, 1981; Schlitz, and Gruber, 1981; Tart, Puthoff, and Targ, 1979; Tart, 1975).[1]

The German word for the entirety of a perception is a *Gestalt*. The *emergent Gestalt* is the *foreground*. The foreground is whatever specific sensation you are attending to at the moment, and it includes those parts or units of perception that become emergent and immediately are perceived. The *background* remains obscure and indistinct during the occurrence of focused perception and provides the larger context within which the foreground can emerge.

Gestalt means the whole is more than the sum of the parts. The perceived Gestalt of a tree includes the trunk, branches, spaces in between, and the relationship among them. The Gestalt also includes the relationship between our perception and the perceived—the entire perceptual attitude and experience. Focusing on the foreground to the exclusion of the larger background context can lead to mistaken conclusions. The following psychotherapeutic example may be useful.

Rick L. was admitted by the Federal Bureau of Investigation (FBI) to the emergency outpatient clinic of the Naval Hospital, Bethesda, Maryland, early one Saturday morning in the late 1970s. Rick claimed he was a Secret Service agent working undercover in Russia for the Central Intelligence Agency (CIA). All evidence confirmed that he indeed had been in Russia and somehow had infiltrated the headquarters in Moscow. As a result, Rick had been captured by the Russian military authorities and released to the U. S. government.

Moreover, Rick claimed he had been ordered to microfilm designated confidential documents and that his life was in jeopardy since both the CIA and the FBI would not acknowledge his existence. Exhibiting delusions of grandeur, Rick appeared paranoid and intermittently exhibited tangential, loose associations. He was determined to have a thought disorder. After a thorough evaluation by the attending psychiatrist, Rick was given a tentative diagnosis of paranoid schizophrenia and admitted to the inpatient service, pending further evaluation.

Myopically, the admitting psychiatrist and attending staff continued to view Rick with the original diagnostic perception. Only one attending, novice psychiatric resident on the ward disagreed. After repeated attempts to convince his supervisors that Rick might be telling the truth, higher level attempts were made to find any extenuating circumstances. Six weeks later, with the help of various political persuasions, confirming data was sent by the State Department. The information revealed Rick was, indeed, an undercover agent who had tried and failed to microfilm classified information for the CIA. Every detail he had mentioned on initial admission was accurate. Eventually, he was released to the protective custody of governmental authorities.

Focusing on the background at the exclusion of the emergent and more obvious foreground also can lead to misleading and mistaken conclusions. For example, Robert B. was brought by a female friend to a private clinic specializing in holistic healing on the California coast. Robert's girlfriend had lived in an ecologically oriented commune on the East Coast with Buckminster Fuller where drugs were forbidden. This was a private clinic, and Robert was evaluated by a young staff clinical psychologist, Dr. Rashna, who was sympathetic to transpersonal and mystical orientations.

Robert held a Bachelor of Science degree in physics from a prestigious Ivy League university on the East Coast. His father was on the board of directors of a large corporation. Being from a family of considerable status and means, Robert had attended private secondary schools and was pressured by his family to succeed. While he respected both his mother and father, his decompensation occurred at the time of common value rebellion in the early sixties.

Robert was dismayed with the upper-class values of his upbringing. He rejected his father's success as a way to self-realization.

Following graduation, Robert traveled to an ashram in India to study yoga and mysticism. There he became an adept student of yoga. After two years, the rights of teacher were conferred on him by his mystical mentor. Returning to the West Coast of the United States, he became involved in hallucinogenic drugs, specifically mescaline, LSD, and psilocybin—the synthetic derivative of magic mushrooms, reportedly for experimental purposes and to extend his mystical studies.

In the evaluation, the girlfriend reported Robert had been complaining his "powers were becoming out of control." On questioning by the clinical psychologist, Robert quite rationally agreed. He reported that during his meditations in full lotus position, he could not help but view his neighbors' activities through the walls, and that sometimes his physical body, without intent, dematerialized and moved through the walls for mere observation. He also was concerned that "the negative vibrations of their karma might be entering his domain" because he was not invited. Irrational and disconcerted about the state of his mental well-being, he was upset about the emotional frustration this unexpected lack of control was creating.

An adept student of yoga himself, Dr. Rashna was sympathetic to Robert's circumstances; he viewed Robert's difficulties as a *spiritual emergency*. In a more conventional framework, he wondered whether Robert's descriptions might be further limiting and endangering him. From a developmentally conventional perspective, Robert was clearly delusional. However, in the consideration of a larger background perspective, Robert was spiritually elevated and was encompassing the evolutionary costs of transcending beyond an ego-determined and personally exclusive orientation.

Knowing that Dr. Chan did not know him well, and that it was a professional risk, Dr. Rashna nevertheless decided to seek consultation from Dr. Chan. Cautiously, he introduced himself in his initial remarks on the phone by giving a summary of his credentials and training, which were extraordinarily impressive. Dr. Rashna told Dr. Chan he was consulting him because he had heard he was both a reputable, conventional psychotherapist, and sympathetic and knowledgeable in mystical traditions.

Dr. Rashna presented Robert's special case and his valuative dilemma, acknowledging that his professional opinion favored substantiating Robert's clairvoyant powers. His evidence was that a variety of these paranormal and unusual events occur when one is on a mystical path. They do not necessarily represent ordinary delusions or craziness that requires alarming intervention. His yielding consideration was that these paranormal events would pass and he didn't think Robert should be subjected to the unsympathetic and traditional incarceration of a psychiatric inpatient hospitalization. Then, he asked for Dr.

Chan's professional opinion. The following is a summary of the phone conversation that occurred.

DR. CHAN: I think that you are missing the obvious in favor of the larger picture that represents conventional reality rather than the mystical reality you and I both believe in.

DR. RASHNA: This is true and why I am calling you, but I don't understand what you are specifically saying.

DR. CHAN: I am saying that Robert has an ethically respectable delusion but a current delusion nonetheless.

DR. RASHNA: How do you arrive at this conclusion from the information I have given you?

DR. CHAN: First, I believe you may be diminishing Robert's recent drug abuse for an interpretation of hallucinogenic experimentation.

DR. RASHNA: How do you know his usage of hallucinogenic experiences is drug abuse related rather than experimental?

DR. CHAN: I don't know the intent of his use of hallucinogenic drugs. All I know, from what you have said, is that his ingestion of mescaline and LSD are, more likely than not, contributory to what I am hearing as a clear delusion.

DR. RASHNA: How do you know it is a delusion rather than a legitimate mystical experience?

DR. CHAN: I don't know his experiences and neither do you. We both know he is complaining, if not directly then obliquely, through his girlfriend or he would not have been willing to visit your office. Additionally, he complained about losing control of the mystical experiences he maintains he is having.

DR. RASHNA: Then, by the way you say this, you don't believe him.

DR. CHAN: Yes! I do believe him. From all that you have said, I believe he is accurately representing his experiences.

DR. RASHNA: Okay, but if this is true, is it not possible that these experiences are a result of his advanced metaphysical training? Do you not agree?

DR. CHAN: No! Not when he complains. According to your report, Robert complained his powers were becoming out of control. He complained that during his meditations his physical body involuntarily dematerialized, and he was receiving unwanted vibrations.

DR. RASHNA: Yes. However, these kinds of occurrences often accompany people dedicated to a spiritual path and mystical awareness.

DR. CHAN: What is your point?

DR. RASHNA: My point is that these delusional experiences represent a transformational development rather than indicating conventional pathology.

DR. CHAN: I understand your sympathetic concerns. However, the problem here is that neither Robert, you, nor I know whether his delusions and complaints of being out of control are temporary intrusions or whether they indicate a larger departure. This larger departure could be away from either ordinary reality or even a separate reality.

DR. RASHNA: What do you mean when you say they might even be a departure from separate reality?

DR. CHAN: I mean that within cross-cultural and transpersonal mystical orientations, and similar to ordinary reality, there are rules for being on a spiritual path or being wayward. These rules occur regardless of culture, tribe, or stylized spirituality. This is how a medicine man knows whether an apprentice is in line or not. It is also how a medicine man can discuss matters of importance with a Zen master if it becomes necessary. In Robert's particular case, he is breaking the rules of even unordinary reality. In this case, I think we need to attend to the obvious.

DR. RASHNA: How so?

DR. CHAN: First, clairvoyance occurs either intentionally or unintentionally. When it occurs unintentionally, it is more suggestive that his delusions are not in the service of either his ordinary personal ego or supportive of his attempts to transform beyond his self-desires. Second, regardless of paranormal abilities, people rarely dematerialize physically to "go through walls." Assuming *out-of-body* travel occurs, it occurs with the ethereal body, not the physical body itself. Therefore, his metaphor shows he is breaking both ordinary and unordinary rules. Third, negative karma, within both Hindu, Buddist, and yogic traditions, is a result of the owner and does not transfer to others. This misperception on the part of Robert is another sign that his delusions are neither self nor beyond-self serving.

DR. RASHNA: I understand. How would you suggest I proceed?

DR. CHAN: I don't know what you should do, nor do I know what Robert should do. If Robert were my client, I would proceed by telling him the results of our conversation and then ask him for his preferences for treatment.

DR. RASHNA: Thank you. I very much appreciate your feedback. I will take our conversation into serious consideration and likely proceed accordingly.

DR. CHAN: This has been a valuable conversation for me as well. Please call me in the future if you wish further consultation on this case or similar others.

Especially important in the two examples above is that perceptual attitudes always reflect an individual's interpretative experience about themselves. Our perceptual attitude remains a point of reference for understanding the information we receive from our world. All people apply their personal perceptual attitudes to others. After all, this is the only way people can try to make sense of their world. In the last example, quite obviously, Robert's perceptual attitude is a reflection of Robert. Almost as obvious, Dr. Rashna's perceptual attitude is about Dr. Rashna, not Robert. Reasonably obscure, Dr. Chan's perceptual attitude is a reflection of Dr. Chan, not Dr. Rashna or Robert. Regardless of psychotherapeutic knowledge, perceptions are always a personal interpretation of the world based on personal experiences. That is, psychotherapists apply their perceptual attitudes first to themselves. Later, they apply them to their clients.

When psychotherapists are unaware of their personal perceptual attitude, obviously the application will be applied automatically. The primary disadvantage of unaware application is that it may not match the client's perceptual attitude and thereby decrease effective psychotherapy. If the perception of the psychotherapist does match that of the client, it is an accidental, unplanned treatment. Also, if psychotherapists are unaware of their own perceptual attitudes, they believe their perceptual attitudes are the only valid causal interpretations of experience.

Perceptually, people experience either a foreground or a background. For example, when people view the branches of a tree or the spaces in between them, it is highly unusual for them to see both the foreground (branches) and background (spaces in between) at exactly the same time with a separate identification and understanding of each part (Kohler, 1947). Just as it is highly unusual for people to attend to both the perceptual foreground and background simultaneously, it is unusual for anyone to attend to variant attitudes.

Attitudes

We are stipulating *attitude* to mean a predetermined position or belief originated for a specific purpose, whether currently conscious or unconscious. Attitudes that are made by stereotypes often are called *prejudices*. Such attitudes are prejudicial in the sense that the believed interpretation is determined by unevaluated sentiments or uninformed persuasions. Attitudes that are made up of either scientific fact or carefully evaluated personal experiences often are called *informed opinions*. All personal development and human evolution of consciousness demands continuous, prudent evaluation. For professional psychotherapists to be effective, they need to delineate attitudes so they can implement them for the life-enhancing benefit of themselves and thereby their clients.

Cognitively, it is impossible to attend to two or more conflicting attitudes in consciousness simultaneously. The usual pattern is to shift between or among dissonant beliefs in an attempt to resolve a conflict. This occurrence is similar to Festinger's theory of *cognitive dissonance* (Festinger, 1957). Festinger described cognitive dissonance as an incongruence between beliefs and behavior. Briefly, his solution for resolution was either to change incongruent beliefs to match desired behavior or change behavior such that it is consistent with desired beliefs.

Our interpretation is that behavior also represents a belief that is either congruent and compatible with other beliefs or incongruent and incompatible. Therefore, we interpret cognitive dissonance to reflect an incongruence between incompatible beliefs. More specifically, this incongruence reflects disparaging methods to satisfy different basic needs. Another way of saying this is that in satisfying one basic need, the satisfaction of at least one other basic need is met by a life-limiting solution.

For example, if John Q. wants to maintain the quality of his marriage and have an affair with his secretary, there is usually a conflict of interests. Festinger would say that his beliefs about his marriage conflict with his flirtatious behavior with his secretary. John Q. could resolve the cognitive dissonance by changing the beliefs about his marriage, which might require open discussion or a divorce, such that his marital beliefs coordinate with his behavior in pursuing a relationship with the secretary. Or, John Q. could resolve his conflict by changing his behavior toward his secretary such that it is congruent with his initial beliefs of fidelity within a marriage.

Our interpretation of this example is different but with similar results. To our way of thinking, the primary conflict of attitude is not John's behavior, but his belief that the wishful affair is not morally acceptable. John Q. holds two incongruent and incompatible beliefs. One belief is about his moral issues of personal integrity and fidelity within the relationship with his wife—this belief satisfies his need for belonging. Here, his wife is the object of his belonging need. Second, John Q. believes he is approaching a mid-life crisis (evidenced, of course, by buying a flame red Porsche) and should be able to do anything he wants, with whomever he wants, particularly since he has earned it. This belief of John Q. satisfies his need for autonomy. Here, his secretary is the object of his autonomy need.

Obviously, the way John Q. is attempting to satisfy these two attitudes now is both incongruent and not working. The way John Q. has his attitudinal beliefs arranged, he cannot satisfy both basic needs in this situation and be morally respectable. It is likely John Q. believes that to satisfy one need, he must give up the other. His interpretation is probably that either he meets his need to belong at the cost of autonomy, or he becomes autonomous at the expense of failing to satisfy his belonging need.

Not so obvious, particularly to John Q., is that basic needs are not incompatible. Indeed, the reason these five needs are basic is that all five are required for human development and the evolution of the species. What becomes incongruent are our beliefs through the life cycle of how to satisfy these needs. John Q.'s beliefs about satisfying them, and the incompatible methods he is using to satisfy both of them, compromise one at the expense of the other. His belief system is therefore life-limiting.

Our perceptual attitude would suggest the following resolution—he must find a compatible means of satisfying his basic needs that by definition is not in conflict. John Q. needs to focus on his basic needs and not his temporary desires. First, he needs to realize that while satisfying his autonomy need to be rebellious, it does not need to be morally rebellious. Second, he needs to prove to himself that this new attitude is true. While there might be a multiplicity of possible solutions, we are choosing two that represent common situations in our experience.

John Q. could divorce his wife and respectably marry his secretary. In this scenario, he would transfer his belonging need from his current wife to his secretary and ensure its fulfillment by marrying her. His autonomy need for rebellion would be temporarily satisfied by divorcing his wife. He could justify his rebellion, in the sense of being morally respectable, by marrying the secretary. The immediate difficulty with this choice is that he has not recreated a new solution for satisfying his autonomy need; he has not disassociated rebellion from moral discrepancy. That is, the most frequent occurrence is that, with time, he will again believe his autonomy need is not being satisfied because he believes autonomy means *moral* rebellion. He will likely need to act out again to prove to himself that he is autonomous. This method will work, but only for temporary satisfaction as it did before. For this choice to work completely, John Q. would need to: (1) redefine autonomy such that it does not include rebellion—a tough task, or (2) satisfy autonomy by being rebellious in a way that does not compromise his moral integrity.

The other solution for John Q. is to find a way of satisfying his autonomy need by being rebellious in a way that is morally satisfying to himself. For example, he could make love to his wife on the dining room table or in Times Square. In this scenario, his belonging need remains intact and satisfied. Additionally, he could do what he considers rebellious with his wife and still maintain his moral respectability. The difficulty with this choice is that John Q. needs to understand and separate rebellion from self-interpreted moral infractions. This leap of attitude cannot be accomplished by him believing that he either is being a good boy or has compromised his autonomy. While this option has a greater likelihood of lengthy satisfaction, it demands more immediate awareness and responsibility. This example illustrates that people cannot attend to conflicting attitudes in consciousness simultaneously.

Perceptual Attitudes

Perceptual attitudes are the ways we receive and interpret incoming information. They are prearranged interpretations of the causes of experiences. Using a prearranged interpretation as a base for understanding our experiences, typically, we further interpret additional experiences in a similar fashion. Perceptual attitudes are based on beliefs about the etiology of either life-enhancing or life-limiting experiences, about either our well-being or our conflicts.

Whether currently known or unknown, perceptual attitudes are based on predetermined beliefs originated for a specific purpose. This specific purpose is based on the causal interpretation of our experience. Considerations and interpretations of experiences are based on beliefs that determine the result of our experiences. These beliefs and the systems that reinforce them include screened information that may or may not be accurate representations of actual or reported experiences.

Regardless of the particular perceptual attitude, the underlying belief that substantiates it is a result of one or more of the following:

- Scientific fact
- Carefully evaluated personal or professional experience
- Unevaluated or limited experience
- Personal prejudicial values
- Unresolved personal conflict
- Narrow professional education
- Biased professional training

Perceptual attitudes are interpretative filters. Filters screen and shade the information we receive thorough our senses. Like perceptions, they are the cognitive ways in which people process and interpret incoming information through their five organismic sensations. Like attitudes, filters alter the interpretation of the content of experiences.

Perceptual attitudes function similarly to different camera lenses professional photographers use for various interpretative effects. In particular, perceptual attitudes function similarly to the various field of vision lenses that photographers implement. Cameras are mechanical instruments and, like computers, perform according to the dictates of the way we program their focusing capabilities. Lenses are created for a specific interpretative purpose. Cameras deliver a perceptual impression according to the design and creativity of the photographer.

Here, we are using people's *field of vision* as a metaphor to help explain perceptual attitudes. Professional photographers have the option of using a close-up, telephoto, mid-range, or fish-eye lens (see Figure 3–1 on page 74). A close-up lens provides intricate detail and magnification but excludes the background and the larger context in which we view and understand an object. A telephoto lens extends moderate detail at a distance but at the cost of the actual and nearer-reality context of observation. A fish-eye or omni lens for the camera provides the most global representation of our experience. It transfers the most inclusive interpretation of the entirety of human experience. However, it has the disadvantage of decreasing visual acuity and distorting images outside the range of conventional perception. A mid-range lens is the most common compromise and the standard to which most automatic cameras are preset. It favors creating images that most people conventionally are accustomed to at the expense of breadth of the field and magnification of detail.

As it is impossible to use two field of vision lenses at exactly the same time, people cannot employ two perceptual attitudes simultaneously. "Valued experiences depend on the voluntary focusing of attention on a limited stimulus field (Pope and Singer, 1978). The same process happens in psychotherapy. All fields of creative and scientific achievement dictate that concentrated attention is required at the exclusion of other distracting perceptions and attitudes (Getzels and Csikszentmihalyi, 1976).

At any given moment, people receive information with one of four perceptual attitudes or some vague and disoriented combination of these four. Similar to the professional photographer's field of vision lenses, from close-up to fish-eye, these perceptual attitudes are: *intrapsychic, interpersonal, organizational,* and *universal.* As with professional photography lenses, each perceptual attitude serves a different function and each has advantages and disadvantages. The intrapsychic, interpersonal, organizational, and universal perceptual attitudes all agree that life-enhancing or life-limiting experiences are a result of two or more parts that are either in agreement or disagreement with one another respectively. The difference in these four perceptual attitudes is the interpretation of the dynamics involved in generating life-enhancing or life-limiting experiences.

Intrapsychic

People who receive information with an intrapsychic perceptual attitude interpret harmony or conflict as originating from various hypothetical, internal dynamics of personal development. The model of psychoanalysis hypothesizes the ego, id, and superego. Similarly, transactional analysis hypothesizes the adult, child, and parent. Gestalt psychotherapy uses the concepts of *top dog* and *under dog.* Recent hypothetical metaphors are the *inner child* and the *wounded child within.* There is even a comic strip by Jeff MacNelly using the metaphor of the *inner grown-up.* Harmony within the intrapsychic perceptual attitude is defined by two or more parts being in agreement. Conflict, here, is when two or more parts disagree or oppose one another. In this latter case, the hypothetical constructs represent manipulations between various dynamic aspects of the whole person.

Compared to other perceptual attitudes, the advantage of assuming an intrapsychic perceptual attitude is that the responsibility for understanding, acceptance, and validation remains the exclusive property of the individual. There are no scapegoats. The responsibility is for either harmony or conflict. When in harmony, there is the advantage of self-credibility and internal validation; when in conflict, the individual has the advantage of self-determining resolution.

The collective disadvantages, as interpreted by proponents of the other three perceptual attitudes, include the following. The first essential disadvantage is that intrapsychic perceptual attitudes require hypothetical evaluation, abstract reasoning, and intellectual insight. As a sole perceptual attitude, we consider it reductionistic and deterministic. From this perspective, personal harmony is an unrealistic, idealistic, and extraordinary exception. That is, it is not expected that most people have the inclination, means, or understanding to take advantage of this perspective in an effective and enduring manner.

An additional disadvantage is that the intrapsychic perceptual attitude about resolution of conflict is an adjustment to the frailty of the human condition. That is, it accepts a limiting and pessimistic worldview that diminishes possibilities of expanding beyond self-absorption. The intrapsychic definition of resolution includes a reluctant acceptance of anxiety, pain, fear, and death. Thus, the human condition is expected to be a difficult process, and the best people can hope for is an understanding and acceptance of this actuality.

Interpersonal

People who receive information with an interpersonal perceptual attitude interpret harmony or conflict as originating from socially compatible or incompatible relationships between two or more people and their presentational roles. Here, each person is a separate self. Self-identity becomes refracted through different inflections of other people. As a result of this process, each self undergoes a change by its perception of the awareness and evaluation of others. First, the self's view of the other, and the other's view of the self starts the process of change. Second, the self's awareness of this awareness, and view of the other about the self, completes the process of experience (Laing, Phillipson, and Lee, 1966).

Here, harmony is defined unidirectionally from the perspective of individuals as they socially relate to others in their environment and become satisfied with their expectations of a compatible or agreeable relationship. Conflict is defined here by a combative or disagreeable relationship from the perspective of individuals in which there is a lack of resolution. It occurs as a result of either constrictive personal roles or inappropriate social role expressions.

Resolution is demonstrated by the acceptance of the engaging individual interfacing in a social environment. The primary means of establishing agreeable or disagreeable compatibility is effective communication, which includes accurate and effective expression, interpersonal listening, and comprehension. Accurate and effective expression may or may not include affective or emotional expression, depending on the desires of the people involved. Accurate and effective interpersonal listening and comprehension is defined by the delivering person. This occurs after evaluating the results of the receiving person, the awareness of this event, and the view of the other about communication.

Compared to other perceptual attitudes, the advantage of interpersonal perceptual attitudes is that they are concrete, observable, and publicly accepted. They are easily identifiable and understandable. People can more simply identify responsibility as a result of interpersonal role presentation and ineffective communication than as originating from unknown and hypothetical dynamics within themselves. When in harmony, there is the advantage of a vacation from self-absorption. When in conflict, there is an identifiable party with whom the conflict occurred, providing an obvious means by which to reconcile differences.

The collective disadvantages, as interpreted by proponents of the other three perceptual attitudes, include the following. The first essential disadvantage is that interpersonal perceptual attitudes limit a dynamic understanding of previous developmental patterns and contributory responsibility. This means the proponents of alternative perceptual attitudes believe that what is being resolved is a temporary situation. The criticism is that resolution is symptomatic and does not resolve the original cause. Therefore, regardless of immediate resolution with the object of conflict, symptoms likely will recur when similar originating issues surface at a later time from different people. The interpersonal perceptual attitude, then, is often considered a superficial compromise and not a solution.

A second disadvantage is that the interpersonal perceptual attitudes provide little encouragement for extending beyond appropriate social interaction. These evaluations offer little motivation for reaching beyond a mundane acceptance of everyday self concerns. With a solution exclusively focused on interpersonal expression, compromise, or negotiation, it diminishes the human experience to the pleasure and satisfaction of ordinary life.

Organizational

People who receive information with an organizational perceptual attitude interpret harmony or conflict as originating from the entire organization of which a person is a member. The organization itself is the whole, and all parts of the whole contribute to the harmony or conflict. Frequently, an organizational perceptual attitude is equated to family therapy models. However, this is misleading in that perceptual attitudes, theoretical structures, and applied methodologies are different functions.

Within the organizational perceptual attitude, each member is a contributory part of the organization. Each member affects the organization and is affected by it. Organizations include all constellations of people within any collective designed for a distinct purpose. Examples include marriages, families, clubs, associations, corporations, countries, and, inevitably, the emerging international world community. Here, harmony is defined by whether the entire organization is functional according to the dictates of its designed purpose. Functional is evaluated and determined by whether the goals of the entire organization are achieved. This determination is made by either the ruling authority or most of the subscribing members. Conflict, then, is defined when either the ruling authority or majority of the subscribing members of the collective believes that the initiating goals of the organization are not being met. When this occurs, the organization is both defined as and determined to be dysfunctional.

Compared to other perceptual attitudes, the advantage of assuming an organizational perceptual attitude is that harmony and conflict are defined by a predetermined goal and represented by a predetermined ruling authority or a majority of members. This assumes that the evaluation of harmony or conflict is not object specific and merely reflects the collective functioning of the organization. There are two specific parts to this advantage. First, harmony and conflict criteria are determined by a collective objective, either by majority selection or by the initially accepted authority. Second, this determination is made before an evaluation of results. Should conflict occur, there are established criteria for evaluation of utilitarian satisfaction.

When responsibility is with an elected or accepted elite (republican), the entire collective knows who is creditable or needs to resolve the conflict. When responsibility is with a majority of members (democratic), regardless of individual participation, all ascribing members are equally responsible for successful harmony or conflict and dissension. All parts share equal responsibility for making the organization functional. Individuals don't feel isolated, as if they were the only ones with a problem.

The collective disadvantages, as interpreted by proponents of the other three perceptual attitudes, include the following. Regardless of assumed justification by scientific evidence, functional and dysfunctional are concepts that refer to authoritatively dictated definitions of malfunction. The determination of functional is always defined as an absence of dysfunction. Harmony and wellness are defined by an absence of disease and conflict. Harmony is rarely recognized as a quality on its own. Dysfunction is the rule of observation and acknowledgment.

These concepts suggest that people grant authority for evaluation to an external referent outside of self-determination. While there is nothing essentially wrong with granting or deferring personal responsibility to external authority, the difficulty occurs when: (1) without continuous monitoring, the individual assumes that the organization will act in the best interests of the individual, or (2) the individual is unaware of essential, individual contributions and abdicates responsibility to the organization. All parts of an organization are mutually responsible. So the saying goes, "a chain is only as strong as its weakest link." When this process occurs, political sociology replaces personal responsibility.

Universal

People who receive information with a universal perceptual attitude interpret harmony or conflict as originating from an interpretation of metaphysical lessons and tests that are opportunities to enhance personal and spiritual development. By spiritual, we do not necessarily mean any identification with an identified religious order or movement, not that such would be preclusive or prohibitive. We merely mean to indicate that people who say they identify and function from this perspective often identify themselves as spiritually oriented. Among others, this paradigm has also been referred to, associated with, or defined as including *peak experiences* (Maslow, 1962), *religious experience* (James, 1929), *cosmic consciousness* (Bucke, 1923), *choiceless awareness*, (Krishnamurti, 1962), *no-mind* (Suzuki, 1949), and *the fourth way* (Ouspensky, 1971).

Different from the other three perceptual attitudes, harmony is assumed to be a law of nature and evolution and to represent the unaffected and actual state of the workings of the universe. This force and evolutionary tendency of physical and nonmeasurable energy is implicit with all individual components and motivational development. Harmony is a coordinated symmetry of all forms of life contributing to a global world and an infinite universe (Wilber, 1979).

However, personal separation from the rest of the world and universe is necessary for development of self-identity. Within our personal development, separation also creates conflict. Viewing ourselves as encapsulated and self-determined entities, by definition, places us in the position of having to either compete or cooperate with the universe. Without attending to universal considerations, separation, and the quest for personal harmony create as many conflicts as the same process resolves. Conflict is considered a result of individual inattentiveness to natural principles and a wayward regression from universal observance. Conflict is merely an alert sign to get oneself back on course.

Human experiences, interpreted as conflicts from this perspective, are actually predetermined tests and lessons we would expect to encounter in personal development. Within a universal perceptual attitude, people anticipate that tests and lessons will continue to occur. Therefore, conflict is inevitably positive and not negative in the service of both individual and therefore collective evolution. In the broadest perspective, this perceptual attitude includes the plant and animal kingdoms of interplanetary life. Indeed, this is the reason for referring to this perceptual attitude as universal. Resolution of conflict occurs as people learn to transcend the importance of self-identity.

Compared to other perceptual attitudes, the advantage of assuming a universal perceptual attitude is that it is the most inclusive way to experience the world. Exclusive belief systems increase conflict when they define conflict in its usual meaning, implying negative opposition. Opposition implies, if not explicitly demands, control of a part of self, a whole self, an interpersonal situation, or an organizational unit. That is, when conflict exists within the other three perceptual attitudes, there is something wrong with somebody or something. When harmony exists within the other perceptual attitudes, it does not indicate life-enhancement, happiness, contentment, or well-being.

With the universal perceptual attitude, this is not the case. Right and wrong, healthy and unhealthy, and good and bad are all merely interpretations and not statements of an assumed objective or scientific fact. Harmony is, and conflicts are, interpreted like interactive seasons or changes in the weather and is expected to be the most frequent experience. However, when conflict occurs, as it inevitably does, it is not negative. It is merely an opportunity to learn and refine previous beliefs and evolve both self-development and consciousness.

The collective disadvantages, as interpreted by proponents of the other three perceptual attitudes, include the following. The essential disadvantage of the universal perceptual attitude is that it is extremely uncommon, if not spiritually idealistic. It is abstract and not so easily prone to consensual validation. As such, it is not an easy perceptual attitude with which to identify. Well-intended expectations easily may become a disappointment in either psychotherapeutic process or in communication. When communication is difficult, rapport is restricted. Many people fail to separate and individuate from their parents or the substitutes they have incorporated into their belief systems. We need to have a self-identity before we can transcend it. Most people struggle most of their lives to define a self-identity.

Another disadvantage of the universal perceptual attitude is that it requires specialized training, which is not as easily discernable or available as with other perceptual attitudes. While such training is available through a myriad of Eastern and Western spiritual and mystical orientations, apprentices frequently become attached to the specific values and beliefs of a particular practice rather than the global perceptual attitude they similarly employ.

Psychotherapeutic Implications

Psychotherapists' perceptual attitudes influence how they perceive the origination of harmony and conflict. Their beliefs about wellness and conflict determine the way they experience, diagnose, and relate their interpretations to their clients. The following case serves to illustrate the difference in perceptual attitudes.

Sharon was an attractive thirty-two year old Portuguese female. As a senior administrator for a large corporation, she was bright, aggressive, and charmingly witty. After ten years of a first marriage and a ten-year-old son, she decided to separate from her husband because she missed passion and romance. Sharon stated that she was aware this reason for leaving her husband appeared superficial. However, she still did not want to live the rest of her life without the passion she continued to desire in an intimate relationship.

While her husband was successful in his own construction firm, he was emotionally devastated by her decision and had extreme difficulty understanding her reasons. Sharon confirmed that her husband was remarkably devoted, caring, and a responsible family man. After mutual consideration and careful negotiations in favor of their son, they agreed the boy should remain in the home of the father with joint custody.

Sharon moved into a luxurious apartment. Within four weeks, she started dating Tony, the man next door. This was her first and only dating experience after separating from her husband. Tony was divorced and her senior by a few years. He owned a sporting goods store and a twenty-eight-foot fishing boat. Sharon reported her relationship with Tony contained passion and romance.

After two months of dating, Sharon became pregnant by Tony while on vacation in Cabo San Lucas, Mexico. She said she was surprised because she had been using a diaphragm consistently, but one time she neglected to use the accompanying spermicide. Neither Sharon nor Tony practiced any orthodox religion. Tony was delighted with the news of her pregnancy and wanted the child but was unwilling to attend psychotherapy. He offered promises of marriage after the completion of Sharon's divorce. In fear of raising a child alone, when six weeks pregnant, Sharon scheduled a legal abortion.

Sharon's stated reason for seeking psychotherapy was not to question her decision for separation and impending divorce but, rather, to become clear about new male relationships. More immediately, however, she wanted to clarify her decision about the abortion that was scheduled for the following week. On the day of her therapy session, she was upset and tearful. While affirming her decision to abort, she felt irresponsible and guilty.

The following sections are examples of how four psychotherapists representing each of the four perceptual attitudes might interpret and understand this case by evaluating the information available. The focus is on the perceptual attitude of understanding Sharon's conflict and not specifically on application, though implications for intervention are unavoidable.

Evaluation 1: Using an Intrapsychic Perceptual Attitude

Sharon is, indeed, in the bloom of love and romantic adventure. I am immediately struck by the convenience of Sharon dating the "man next door." It seems that she put herself in the position of being not quite married and yet not actually free. That is, where before she felt emotionally separated from her husband, she now has a symbolic physical wall between her living space and her new boyfriend's living space. Emotionally, she is neither married nor single. Neither is she completely separate from her husband or boyfriend, nor individuated from what appears to be parental substitutes.

The pregnancy represents her ambivalence by the attempt to distance from her husband and also an attempt to connect with the boyfriend. Conveniently, however, emotional and financial bonding is outside the immediate possibility as customarily declared by marriage. Interestingly, the child represents the only safe object of bonding for Sharon. However, she is even ambivalent about whether she wants to make this commitment, both in her mild negligence of birth control and her strongly mixed feelings about the abortion.

Clearly then, the burden of responsibility for the immediate crisis of whether to continue with the abortion must rest with Sharon. After all, we don't know whether Sharon will actually file for divorce, or whether the relationship between Sharon and Tony will grow into the mature status that would create a marriage demanding responsibility and commitment. Indeed, Sharon needs to resolve her ambivalence with the abortion decision immediately and deal with Tony later. Should she decide to deliver and keep the child, she could be faced with a lifelong commitment as a single mother. On the positive side, and giving her the benefit of doubt, this unforeseen pregnancy may serve as the motivation for Sharon to grow up, negotiating a resolution between the nurturing and the rebellious parts of herself—between mother-Sharon and little-girl Sharon.

Evaluation 2: Using an Interpersonal Perceptual Attitude

Admittedly, I am somewhat annoyed and unsympathetic regarding Sharon's irresponsible adventures into what I view as "Lala Land." For whatever personal reasons, she has clearly abandoned her husband and son. She now is "going steady" with the first and nearest kid on the block after leaving home. Completely aware of birth control practice, and within two months, she became pregnant by her boyfriend while still married to her husband. Now, she would rather kill the baby than go ahead and deliver it and give it to Tony or even someone else. This is unpardonable and irresponsible behavior that is quite understandably distressing to other people besides herself. The husband doesn't know what he is doing wrong and probably was doing exactly what he did ten years ago when she married him. The son cannot understand the emotional turmoil and loss and now doesn't have his mother in the home.

The concern is that Sharon wants to conveniently dismiss her responsibility, regardless of whether she likes it or not. The decision has already been made, by negligence or secret desire. An abortion is out of the question, not because of the pro-life issue, but because there are absolutely no extenuating circumstances that justify a change of menu in the middle of the meal.

Obviously, Sharon believes she has a compatible relationship with Tony, at least for now. The responsibility of pregnancy demands time for her to learn whether to continue it. There is nothing terrible about Sharon's case. It happens every day, and people learn to deal with it. This is what life is all about. Wasn't it John Lennon who said, "Life is what happens when you have other plans."? So, I would say to Sharon, "Congratulations, now you get a chance to get on with the living of life."

This time, however, Sharon needs to learn to consider the social consequences of her actions with each of the other people with whom she is interfacing. She needs to learn to relate in grown-up ways that include responsibility, genuine intimacy, clear communication, and maintaining passion. Fires extinguish naturally only when you stop fueling them. And, part of growing up in relationships is learning how to do that as well. Sharon needs to learn how to express her boundaries of both autonomy and belonging. She can do this! She is well-educated, affluent, healthy, and well into middle age. It's about time she learns that responsibility and fun don't have to be opposed.

Evaluation 3: Using an Organizational Perceptual Attitude

It may sound strange, but I really enjoy working with these kinds of enmeshed and complex dysfunctional families. Everybody in the family is in relationship to everyone else. It's like a daily domino effect where everyone trades pointing the finger at everyone else so they don't have to end up as the scapegoat. There is no one person at fault or to blame. Everyone in this case has a contribution to the immediate crisis and is equally responsible for resolution.

The organizational dilemma is that Sharon doesn't feel Tony is committed to the relationship. Because of that, she is uncertain whether to continue the pregnancy. Since she is indecisive about the pregnancy, Tony is not sure he wants to further commit to the relationship. Therefore, he behaves as though and demonstrates that he is not committed. Then, the cycle starts all over because Sharon doesn't feel Tony is committed to the relationship.

Sharon is not sure that this relationship is going to work because it doesn't appear stable to her. Consequently, she is not sure she wants to raise the child on her own. Tony's demonstration of ambivalence fares no better. His promises of marriage are circumstantially far enough away that he doesn't have to immediately demonstrate commitment. While he claims desire for the birth of the child, it is within a situation where he has not committed physical, legal, or financial responsibility. The circumstances of the relationship could easily change as they have in the past. Because Tony is not demonstrating commitment to the relationship, Sharon does not feel committed to the relationship to bear the child.

I would bring everyone into an extended family therapy session if possible. This means everyone, including the previous husband, her son, and the parents of both Sharon and Tony. It's time for everyone to learn they have an equal contribution and that each person's cause is another person's effect, and similarly, each person's effect reinforces origination of cause.

Evaluation 4: Using a Universal Perceptual Attitude

Native Americans have a profound reverence and respect for all of life—for people, animals, plants, weather, and mother earth. They believe that each part of life affects all others. No living animal or plant, or even the earth, should be abused, lest it change the whole. Before buffalo and deer were hunted, prayers were offered to request forgiveness as well as success for the hunt. Only what was absolutely needed for survival was hunted. Following the kill, further prayers were offered for forgiveness as well as in gratitude.

Native Americans assumed that the success of the hunt was favored by the Great Spirit for the survival and well-being of the tribe. Similar prayers still frequently are offered for the harvest of trees, plants, and medicinal herbs. Even today, harvesting any plant must be absolutely necessary. Even then, such a decision is conducted in the spirit of appreciation, not convenience. This spirit of reverence includes both the attitude before the decision to change a life and after in a continuing attitude of appreciation for the harvest or hunt.

The buffalo dies in service of the tribe. Its pelt provides insulation to the tribe from cold winters and its body maintains the tribe from starvation. From its bones and horns are made knives, eating utensils, and needles. If a loss of life is to occur for the sake of emotional or physical survival, full appreciation must continue to be demonstrated. If Sharon chooses to abort this life, I would invite her to do so with this attitude.

Should Sharon decide to abort, I would suggest that she and Tony conduct a ritual—a ceremony before the abortion. If nothing else, on a clear night, both of them need to look at the sky and the stars, and with a sense of reverence, apologize for the decision they decided they needed to make. That's the first part. Second, I would tell them they need to give back to the universe what they have borrowed in some way. The poet Gibran once said that our children are not our own; they are life longing for itself. Giving back to the universe is not a payback for being bad. It is not to be a reaction from feeling guilty. This act is simply an offering of compensation. It is a compensation for what they have borrowed for the purpose of learning a lesson in life. Whatever they choose to give back will be demonstrated by their actions and thoughts after the abortion.

Should they ask how much they need to give, I would know they are missing the point and taking self-advantage for the sake of convenience. Their later actions are not to be a matter of repentance. Offerings are not a matter of morality, where people do something wrong and need to pay a debt. This offering is a simple and obligatory matter of rebalancing life forces by giving to the universe in some way that you alone determine compensates for what you have borrowed.

Third, Sharon and Tony need to decide ahead of time what they will offer to the universe so they will know when they have completed the offering. I would tell them that their offering could take one hour or a lifetime. Part of the responsibility of subtracting life from the universal force is deciding on the parameters of how you will return it; and this needs to be decided before changing life forms. Last, I would remind Sharon to make a decision she can live with the rest of her life and that will work for her, Tony, and the universe.

This case illustrates how psychotherapists apply distinct perceptual attitudes, and how these different attitudes inevitably influence their understanding and application of process. Psychotherapists are monoperceptual at any given moment with an intentional ability to be multiperceptual. Knowing the perceptual attitude through which we perceive clients' conflicts enables us to clarify our theoretical understanding and psychotherapeutic goals. It allows us to establish more effective rapport, communication, and methodology. Within any apprentice-mentor relationship, a student learns only as much as a mentor knows (Zeucher, 1982). A good student reflects a wise teacher. Within the psychotherapeutic relationship, psychotherapists limit their clients' healing to the adaptability of their own personal and professional development.

Maintaining an awareness of our perceptual attitudes allows us, within the limits of our preferences and developmental evolution, the ability to select varying perceptual attitudes in alignment with personal, developmental growth. With this ability, we can select psychotherapeutic attitudes that are more appropriate in meeting clients' needs and circumstances. These choices allow us to use perceptual attitudes that are congruent with our theoretical structure and methodology. It also allows us to use different perceptual attitudes for countering clients' resistances with effective mobilization.

Selecting appropriate perceptual attitudes by clients' needs requires deliberate implementation. Some people learn to be multiperceptual at a very early age; they can easily select two or more perceptual attitudes. For these multiperceptual people, selection occurs automatically and without conscious thought. Most of us, however, grow up with a singularly dominant perceptual attitude inculcated from family and subculture. We then continue to perceive through these corresponding symbols and attitudes. Like all people, psychotherapists usually favor one perceptual attitude in dealing with both life and clients.

These favored beliefs limit psychotherapeutic effectiveness when either they do not match clients' beliefs or it might be useful to employ a different perceptual attitude for client mobilization. The better equipped psychotherapists are aware that different perceptual attitudes are for different objectives. They also know that any one perceptual attitude cannot encompass all dimensions of human experience.

It is possible to expand our adaptability and use different perceptual attitudes for different purposes. Like the photographer, we can obtain new lenses for our personal and professional cameras. Learning different attitudes later in life requires expanding our beliefs. Selecting perceptual attitudes means being able to choose perceptual attitudes through changing symbols of meaning. The knowledge of these perceptual attitudes allows us to translate human conflict, or difficulties of personal development, into different perspectives.

When a client, John, presents a conflict about his wife, we can perceive and translate this conflict through any of the four perceptual attitudes. Intrapsychically, we would experience John's conflict as a result of internal dynamics or with his self-development. Interpersonally, we would experience John's conflict as originating in relationship to his wife. Organizationally, we would experience John's conflict as subsumed in the entity of dysfunctional family relationships. Universally, we would experience John's conflict as unwillingness to extend his awareness beyond self-concerns.

Selecting among perceptual attitudes allows considerable flexibility. We have multiple ways to consider clients' resistance, need for support, and intellectual insight. Suppose John's conflict is his anger with his father who just died. Intrapsychically, we could interpret John's difficulty as projected anger and introjected victimization. Interpersonally, we could interpret his difficulty as unresolved anger with his father whom, although deceased, John is still carrying around with him. We could even use role-playing to resurrect his father for a dialogue of resolution. Both perceptual attitudes are proper for John's immediate pain, conflict, and crisis. However, if we attach to an organizational position, we block easy implementation because it is impossible to bring his father back to life in the actual setting unless we use a multigenerational process (Kerr and Bowen, 1988; Minuchin, 1974). A universal position might be valuable later to place a new perspective on life and death but is inappropriate at the time of immediate grief. If for no other reason, it is difficult to experience the largest and most abstract of perspectives when the more conventional, finite, and concrete perceptual attitudes are demanding immediate attention and relief.

As we increase our attention and learn to use various perceptual attitudes, we become multiperceptual. We can strategically select attitudes for various treatment plans. A convenient way to remember all this is that the interpersonal attitude is a microcosm. A microcosm is the small picture; it is the close-up lens. The universal attitude is a macrocosm—the big picture. It is the fish-eye lens. The interpersonal and organizational are sequentially global attitudes between microcosm and macrocosm.

The dynamic process within one perceptual attitude is identical to the process in another. John's interpersonal conflict incorporates the same dynamics as his universal alienation. John's disappointment in himself, on an increasingly larger scale, reflects disappointment with his father, his marriage, and his expectations of the world.

Another example is Mary, a good Catholic who can't understand why God took her child at birth. Her specific conflict with God is the same as the conflict with her family of origin, her marriage, and her self-development. Selecting perceptual attitudes allows us to relate to Mary in a multiplicity of ways so she can understand right now. Selecting a different perceptual attitude later will allow Mary to resolve her grief, assume responsibility for her anger, and even forgive her God. Each perceptual attitude allows each client to take responsibility within the parameter of their perceptual dimension.

Levels of responsibility are similar to the expansive parameters of perceptual attitudes. Intrapsychically, we are responsible for our dynamic personal

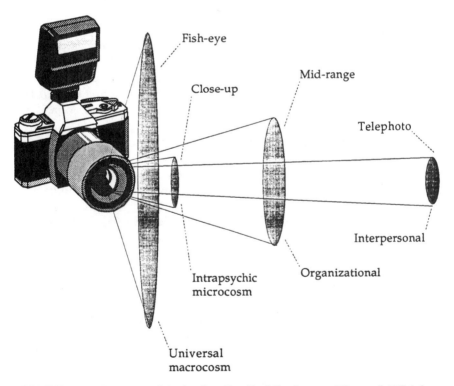

FIGURE 3–1   Perceptual Attitudes Can Be Like Lenses Through Which We "View" Our Experiences.

development. Interpersonally, we are responsible for our self-identity in relationship to others. Organizationally, we are responsible to our family groups, society, and cultural institutions. Universally, we discover that we are responsible as an integral part of the ecology and evolution of the universe.

Note

1. The function of extrasensory perception in relation to intuitive feelings is further discussed in chapter 5 under the subheading Intuitive Feelings.

References

Bucke, R. (1923). *Cosmic consciousness.* New York: Dutton.
Festinger, L. (1957). *The theory of cognitive dissonance.* Stanford, CA: Stanford University Press.
Getzels, J., & Csikszentmihalyi, M. (1976). *The creative vision.* New York: Wiley Interscience.
Kerr, M., & Bowen, M. (1988). *Family evaluation.* New York: W. W. Norton.
Kohler, W. (1947). *Gestalt psychology.* New York: New American Library.
James, W. (1929). *The varieties of religious experience.* London: Longmans & Green.
Krishnamurti, J. (D. Rajagopal, Ed.). (1962). *Commentaries on living* (Third Series). London: Victor Gollancz.
Laing, R., Phillipson, H., & Lee, A. L. (1966). *Interpersonal perception.* London: Tavistock.
Maslow, A. (1962). *Toward a psychology of being.* Princeton: D. Van Nostrand.
Minuchin, S. (1974). *Families and family therapy.* Cambridge, MA: Harvard University Press.
Ouspensky, P. (1971). *The fourth way.* New York: Vintage.
Pope, K., & Singer, J. (1978). *The stream of consciousness* (p. 344). New York: Plenum Press.
Schlitz, M., & Gruber, E. (1981). Transcontinental remote viewing: A rejudging. *Journal of Parapsychology, 45,* 233–237.
Suzuki, D. (1949). *The Zen doctrine of no-mind.* London: Rider.
Targ, R., & Harary, K. (1984). *The mind race.* New York: Villard Books.
Tart, C., Puthoff, H., & Targ, R. (Eds.). (1979). *Mind at large.* New York: Praeger.
Tart, C. (1975). The physical universe, The spiritual universe, and the paranormal. In Tart, C. (Ed.), *Transpersonal psychologies* (pp. 113–151). New York: Harper & Row.
U. S. House of Representatives/Committee on Science and Technology. (June 1981). *Survey of science and technology issues: Present and future.* Washington, DC: 97th Congressional Record.
Wilber, K. (1979). *No boundary.* Boulder, CO: Shambala.
Zeucher, D. (1982). *The mentor/protege relationship: A phenomenological inquiry.* Unpublished doctoral dissertation. Professional School for Humanistic Studies, San Diego, CA.

4

Identifying Theoretical Structures

Psychotherapeutic effectiveness and satisfaction require identifying theoretical structures based on beliefs about the origination of human wellness, conflict, and pain. These beliefs include applications for the reduction of human pain and the restoration of wellness. They differ from perceptual attitudes by focusing on applications of theory, rather than on perceptual attitudes for receiving and interpreting information.

Theoretical structures form the foundational structure of our professional home. They are the supportive rationale of psychotherapeutic beliefs and applications. Theoretical structures establish justification and orient goals for implementing our methodology. Although different, each theoretical structure employs accepted principles explaining human harmony, conflict, and change. Each explanation justifies an application. Theoretical structures, then, are the underlying beliefs by which we personally and professionally interpret human behavior.

By definition, theoretical structures include beliefs and implied applications about the origin of wellness, disease, and preferred practices of treatment. Each theoretical structure is defined by a distinct belief of wellness or disease origination and its respective application. Theoretical structures are not a Lockean *tabula rasa*. They are not a neutral slate upon which our observations merely impress themselves for uncontaminated application. They are biased beliefs.

Theoretical structures expose patterns of preconceived professional beliefs. These professional beliefs are supportive and in accord with our opinions, beliefs, and values of previous personal and professional experiences. *During* intentional behavior, people form and filter their sensations such that they often conform to either needs and expectations or to predetermined goal orientations, applied objectives, or ontological evolutionary focuses.

After following their predetermined theoretical structure, people keep what is agreeable to their accustomed functioning. Otherwise, they would meet that which is opposing, threatening, or conflicting. In this way, intentions shape being. They use these filtered defenses against situations they do not fully understand and do not feel they can handle within the time they practically can allot them. However, by relying on a particular theoretical structure, people limit their options within familiar belief systems. Conformity and security must be risked for intentions to have power. When people act with a known purpose, they are intentional. Intentionally, they focus their attention on a limited stimulus field. Intentions set up a life goal and perceived support from personal experiences.

Our observations are that theoretical structures are easily divided into three critically underlying beliefs about wellness and disease and the corresponding applications. We are designating them the *productive, innovative,* and *creative* theoretical structures. Each theoretical structure has a *goal orientation, applied objective,* and *ontological-evolutionary focus.* Additionally, each structure has a presupposition about human development, dysfunction, and the function of the universe substantiated by either Newtonian physics or field theory. Each theoretical structure has a particular value and purpose, and each has advantages and limitations.

Observation shows that people either willingly or unknowingly function within only one theoretical structure. While more educated than the general populace, psychotherapists differ little from this widespread principle. Psychotherapists, who have a greater breadth of worldly experience and educational background, may be more aware of, and even empathetic to, variant theoretical structures. Nevertheless, they also contend a preference. Psychotherapists who commit in depth to a particular structure either negate other possibilities or find a way of assimilating them within their preferred theoretical structure.

Occasional exceptions occur. Generally, people will employ a diverse theoretical structure when their dominant one does not bring desired results. A dramatic case is that of a confirmed atheist who, when severely injured on the battlefield, prays to a God he has never believed in. Another example is of a pro-life, single female who becomes impregnated by someone known to have a life-disabling genetic disease and then chooses to abort. Although these examples are extreme, the temporary and convenient reasons to adjust dominant beliefs slip through the back door into everyday life and clinical practice. Interestingly, after the stressful circumstance, the dominant theoretical structure is resumed, often with an acceptable excuse for the transient departure.

Each theoretical structure is justifiable within the rationale of its logical domain. Intelligent and reasonable people clearly can disagree, equally supporting and justifying claims within their own frameworks. As a psychotherapeutic example, an intern in clinical psychology who favored a model of Gestalt therapy, sought supervision from a staff psychiatrist who preferred a psychoanalytic model.

The intern's client was a twenty-eight-year-old female diagnosed with anorexia nervosa. The intern had received excellent training and was moderately skilled in Gestalt therapy. The intern accepted the patient from a graduating intern who had also employed Gestalt therapy, so that for the client the continuing theoretical structure was consistent.

During the first session, the new intern used a methodology in which the client was asked to place her stomach in an opposing chair. The intern then asked the client to create a dialogue with that part of herself, an effective methodology when conducted correctly. The session was reported to have gone well. Supervision by the staff psychiatrist who had graciously agreed to provide this intern's training followed. The intern presented the case history and proceeded to explain the theoretical rationale of his intervention strategy. As reported, the case presentation took the following course.

INTERN: (nonchalantly) And, then I ask her to put her stomach in the chair across from her and talk to it.

STAFF: You did what?

INTERN: I asked her to face an empty chair, symbolically place her stomach in it, and then create a dialogue with that part of herself.

STAFF: (completely dismayed and assertive) That is not acceptable. What is your justification for such a procedure? [Note here that the staff is asking for the theoretical rationale that supports the methodology.]

INTERN: (surprised and confident) Within this modality, the procedure is justified by having the client take complete responsibility for owning the disowned parts of self. In this way, the therapist remains a neutral party and allows the client to acknowledge the denied symptom as representative of the part of the self with which she conflicts.

STAFF: (calmer and firmly) Well, that makes sense within the structure that you used, but I don't agree with it. The way I view that procedure is that you robbed the client of any responsibility by supplying her with a parlor room technique within which she could dramatize her pathology and avoid insight into the nature of her histrionic delusions.

INTERN: That's amazing. What you said is exactly opposite of everything I have ever learned.

STAFF: I understand that, but if you are going to continue supervision with me, we are going to do it my way. After all, you are the one that sought additional supervision from me.

INTERN: Okay, we'll do it your way because I want to learn your way.

This example illustrates one difference between two divergent models and reflects the divergent theoretical structures. Both justifications by the intern and supervisor are valid within the context of their respective theoretical structures. To be clear, the example is not about the difference between Gestalt therapy and psychoanalysis as *models* of psychotherapy.

Models of psychotherapy are acknowledged systems of psychotherapy identified by title and specific founders. A few obvious examples that include single founders are: Freudian Psychoanalysis (Sigmund Freud), Adlerian Individual Therapy (Alfred Adler), Jungian Analysis (Carl Jung), Transactional Analysis (Eric Berne), Person-Centered Therapy (Carl Rogers), Gestalt Therapy (Fritz Perls), Reality Therapy (William Glasser), and Rational-Emotive Therapy (Albert Ellis). Other well-recognized models, such as behavioral therapy, cognitive therapy, and existential therapy, have several founders who agree and disagree on aspects of both the theoretical structure and the methodology (Corey, 1982).

When practiced by a wide range of clinicians, models of psychotherapy do not necessarily correspond, nor do parallel theoretical structures. Indeed, this is our reason for employing an expansive theoretical paradigm to examine the underlying principles of theoretical structures that include all models of psychotherapy.

As a result of the differences among theoretical structures, each has advantages and disadvantages. Nevertheless, effective application of any of them also depends on the congruency of their relationship to all other components of a designated orientation. These components include belief systems, perceptual attitudes, methodologies, relationship dynamics, parental roles, and boundaries of imposition. This is true especially when these structures are applied by a psychotherapist to specific clients. Table 4–1 differentiates theoretical structures and provides an overview for reference and clarification. Each component of the table will be discussed in the sections following.

Productive Theoretical Structures

We are designating *productive* to define the originating and furnishing of desired results. Productive means that the results of an act determine, not influence, the value of the act itself. The process is the instrumental activity from which a result occurs. In the ordinary world, this process is best exemplified by those persons who develop and perfect skills, whether that be of a competent

TABLE 4–1   Theoretical Structures

	Productive	Innovative	Creative
Goal orientation	Survive and adjust	Grow and develop	Transcend
Applied objective	Repair Recover Rehabilitate	Prevent Improve Cultivate	Align Shifting consciousness
Ontological-evolutionary focus	Prepersonal	Personal	Transpersonal
Theoretical presupposition	Hole Theory		Whole Theory
Correlative physics	Newtonian Physics		Field Theory

craftsman, surgeon, or psychotherapist. We define productive theoretical structures by the following criteria:

1. The act results in a significantly recognizable alteration of objects or events by a script, formula, or blueprint of established success.
2. The result is defined by either a recognizable authority outside of the self, or by the self, but only when the self has determined that self is the authority.
3. Change of the object or event is emphasized over an awareness of the process of change or the awareness of the self that made the product.
4. The importance of the process depends on the degree to which it serves to obtain the result and confirms the originating theoretical structure.

As applied to psychotherapy, productive theoretical structures equate psychological pain and dysfunction with physical disorders. Psychotherapists are productive when they effectively employ a learned repertoire of techniques. When this is the theoretical structure, it is determined by a recipe for success. As such, they theoretically justify psychotherapy as *treatment*.

The physiological influence in the conceptualization and writing of the *DSM III-R* (American Psychiatric Association, 1987) is obvious. All of the neuroses and behavioral malfunctions are now classified as *disorders*. The physiological concept of disorders ostensibly justifies the use of medication and the need for treatment. Frequently, the implication of treatment is that it needs to be conducted by a licensed medical or behavioral science professional.

While the productive theoretical structure often is equated to a Western-world medical model, productive is a more accurate concept for two reasons.

First, many psychotherapists who adopt a productive theoretical structure are not physicians. That is, many psychologists and clinical social workers apply a productive theoretical structure. Second, many psychotherapists who apply a productive theoretical structure do not believe that the diagnostic etiology of the client is physiologically determined. Their intended application reflects a Western-world medical model. However, this intended application is not justified by their underlying theoretical suppositions which, for example, may be psychosomatically oriented.

The *goal orientation* of the productive theoretical structure is based on survival and adjustment. With major depression and schizophrenia, the goal orientation is survival. Those working on inpatient wards often feel restricted in helping their clients maintain minimal daily functioning. With borderline and other personality disorders, the orientation is behavioral management and social adjustment. Those working in mental health clinics focus on adequate daily functioning that allows their clients to maintain outpatient rehabilitation. Often, the focus is on clients gaining employment or financial and emotional stability. Sometimes the overall orientation is preventing harm by self-infliction or other oriented-violence.

The *applied objective* of the productive theoretical structure is to repair, recover, or rehabilitate. Within this objective, the state of being broken demands fixing. With severe physiological breakdowns, sometimes it becomes necessary to remove worn and broken parts and replace them with new ones, such as blood transfusions, organ transplants, or bone replacements. Physical disease and psychological disorders are considered events that happen to people. The productive assumption is that people are not responsible for either the occurrence of disease or disorder, or for the primary healing. Responsible, here, means that people do not, themselves, make an intentional or active contribution to the dysfunctional occurrence. Thus, they cannot direct an intentional or active contribution to repair and recovery.

Within this theoretical structure, people are not responsible for the common cold, allergies, diabetes, alcoholism, neuroses, and personality and behavioral disorders. People are even less responsible for terminal and major illnesses. Such major illnesses include: cancer, heart disease, diabetes, allergies, schizophrenia, psychotic depression, bipolar disorders, and all other illnesses where there is the assumption of genetic transmission, regardless of family history or predisposition.

Although there is often professional acknowledgment that people could have reduced the risk of incurring some illnesses by exercise, nutrition, or methods of stress reduction, once the disease is diagnosed, the person is absolved of the primary responsibility for healing. Within this framework, the person is never completely responsible for preventing the disease or healing the problem.

In productive healing, diagnosis and healing are based on an evaluation of the malfunctioning symptoms. These symptoms are considered a sign that something is wrong and needs repair. Conventional medical practice repairs by invasive procedures such as surgery, chemotherapy, radiation and non-homeopathic medication. Antidepressant medication is given to depressed people. Antianxiety medication is given to people who are anxious and fearful or prone to panic attacks. However, both surgery and medication are invasive procedures with the theoretical assumption that these methods will arrest or cure an illness defined by symptoms.

At this point, wellness is defined by an absence of disease. In much of medicine, people are never cured. Even when surgery and medication are effective, people are not necessarily cured. In this structure, people are in remission. The assumption is that while their symptoms are temporarily alleviated, sometime in the future they are likely to regain similar or worse dysfunction. This belief conventionally holds true with all major physical and psychological diseases and most minor diseases and disorders. Exceptions occur within circumscribed physical accidents exemplified by minor broken appendages and minor dermatological infections. However, even these are substantiated by narrow parameters.

When this belief is adopted by psychotherapists, the same expectation occurs. If a psychotherapist is surprisingly successful in dealing with a personality disorder, the client is temporarily repaired, recovered, and in remission. When medication temporarily alleviates the symptoms of an endogenous depression, the client is in remission. The same frequently is assumed true with minor dysfunctions such as drug addictions, panic disorders, bulimia, and ego-syntonic homosexuality.

The productive theoretical structure's *ontological-evolutionary* focus is *prepersonal* (Wilber, 1982). An ontological-evolutionary focus is the spatial and temporal context of the developmental origination of human harmony and conflict. It is the locus of attention within the evolution of self-development. Prepersonal merely means that the focus of attention is on the alienated self. In a neo-Freudian psychoanalytic model, this is called a poorly defined, undeveloped, or fragile ego. In a behavioral model, a prepersonal focus would be on reconditioning ineffective behaviors learned from conditioning. In a cognitive model, a prepersonal focus would change the illogical and irrational conclusions drawn from experiences. In a hypnosis model (Kroger, 1977), much of prepersonal development is unknown or unconscious. The focus is to uncover originating and alienated experiences relevant to, and therefore causing, the current conflict. All prepersonal modes focus on past thoughts, behaviors, feelings, beliefs, or learning.

The following is a summary of the productive theoretical structure and its implications for application in behavioral science and psychotherapy.

A. Although people are responsible for culturally accepted prevention of extremely minor maladaptation by maintaining reasonable nutrition and exercise, they are not responsible for all major and most minor diseases, disorders, and dysfunctions.

B. Symptoms are a sign of a problem. A problem is a sign of something negative, ill, diseased, disordered, or broken.

C. External authority conventionally is responsible for diagnosis.

D. Diagnosis is empirically observable, measurable, statistically categorizable, and symptom specific.

E. Treatment is symptom specific and disorder oriented.

F. External authority is exclusively responsible for performing treatment.

G. Health is defined as an absence of pain, suffering, dysfunction, disease, or disorder. With a small percentage of exceptions, repair and recovery are considered temporary, and the client remains in remission.

Innovative Theoretical Structures

We are designating *innovative* to define the introduction of a novel idea, thought, method, or device. Innovative means whatever is novel is recognized and acknowledged. This criterion is used by the U.S. Patent Office. Whereas productive theoretical structures are repetitive, innovative theoretical structures must demonstrate originality or novelty. However, the acknowledged novelty is still relative and within the confines of previously established standards or elements. That is, the novelty is merely additive or subtractive. It is only a recombination or rearrangement of known elements. The novelty is represented by a new synthesis of acknowledged components. We define innovative theoretical structures by the following criteria:

1. Beyond reproduction, duplication, or imitation, the quantity of novelty of either an object or event contributes to a new recognized pattern not previously acknowledged by its individual components.

2. The quantitative difference is acknowledged as valuable or meaningful by both the agent of innovation and a recognizable authority outside of self.

3. Change of the object or event is emphasized by either investing a previously uninvested character or by perceiving the experience with a new meaning determined by self.

4. The result and process are equally important to the extent that novelty is obtained and the meaning of the process is interpreted.

The primary difference between the productive and innovative theoretical structures is quantitative. As applied to psychotherapy, innovation occurs when psychotherapists effectively employ a theoretical structure that results in a definitively novel implementation that is meaningful to both the client and the psychotherapist.

An example of an innovative theoretical structure in the medical field is chiropractic medicine, a noninvasive, nonsurgical treatment that often includes giving clients vitamins and occasional herbs instead of medication. In comparison to productive theoretical structures, it is innovative because:

1. Individual treatment is designed according to the experience of the client.
2. The structure is designed to value preventive measures as much as professional treatment.
3. Wellness is focused on rather than disease.

Chiropractic treatment varies from conventional medical practice in degree and not in form. That is, the innovative theoretical structure is quantitatively rather than qualitatively different from the productive theoretical structure and conventional Western medicine for the following reasons:

1. Diagnosis is still symptom specific.
2. Chiropractic diagnosis is based on a Western medical, biological, and biochemical evaluation.
3. Sequential treatment is based on the original diagnosis.

As applied to behavioral science and psychotherapy, the *goal orientation* of the innovative theoretical structure is based on personal growth and development. Innovative goal orientations frequently are based on a health model. That is, health is not defined as the absence of disease but as a state of wellness and well-being. Healthy personality development results from membership in a functional family, properly associated learning, and life-enhancing belief systems. Innovative structures define psychological health by patterns of personal, career, relationship, and family functioning.

The *applied objective* is to build or cultivate function, and to improve and cultivate character and personality. The innovative theoretical structure focuses on prevention of disease and disorders. It does not assume people need to be ill, sick, or diseased to improve. Nevertheless, people need to improve and cultivate personal development and self-realization to take increasing responsibility for self-satisfaction.

The innovative theoretical structure's *ontological-evolutionary focus* is *personal*. Personal within this context means the focus of attention is on self-development and the cultivation of self-satisfaction. In a neo-Freudian psychoanalytic model, personal development would focus on appropriate developmental separation and individuation from the parents or their substitutes. It would strive for balance between a well-developed ego, controlled id, and socialized superego. A behavioral model would focus on dealing with immediate and current undesired habits. A cognitive model would strive to arrive at the reasons for altering ineffective beliefs and consequential behaviors. A reality therapy model (Glasser, 1965) would be compatible because it focuses exclusively on conscious experience. All innovative modes focus on the present and on developmental completion.

The following is a summary of the innovative theoretical structure and its implications for application in behavioral science and psychotherapy.

A. People determine the level of their responsibility for wellness and disease that they want to share with an externally designated authority. The primary orientation is toward preventive measures for wellness. All improvements and cultivation of health and psychotherapeutic functions are assumed by the client.

B. Symptoms are a signal indicating an organismic request for attention. However, they are not necessarily a problem, dysfunction, disease, or disorder by conventional standards.

C. Symptoms are evaluated by the client.

D. Diagnosis is symptomatic, signaling organismic concern.

E. Innovative treatment is focused on the present.

F. People choose the level of responsibility to share with external authority.

G. Health is defined as self-acceptance and satisfactory functioning.

Creative Theoretical Structures

We are designating *creative* to define an imaginative mastery, arising from a shift in consciousness, and resulting in the power to grant new form in thought, action, or behavior. Creative describes the focus of expanding awareness and self-definition beyond self to include others and the world. More accurately, creative, as we are using the term to describe a theoretical structure, is a metaphor[1] for describing a quantitatively inclusive and qualitatively expansive paradigm beyond productive and innovative theoretical structures. We define creative theoretical structures by the following criteria:

1. In the generic, creativity is a qualitatively different state from production and innovation. Creativity is defined in an object, or through an experience that results in an unrecognizable and qualitatively different pattern than previously known. Examples of individually created objects include the caveman's wheel, our everyday scissors, Leonardo da Vinci's Mona Lisa, Michelangelo's Sistine Chapel fresco, Bach's Toccata and Fugue in D minor, Einstein's theory of relativity, and *Don Quixote de la Mancha* written by Miguel de Cervantes Saavedra. Examples of collectively creative objects include the Egyptian, Aztec, and Mayan pyramids; the Declaration of Independence; the Constitution of the

United States; and the automobile.[2] Examples of creative experiences and resultant events include those initiated by major world religious founders such as Buddha, Jesus, and Mohammed. These examples are merely well-known and classically representative. Millions of examples occur in everyday modern life, which are too numerous to mention them here.

2. The qualitative difference of the creative object or experience is acknowledged as valuable or meaningful by the individual creator as the decided authority of self with others representing the same paradigm.

3. When applied to objects, events, or experiences, the creative paradigm results in an expanded shift in consciousness of the creator defined by an identification beyond ego, self, personal concerns alone, or product focus. This is not to say that the self is obliterated or disconcerted. The self merely takes the background of orientation. Again, the verification for this acknowledgment is through individual experience in conjunction with authorities within the designated paradigm and not from without.

4. The creative theoretical structure is a consistent and replicable experience. The defining criteria of its replication are based on self-observation and evaluated knowledge by prearranged principles in accordance with others who are known by the initiator to have made the same shift in consciousness. The process is not only meaningful, it also becomes desirably obligatory through personal commitment.

The creative theoretical structure differs substantially and qualitatively from the productive and innovative theoretical structures. As applied to psychotherapy, creative theoretical structures are based on an optimal transcendence of continuous self-identification. Psychotherapists are creative when they employ a theoretical structure that represents their shift of consciousness with the goal of shifting the consciousness of their client. This is absolutely not to be confused with religious, prejudicial, or political cults that serve to condition, manipulate, or exploit any values that are not inclusive of opposing values.

From the perspective of the productive theoretical structure, an excellent example of creative medical healing is acupuncture—a Chinese and Korean medical practice nearly 5000 years old. In the United States, acupuncturists need to attend about six years of college and must obtain state licenses. Many major medical insurance companies cover reimbursement. An acupuncturist's usual initial question is, "Where does it hurt or where is it bleeding?"

During each session, treatment for the client's complaint considers the entire organism related to the current pain. Diagnosis is made on the basis of the new registered pain each session. Pain, as a perceived experience, may be in a completely different location in the body each session. Therefore, on each succeeding session, the diagnosis may be different. Creative psychotherapists don't know how long treatment is going to be because the diagnosis changes each time. In attempting to restore to wellness the origination of the symptoms, other pains may show up.

Treatment is changed to respond to the new complaint. There is no assumption that the previous illness or disease is in remission. Wellness is defined by patients' observance of their own condition as well as observations of *energy*[3] by experienced acupuncturists. If you ask acupuncturists why their treatment worked, they will tell you that they don't know. They just will tell you that based on your pain, they perform certain procedures with needles and herbs, that have worked for several thousand years. There is no scientific explanation that makes cause-effect sense to Western science, medicine, or even to acupuncturists themselves.

One problem in understanding holistic healing is that this system is not based on Western or scientifically known perceptions of cause-effect diseases of the human organism. Western medicine views the body as a machine with separate problems that occur. Eastern medicine looks at the person as an integrated system in which all parts affect each other. Any disease or dysfunction represents an imbalance of energy. This imbalance of energy means that healing needs to occur with a consideration of the entire body. For this reason, needles many times are inserted at points in the body that appear, according to the Western medical observer, to bear no relationship to the targeted illness, pain, or symptom.

The *goal orientation* of the creative theoretical structure is to transcend self-identity. We interpret *transcend* as meaning to go beyond or exceed the usual or conventional limits of ordinary experience and knowledge. Creative goal orientations often align with mystical or spiritual beliefs. Self-realized functioning results from living life such that the meaning of life is oriented toward a cause, event, or other outside of the organismic self (but not necessarily self-sacrificial or at the expense of the self) (Frankl, 1967; 1969). In his model of logotherapy, Viktor Frankl (1963) uses the analogy of the psychotherapist as an "eye specialist rather than that of a painter" whose goal is to widen and broaden "the visual field of the patient so that the whole spectrum of meaning and values becomes conscious and visible to him."

The *applied objective* is to align self-identity and definition beyond a dualistic separatism between oneself and the universe. James Fadiman (1980) states, "one therapeutic goal is to align the personality within the total self so it functions appropriately." Experientially, it is to shift consciousness such that it becomes qualitatively different from self-focused consciousness. This new consciousness is inclusive of self-enhancement within considerations of events and objects outside the self. The creative theoretical structure is based on a created personal mental manual that directs thoughts and behavior from a preevaluated and committed metaperspective.

The creative theoretical structure's *ontological-evolutionary focus* is transpersonal. *Transpersonal* is defined as a superconscious state focused beyond personal growth and self-development. Abstracting from the original definition of transpersonal psychology, we interpret transpersonal to mean the empirical study and responsible implementation of the results individually interpreted as meaningful and relevant to individual and species-wide metaneeds and synergy, unitive consciousness, mystical experiences, essence, bliss, ultimate meaning, transcendence of the self, oneness, cosmic awareness, cosmic self-humor and playfulness, sacralization of everyday life, and transcendental phenomena (Sutich, 1969). Transpersonal, within this context, means that the focus of attention is beyond self-concerns except when they include life-enhancing influences on others and the environment.

Some models that employ a creative theoretical structure are oriented to the present. For example, James Bugenthal (1980) represents an existential model when he states, "When I begin to realize that my truest identity is as process and not as fixed substance, I am on the verge of a terrible emptiness and a miraculous freedom. . . . Presence, being here, centeredness, immediacy, are all terms to point to a fundamental reality. Only in this moment am I alive."

Other models that subscribe to a transpersonal evolutionary focus are teleological with a future-oriented focus. A transpersonal alignment or a shift in consciousness would focus on establishing a direction or commitment to a purpose beyond either an assumed completion of self-development or self-gratification.

Hall and Lindzey (1978) discuss the particular focus of Carl Jung's perspective of the human dimension is his combination of *teleology* with *causality*. That is, the Jungian model is as focused on people's future direction as it is on their present understanding of experiences. Jung's theory of psychology is future-oriented in that it focuses on the nature of possibilities to which people strive (Schulz, 1981).

Roberto Assagioli (1965), the founder of psychosynthesis, agrees with the advantage of "directing all psychological tendencies toward creative purposes" because they accrue "from the manner in which these tendencies, the very energies themselves, become transmuted and sublimated through being redirected to higher ends" (Assagioli, 1973).

Paradoxically, we need a well enough defined self-identity with which to transcend. John C. Lilly (1972), a physician known for his early research with dolphins and later with altered states of conscious in relation to human beings, is adamant about this requirement for effective self-transcendence. Lilly clearly stated that personality development needs sufficient definition and reference before we can extend beyond its boundaries. Only in this way can we continue both to enhance self-development and transcend beyond self-identity.

To the extent that self-identity is not sufficiently clarified before experiencing transcendent experiences, there is an increasing risk of decompensation or disintegration of the observing ego or self-definition reference. Indeed, our clinical observations support that this was the primary difficulty with even well-intended and sincere experimental use of hallucinogenic drugs in the 1960s. The following actual anecdotal vignette illustrates that we need to have a self-identity before we can expand beyond it in a life-enhancing way and replace it with a different foreground.

Bob Z. was a lean, six-foot, twenty-seven-year-old Vietnam veteran in 1973. He was an outstandingly scholastic senior at a mid-western college. Attractive, bright, and charming, he was invited by several professors to informal faculty gatherings off-campus. Bob was socially appropriate with one exception. All of life was a big joke to Bob. Completely removed from emotional expression or intimate contact, he was always a major contributor to the celebration of the party. One of the professors at the college called him one evening to invite him to a social gathering of the faculty families.

Bob answered the phone, "Good evening, this is the President of the United States. How may I serve you?"

Knowing him, the faculty member responded, "Knock it off, Bob. This is Bill and I wanted to invite you to a picnic we are having Saturday afternoon at the park."

Bob responded, "I am terribly sorry, but I have a scheduled meeting with the Soviet Premier that afternoon, but perhaps I could attend afterward."

"Bob, quit fooling around. We're trying to get a count so we know how much food to make. Are you going to be there or not?"

"Clearly, you do not understand this very important matter of State. I need to take care of this crucial matter to our country first, and then I would be privileged if I have the luxury of having enough available time to honor your family gathering. Please do not expect me because I cannot determine ahead of time how long this important matter will take. However, in all likelihood, it looks as if our meeting will end in time to permit me to appear. I thank you for this sanctioned invitation and only wish that I can meet with you per your gracious request."

Frustrated, the professor ended the conversation. Never on the phone did Bob confess to the unreality of his imaginary role-play. However, Bob was not delusional. Nor was he schizophrenic, bipolar, psychotic, depressed, narcissistic, a multiple personality disorder, or any other *DSM* diagnosis. Bob was every bit as sane, and more mentally aware and healthy than most people. At least that was the view of all the professors of the psychology, philosophy, and religious studies departments, as well as their respective and nonacademically oriented families.

Bare-chested and clad in levis and sandals, Bob arrived at the picnic not more than an hour late, fashionably on time for his previous telephone role-play. He embellished a demur of formality as if he were royalty and had just arrived from the White House regardless of dress. He brought one bottle of Bolla Valpolicella for the host professor, several long-stem white roses for the wives of each professor, and ten kites for the children. Entertainingly and cordially, he met most members of every family, especially the children. Following appropriate introductions, he gathered all the children and took them into an expansive grass field to teach them the art of flying their kites.

Three months later, a professor of religious studies, who had attended the picnic, decided to have an informal meeting at his home to discuss shamanism and altered states of consciousness. Families and children were excluded, except the wife of the host. However, all of the other departmental professors, Bob, and 10 honor students were invited. These 10 graduating seniors were to be divided among the 3 host departments as honored guests and by invitation only.

All of those invited attended this moderately covert meeting that took place in 1973 in an environment of a private mid-western college where the faculties of psychology, philosophy, and religious studies, were sympathetic, if not devoted, to the expansion of consciousness beyond conventional beliefs. After a few presentations, there was a wine and cheese party. One of the students named Willy lit a "number" (marijuana cigarette) and tried to pass it to Bob. Bob just stared at Willy.

Willy responded, "Here, take some man, this is top-drawer stuff," and took a "hit" on the "joint."

Bob politely responded, "No thanks. I don't do that anymore," and looked in another direction.

Willy persisted, "Come on, you never had it this good."

Bob turned around, looked at Willy, and calmly but firmly replied, "Man, I smoked stuff out of a barrel of an M16 in Nam you never even heard of. I've done fresh peyote and mushrooms in the Yucatán and been on acid trips for days at a time. Don't give me that rap! You want to blow your mind, go for it, but don't play it out like you know what's happening."

As Willy walked away, Michael, a professor of religious studies, turned to Bob.

"Talk to me. I overheard your response to Willy and I want your opinion on something."

Bob looked at Michael, and seriously replied, "Sure, what do you want to know?"

"I've read some reasonably good studies suggesting that well-intended and controlled use of hallucinogenic substances facilitates both altered states of consciousness that can serve as rational breakthroughs for mystical experiences. My intellectual understanding of this is there is no free lunch, but I have very little personal experience to substantiate this assumption. What's your experience?"

Bob replied, "I don't know about anyone else, but I am convinced about my experience and I believe it represents an accurate account of what's happening. I agree. There are absolutely no short cuts. There is no doubt in my mind that what I have experienced with hallucinogenic drugs is the same in every way to everything I have read about mystical experiences, with one major exception. My experiences aren't integrated. They are all disorganized. It's like visiting a planet and receiving information that you know is true. However, once you are back home, it doesn't have any unified meaning in relationship to what's happening to you now. I noticed fragmented parts of the experiences at times and some of them are just starting to make sense to me. So, what I'm telling you from my experience is that I got the information, but I'll spend the next twenty years working on integrating it. Meanwhile, because I have experienced pieces of information that I know are true and different from ordinary reality, I feel somewhat alienated and disconnected from this world. Sometimes, I don't know what's real and what's fantasy."

Michael listened carefully, "So, do you think you're crazy at times?"

Bob smiled, "That's the point, isn't it. How would I know, when what I am working on is setting up the framework based on what's real to compare it to. You see, crazy, and the popular notion of conventional reality, and the conception of mystical are all different perspectives. To answer your question, I would need to commit to one of the frameworks, and I can't do that yet."

"So, assuming someone is interested in a mystical framework, you think it might be better to study yoga for twenty years."

"I don't know. I haven't studied yoga for twenty years. My guess is that we'll both get there at the same time, but Mr. Yoga is going to have a lot easier time along the way. He'll be ready for it when it happens. I wasn't, but I don't have that choice now."

In addition to the point that a well-defined ego is necessary for transition, and relevant to the above story, there is sometimes a well-intended but completely mistaken belief that mystical experience is similar to or identical with psychotic or schizophrenic experiences. This is a profound error of understanding. It is about as accurate and foolish as saying that because a tennis ball and an onion are both round, reasonably firm, and roughly the same size and color, they are both members of the vegetable kingdom.

The difference between the mystical and the schizophrenic experience is primarily one of preestablished self boundaries.

1. Regardless of culture, mystical observations of the workings of the universe are understood and agreed upon in structure and beliefs by other mystics.

2. The mystic experiences life beyond self-identity by choice.
3. The mystic is clear on the boundaries of self-definition and mystical understandings of both conventional and separate realities.
4. The mystic is self-fulfilled with his experience and contributes to others on similar paths.
5. In the application of observations, both mentor and apprentice experience life-enhancement by mystical experiences.

Contrary to all these positions is the experience and reality of the schizophrenic.

1. Specific to culture, schizophrenic observations of the workings of the universe are misunderstood compared to both conventional reality and reality as experienced by collective mystics. Individually understood structure and beliefs vary remarkably.

2. The schizophrenic experiences life within a disoriented self-identity through any combination of genetic transmission/predisposition and ineffective social learning. Self boundaries are poorly defined. Elements of the outside world enter without choice. Admittedly, there are schizophrenics who may have had mystical experiences, just as there are mystics who have had schizophrenic experiences. However, to equate the two is both an inductive and deductive fallacy (Wilber, 1989).

3. The schizophrenic is confused about any continual boundaries of self-definition, conventional reality, or mystical experiences.

4. Although exceptions exist, the schizophrenic is usually dissatisfied with his experience. While usually he can sympathize with other people classified as having major and minor psychiatric disorders, the contribution serves only to confirm self-limiting options.

5. In the application of observations, the schizophrenic is self-serving rather than oriented toward metaneeds.

In summary, self-identity and a socially developed personality need to be well established to provide a reference for continuous integration. Otherwise, any attempt to extend beyond oneself will add conflict to the functional personality development. Additionally, there is a significant difference between transcendent shifts of consciousness and psychotic experiences.

Creative theoretical structures work well with clients and psychotherapists who are high functioning and inclined toward this orientation. Some clients are extremely well adjusted, successful, and socially contributory and may function at a higher level of consciousness than their psychotherapists. Thus, an appropriate match between psychotherapist and client, or mentor and apprentice, at this level of functioning is more difficult and crucial.

The following summarizes the creative theoretical structure and its implications for application in behavioral science and psychotherapy.

A. People assume complete responsibility for their well-being and wellness. Focus is on the person and not the disease or disorder. Wellness is considered a state of being and not an absence of disease.

B. Dysfunctional symptoms are defined by the person. Dysfunctional symptoms indicate an ineffective solution to a basic need.

C. The person evaluates the discerned dysfunction and usually chooses wellness-oriented external authorities for evaluations and opinions.

D. Diagnosis is organismic, including all spiritual, mental, and physical aspects of the organism.

E. Wellness is assumed by living life-enhancing strategies of both conventional and unconventional wisdom.

F. People assume complete authority for evaluation and practice of wellness and well-being and frequently bond with others who support this belief.

G. Wellness and well-being are defined by an evaluation of self, of all others, and of ecological and planetary considerations.

From the perspective of productive and innovative theoretical structures, the disadvantage of employing a creative theoretical structure is that the process demands more personal responsibility than most people are willing to assume. In the productive and innovative theoretical structures, there is a fear of success and thereby fear of separation of self from others. In the creative theoretical structure, there is only less success. What the productive and innovative structures call a fear of failure is considered a convenient block to avoid increased responsibility that would be assumed in the creative structure. The fear of failure is only an excuse to avoid increased success, self-responsibility, and the awareness of those options.

After all, everybody knows all about the fear of failure. People are well practiced and familiar with the fear of failure. They started learning about the fear of failure when they were ejected from the womb and had to take a breath. In the early developmental years, they learned about eating without choking, walking without falling, and talking so other people could understand. The fear of success is less familiar and less frequently experienced directly. It is so because more people believe they have failed than those who believe they have succeeded. It is so because people are accustomed to focusing on their failures rather than crediting themselves with their successes. The fear of success is more difficult because it demands complete responsibility. When people try one hundred percent and the results do not meet their expectations, they become afraid of what really might happen with success.

Confronting the fear of failure is facing possible physical or emotional injury. Facing the fear of success is meeting the fear of aloneness. Within the perspective of the creative theoretical structure, the fear of success is not a fear of actual success at all. It is a mistaken notion that complete success would demand a level of responsibility beyond people's acknowledged and known abilities. Of course, the trick is to know that the fear of being responsible is a product of current limited beliefs.

From the perspective of the creative theoretical structure, the fear that success requires, rather than invites additional responsibility, is false. It results from patterns of experience only functional in productive and innovative structures. Believing that if people become completely successful, they will have to be responsible in ways that will be unpleasant to them, makes complete satisfaction or success extremely difficult, if not impossible. Within the creative theoretical structure, people do not have to be more responsible, with their current definition and understanding of responsibility, when they become more successful. They will develop a definition of responsibility that is not burdening with a shift in consciousness. The paradoxical difficulty is that people cannot know this until they take the risk of being completely successful according to their self-defined expectations.

Hole Theory and Newtonian Physics

Metaphorically, the productive and innovative theoretical structures are based on a presupposition we designate as *hole theory*. Hole theory is a global metaphor for discussing the etiology and resolution of diseases, disorders, malfunctions, disintegration, conflicts, and pain in human growth and development. The theory presumes that breakdowns or malfunctions of the self or personality are the result of various deficits. Hole theory starts from a negative assumption that is pessimistic and realistic. Within the productive theoretical structure, the belief is that people need to repair, recover, or rehabilitate the problem. Within the innovative theoretical structure the belief is that people need to cultivate their personality development or improve some aspect of dissatisfaction. Even *wellness* presumes a negative motivation. That is, people who are well do not attend wellness support groups.

Hole theorists postulate that people always need to try to repair and improve themselves. People attempt to improve their developmental fixations and dislodge their primitive defenses and replace them by those that are socially appropriate and contributory. Life must be a struggle. People are always trying and failing to climb out of the hole. As people have one good day, or actually accept themselves in a moment, something else must go wrong. Life is a series of conflicts and problems to solve.

However, people really are not expected to meet their expectations, assuming they even know them. Met expectations are news and the kind of recognized exceptions monitored in *Time* magazine and *Sports Illustrated*. Disappointments also are monitored. Hole theorists expect continued suffering and conflicts not only to occur but customarily to be insurmountable. Maturity is defined as learning to accept this as an existential reality. Nevertheless, people are strongly encouraged to keep trying. Completion is defined by the adaptive options of the cultural, social, or conventional reality as usually defined by hole theorists.

Fritz Perls (1969), the founder of Gestalt therapy (Hatcher and Himelstein, 1983), referred to *holes* in the personality. Holes represent deficits or areas of incompletion in self-development. Using this helpful analogy, people fill in these various deficits with either life-compromising or life-enhancing thoughts and behaviors. Examples of life-compromising methods include addictions, the lack of a nutritious diet, and inadequate exercise.

Other people try to provide what is missing in their lives with life-enhancing behaviors. Health-oriented people enhance personal growth and self-development by exercise, diet, creative expression, meditation, communication, intimacy, working, and sharing avocations with other people. People define their completeness as a result of either feeling good, thinking logically, or behaving effectively. When the current need is fulfilled or the conflict is resolved, it ceases to be a distraction demanding attention.

From a theological perspective, hole theory is similar to the Christian belief in original sin. Original sin in conventional Christian doctrine is a negative and assigned event of the human condition. Sin is automatic until redemption and salvation. Sin is forgivable, but only by the grace of God. That is, people can be saved, but only through transcendental penitence and externally referenced grace. Important to note within this presupposition is that people are also discouraged to make the transcendent God imminent. This presupposition supports a theological distinction between the human soul and the divine spirit. People are discouraged from believing they are a reflective part of the whole as an imminent God themselves.

Psychoanalytic, behavioral, and most existential models are based on this presupposition. Psychoanalytic models presume developmental pathology. With a focus on developmental fixations, complexes, and defenses, the entire model is bereft of healthful expectations. When theory is applied, the same negative expectations occur with a focus on resistance and transference. The belief is that, within the confines of accepting the inevitability of human tragedy, we need to adjust ourselves to accepting the *reality* of this developmental realization.

Representative of a behavioral model, B. F. Skinner (1971) believes freedom and dignity of the individual are misguided fantasies. Behaviorism contends that people make choices predetermined by a complex series of previous reinforcements, programs, schedules, learning, and conditioning. The only option is to repair the dysfunctional aspects of ineffective associations, conditioning, and learning such that they can be productive and effective in everyday life.

Existentialism is a philosophy initiated by Friedrich Nietzsche and Sören Kierkegaard in the nineteenth century. It was further developed by Jean-Paul

Sartre, Karl Jaspers, Albert Camus, and Martin Heidegger in the twentieth century. According to Shaffer (1978), four existential themes emerge as primary:

1. People are confronted with the unavoidable uncertainty of a world without any fixed meaning and with the certainty of their eventual nonbeing or death.
2. In the face of a potentially meaningless situation, they become aware of their inherent freedom to choose attitudes toward situations and to choose their actions.
3. There are constraints, both biological and environmental, on human freedom, yet within these limits there is always a choice.
4. People cannot evade responsibility for choosing for themselves, for they are constantly creating themselves by the choices they make or fail to make. It is this awareness of personal freedom and responsibility that leads to anxiety. How to deal with this anxiety is significantly related to identity.

Fundamentally, existentialists believe that people can become a whole self only by accepting their inadequacies and adjusting to the given human conditions of pain, anxiety, fear, and death. The existential view of the world is that it is a cosmic tragedy.

Hole theory correlates with classical Newtonian physics, which focuses on cause-effect relationships—where, when one event happens, it causes a seemingly separate event to occur. The explanation of events is associative and linear. Events occur in a past, present, and future sequence. Newtonian physics focuses on "the individual unit of being, separate in recognition from the rest of reality, and this individuality is considered most real. The placing of it in classification is only for the purpose of making it easier to think about and to remember" (Leshan, 1974).

In summary, according to hole theory, events occur as time moves from the future through the present and into the past. Human development is perceived as beginning at birth and ending at death. For most people's daily life, Newtonian physics is absolutely necessary and valid. People use this structure for stopping at red lights, making breakfast, tying their shoes, and other such task-oriented behaviors. It is essential for daily behaviors that most people must perform routinely.

Whole Theory and Field Theory

Metaphorically, the creative theoretical structure is based on a presupposition we designate as *whole theory*. Whole theory is an alternative and qualitatively different metaphor for understanding harmony and dysfunction in human growth and development. The theory presumes that self-compromising or self-limiting events occur as a result of disharmony with the larger phenomenal field. This field of experiences includes all other living entities. It even includes forms not considered as living with hole theory such as rocks and man-made objects.

Malfunctions are interpreted as an imbalance of forces, incongruence, or a lack of metasynchronicity. Different from problematic symptoms, these malfunctions are positive signs for correcting imbalance through personal alignment of increasing responsibility and contributing effect. Whole theory starts from a positive assumption that is optimistic and idealistic. Within the creative theoretical structure, the belief is that life-enhancement inevitably demands responsibility for aligning self beyond immediate self-concerns in favor of valuing the phenomenal field (Welch, 1983).

Personal evolution is assumed as a natural course of events within the field. There is not necessarily a need to improve the self, except in consideration of realignment with the field beyond self. Even in this case, such shift of consciousness is not a quantitative improvement where *better* means *more* and *more* means *better*. The belief of improvement is a measurable and valuative term interpreted within hole theory. It is inaccurate to describe processes with whole theory because it is self-referential at the exclusion of the field.

Whole theorists postulate that life is just life. The force of life is neither a curse nor a blessing. Physical life does provide opportunity—opportunity to transcend beyond confined self-concerns. Within whole theory, when problems are self-exclusive, personal problems will continue to exist by the basic process of self-referential interpretation. People are optimistically expected to meet their expectations, either sooner or later, but only with a shift from conventual field-limited consciousness. Otherwise, they are expected to continue functioning within the limitations of hole theory. A shift of consciousness is defined as learning to accept the force of field as an inevitability.

In modern field theory (Oppenheimer, 1966), personal reality is the role individuals play in the larger phenomenal field. Self-experience, within the phenomenal field, is *of* the field of experience. Individual experiences, separate from the whole field, are experiences of an artificially separate part of the field. Field experiences are similar to *near-death* (NDE), or *out-of-body* (OBE), experiences (not to be confused with delusions). The experience is as an observer outside of self. "Thus, from a field-theory viewpoint, we cannot legitimately say, 'Here is an electron,' but can say it best, 'Here is an area where the field is strong,' or else we must switch back to the point of classical physics and say, 'Here is a place and time where an instrument registered a reaction'" (Leshan, 1974).

Einstein's theory of relativity assumes geometry is a construct of the human intellect (Margenau, 1959). Our intellect separates and classifies experiences as a way to understand them, providing a different perspective for application. Also, our intellect can experience beyond the geometrical structure and conceive reality outside of conventional categories. Rather than focusing on structure, whole theory focuses on function (King, 1973). Field theory is outside the linear dimension of usual experience. The Newtonian categorization of past, present, and future delineations is irrelevant. All experience is encompassed in the present.

The phenomenal field consists of energy in continuous motion. Change is the constant. This motion, however, "is not chaotic and haphazard though it includes an element of randomness. It is ordered motion—motion within boundaries, within more or less clearly defined and relatively permanent *fields*" (Rudhyar, 1970).

Not only is the phenomenal field *in order*, but it maintains a structure that pervades all function of energy, particularly observable in the living human organism. We create continual dispositions and do so by intentionally acting on our environment. We do so by selecting particular situations and by applying the results. Action is either intentional or unintentional. Action without a conscious purpose in mind is means-oriented and usually occurs as unconscious reactivity. To say that the latter is purposeless is true only in the sense there is no predetermined goal known to the conscious mind. It is purposeful in and of the moment. Later it can be judged to have or have not been purposeful for some other end.

Methodological Implications

Each of the theoretical presuppositions has advantages and disadvantages for practical implementation. The effective advantage of hole theory is that it operates within the public domain of identifiable experience. It focuses on concrete problems and within what most people experience as cause-effect relationships. It is symptom specific and often offers immediate results for resolution of symptomatology. It focuses on the past and the present with which people can easily identify and associate their cause-effect activity.

Hole theory focuses on development, from prepersonal to personal. Adults can identify conflicts as associated and linked to patterns in childhood. For example, those growing up in a dysfunctional family of origin can see how patterns learned in childhood predetermine the conflicts they experience in their current families.

The advantage of whole theory is that it operates outside our usual belief limitations. It provides an opportunity for an expansion of self-identity and redefinition regardless of the limitations associated with particular diagnoses. It is frequently more therapeutically effective than hole theory because it circumvents and transcends the expected limitations of cause-effect relationships. It focuses on the present and the future. Within the range of personal development, whole theory focuses on the personal and transpersonal. It focuses on the definition of self and the greater universal experiences that bind people together.

An ideal example of the practical implications of these different theoretical structures is the use of clinical hypnosis. Clinical hypnosis can facilitate weight change and heal physical disease and injuries. Suppose we want to help a client (Example 1) lose weight and (Example 2) to help another heal an arthritic or injured hand.

Using clinical hypnosis within hole theory, we would want the client to repair or improve the disease or damage. Hole theory states that once we repair or restore structure, then the client can accept it. In clinical hypnosis, the process to repair or restore blocks, problems, diseases, or conditions to their original functioning or desired state is known as *process imagery*.

As applied to weight loss, one such process imagery is *jungle doors* (Stern and Hoch, 1976). In this imagery, the client visualizes walking through a jungle and finding a door. Behind the door is a barrier to the desired achievement. By opening the door, the client can study the nature of the block and as a result can program success. This imagery facilitates discovery of hidden psychological blocks to losing weight.

In Example 2, healing an arthritic or injured hand, the process is to visualize the specific nature of how the hand is damaged. The psychotherapist asks the client to draw pictures of the damaged part and visualize every facet of the damage. The client is then directed to bring forth some image of repairing the disease or damage. Images could include a fixing crew or a water hose to cleanse it. The process is to repair the wound and restore the hand to its original functioning.

Using clinical hypnosis within whole theory, we would want the client to visualize the desired state of being or goal. Whole theory states that as people imagine a desired state, they intentionally facilitate its occurrence. In clinical hypnosis, this process is known as *end-result imagery*.

As applied to weight loss, the client in Example 1 is encouraged to visualize being thin, which is more powerful than merely thinking thin. Regarding weight loss, there is evidence to suggest that end-result imagery is more powerful than process imagery (Korn and Johnson, 1983).

In Example 2, whole theory focuses on the client experiencing the hand as already well. It starts with acceptance. Whole theory focuses on the hand in its functional completeness. Within clinical hypnosis, this imagery pulls from the future, but within the belief that has already occurred. Following an introductory trance, the client visualizes the hand in its perfect state of wellness.

An extremely small sample of research studies in hypnotic altercations and healing within the autonomic nervous system indicate that people can:

1. Cure warts (Johnson and Barber, 1978; Ullman, 1959).
2. Alleviate conventional headaches (Barabasz and McGeorge, 1978).
3. Cure diverse forms of dermatitis (Barber, 1984).
4. Aid the coagulation of blood in hemophiliacs (Banks, 1985).

5. Relieve hypertension and cardiac difficulties (Gruen, 1972; Wain, Amen, and Oetgen, 1984).
6. Enhance the immune response (Hall, 1982–83).

Additionally, there is increasing evidence that people can significantly contribute to prevention and modulate more severe diseases such as those involving the endocrine system which affects hormonal rhythms, postpartum depression, the aging process (Rossi, 1986), and the immune system which affects cancer, asthma, allergies, and arthritis (Rossi, 1986; Rossi and Cheek, 1988; Siegel, 1986). The more severe the disease, the more reluctant hole theorists are to admit cure. In contrast, previous diseases, even when cured, always are considered in remission by hole theorists.

Newtonian physics can only go so far to explain curative results within cause-effect relationships. Some hole theorists might accept that people can get rid of their warts. However, when another client states he or she removed a mole, hole theorists would more likely say, "You can't do that." Moles are outside the possibility. Or, they might say the client only thought it was a mole, but it was a wart. There are many boundaries and impossibilities in the hole presupposition. From the presupposition of whole theory, most anything is possible. The limits of whole theory are the self-imposed ones.

Parents may remember when their children were very young. They may have demonstrated strange abilities, when considered within a cause-effect structure. Children, of course, think nothing of such things. At some point, children start to hear they are not supposed to be able to perform these *miracles*. They start thinking maybe it cannot be done. They may start believing they dreamed it or just imagined it. Or, maybe they hallucinated the experience. Phenomenologically, children start removing themselves, at this point, from identifying as a part of the field. Self-identifiably outside the field, they start thinking by the rules of classical physics. Associations and relationships now become cause-effect occurrences. Something or someone always makes events happen by a chain of events.

Another example of how different theoretical structures imply methodological differences is a client diagnosed as a having panic disorder with agoraphobia. Jane has difficulty driving. Everytime she drives, she becomes terrified of hearing sirens. The sirens remind her of when she needed to take her two-year old child to the hospital. The child was fine. However, all later events that Jane associates with her previous fear elicit panic. Her anxiety now makes it difficult for her to go to the market and shopping mall, and even continue to drive to psychotherapy sessions.

The theoretical implication of hole theory is to repair or rehabilitate the immediate symptomatology. The behavioral model is an excellent choice within this structure. From a whole structural view, her difficulties are within a global field. This client was passive dependent. She did not want to grow up.

From a whole structure we might say, "Look, you have all these difficulties. You have multiple limitations. You can't go to the market. You can't do this and you can't do that. You tell me you don't feel very grown up. Everyone treats you as pretty and you don't think you have a brain."

As the client acknowledges this, the whole theorist orients her toward a responsible adult image in the future. She can focus on the picture of how she would want to be if she were an ideal adult of her choice. We start by working with what "adult" looks like to her. We then set incremental goals. For example, starting to grow up might mean she can run in the park with her dog for fifteen minutes without her husband. This is an initial step toward achieving her image of an adult. She starts thinking and behaving with the structure of her idealized adult image. She acts *as if* this image were already occurring. She approximates fulfillment. She starts behaving in ways that agree with her idealized image. She thinks in that way and the panic subsides. The agoraphobic behavior occurs less often. She begins driving and going to the market. Whole theory, here, is pulling from the future rather than repairing the phobic symptom. Defining our underlying theoretical structure and its implications allows us to determine a congruent methodology.

Notes

1. The use of metaphors, as one example of applied observations, are thoroughly discussed in chapter 7, Boundaries of Imposition.
2. Several nineteenth-century engineers, including two Germans—Gottlieb Daimler and Karl Benz—actually are responsible for creating the automobile. Henry Ford innovated mass-production and convenient servicing of the product.
3. The concept of *energy* is defined here as an electromagnetic or biochemical event of power and force. This definition includes the Indian (yogic) concept of *prajna* or *prana* (Garrison, 1964; Vishnudevananda, 1960), the Chinese (Taoist) and martial arts concept of *chi* (Man-ch'ing and Smith, 1971), the Japanese (Zen), and martial arts concept of *ki*, (Westbrook and Ratti, 1977). All of these multicultural concepts are nearly identical (Frager, 1970). These concepts translate into the English as vital energy, vital air, vital force, and intrinsic energy. They include the implication of mental direction or discriminative knowledge (Goleman, 1977).

References

American Psychiatric Association. (1987). *Diagnostic and statistical manual of mental disorders* (3d ed., rev.) (*DSM-III-R*). Washington, DC: American Psychiatric Association.

Assagioli, R. (1965). *Psychosynthesis*. New York: Hobbs & Dorman.

Assagioli, R. (1973). *The act of will*. New York: Viking Press.

Banks, W. (1985). Hypnotic suggestion for the control of bleeding in the angiography suite. *Ericksonian Monographs, 1*, 76–88.

Barabasz, A., & McGeorge, C. (1978). Biofeedback, mediated biofeedback and hypnosis in peripheral vasodilation training. *The American Journal of Clinical Hypnosis, 21*(1), 28–37.

Barber, T. (1984). Changing unchangeable bodily processes by (hypnotic) suggestions: A new look at hypnosis, cognitions, imagining, and the mind-body problem. *Advances, 1*(2), 7–40.

Bugenthal, J. (1980). *The search for authenticity* (pp. 191–92.) New York: Holt, Rinehart, and Winston.

Corey, G. (1982). *Theory and practice of counseling and psychotherapy*. Monterey, CA: Brooks/Cole.

Fadiman, J. (1980). The transpersonal stance. In R. Walsh & Vaughn F. (Eds.), *Beyond ego* (p. 177). Los Angeles: J. Tarcher.

Frager, R. (1970, December). On vital energy: Some Eastern and Western conceptions. Paper presented at the World Conference on Scientific Yoga, New Delhi, India.

Frankl, V. (1967). *Psychotherapy and existentialism*. New York: Washington Square Press.

Frankl, V. (1969). *The will to meaning*. New York: World Publishing.

Frankl, V. (1963). *Man's search for meaning* (p. 174). New York: Washington Square Press.

Garrison, O. (1964). *Tantra: The Yoga of sex*. New York: Julian Press.

Glasser, W. (1965). *Reality therapy: A new approach to psychiatry*. New York: Harper & Row.

Goleman, D. (1977). *The varieties of meditative experience* (p. 77). New York: Irvington Publishers.

Gruen, W. (1972). A successful application of systematic self-relaxation and self-suggestions about postoperative reactions in a case of cardiac surgery. *International Journal of Clinical and Experimental Hypnosis, 20*, 141–151.

Hall, C., & Lindzey, G. (1978). *Theories of personality*. (3d ed.). New York: Wiley.

Hall, H. (1982). Hypnosis and the immune system: A review with implications for cancer and the psychology of healing. *The American Journal of Clinical Hypnosis, 25*(2–3), 92–103.

Hatcher, C., & Himelstein, P. (Eds.). (1983). *The handbook of Gestalt therapy*. Northvale, NJ: Jason Aronson.

Johnson, R., & Barber, T. (1978). Hypnosis, suggestion, and warts: An experimental investigation implicating the importance of "believed-in efficacy." *The American Journal of Clinical Hypnosis, 20*, 165–174.

King, C. (1973). *The states of human consciousness*. New Hyde Park, NY: University Books.

Korn, E., & Johnson, K. (1983). *Visualization: The uses of imagery in the health professions* (p. 162). Homewood, IL: Dow Jones-Irwin.

Kroger, W. (1977). *Clinical and experimental hypnosis* (2d ed.). Philadelphia: J. B. Lippincott.

Leshan, L. (1974a). *The medium, the mystic, and the physicist: Toward and general theory of the paranormal* (p. 234–235). New York: Viking Press.

Lilly, J. (1972). *The center of the cyclone*. New York: Julian Press.

Man-ch'ing, C., & Smith, R. (1971). *T 'ai-Chi* (p. 5). Rutland, VT: Charles E. Tuttle.

Margenau, H. (1959). Einstein's conception of reality. In Schilppi, P. (Ed.) *Albert Einstein: Philosopher–scientist*. New York: Harper & Row.

Oppenheimer, J. (1966). *Science and the common understanding*. New York: Simon & Schuster.

Perls, F. (1969). *In and out of the garbage pail*. Moab, UT: Real People Press.

Rossi, E. (1986a). *The psychobiology of mind-body healing* (pp. 125-148, 149–181). New York: W. W. Norton.

Rossi, E. (1986b). *The psychobiology of mind-body healing* (pp. 149-181). New York: W. W. Norton.

Rossi, E., & Cheek, D. (1988). *Mind-body therapy: Methods of ideodynamic healing in hypnosis*. New York: W. W. Norton.

Rudhyar, D. (1970). *The planetarization of consciousness* (p. 120). The Netherlands: Servire/Wassenaar.

Schulz, D. (1981). *Theories of personality* (2d ed.). Monterey, CA: Brooks/Cole.

Shaffer, B. (1978). *Humanistic psychology*. Englewood Cliffs, NJ: Prentice-Hall.

Siegel, B. (1986). *Love, medicine and miracles*. New York: Harper & Row.

Skinner, B. (1971). *Beyond freedom and dignity*. New York: Knopf.

Stern, F., & Hoch, R. (1976). *Mind trips to help you lose weight* (pp. 93–95). Chicago: Playboy Press.

Suitch, A. (1969, Spring). Inside flap. *Journal of Transpersonal Psychology* (1st issue).

Ullman, M. (1959). On the psyche and warts: I. Suggestion and warts: A review and comment. *Psychosomatic Medicine, 21*, 473–488.

Vishnudevananda, S. (1960). *The complete illustrated book of yoga* (p. 356). New York: Bell Publishing.

Wain, H., Amen, D., & Oetgen, W. (1984). Hypnotic intervention in cardiac arrhythmias. *The American Journal of Clinical Hypnosis, 27*(1), 70–75.

Welch, G. (1983). A phenomenological study of the transpersonal experience of "acting from field": Three case studies. Unpublished doctoral dissertation. The Professional School for Humanistic Studies, San Diego, CA.

Westbrook, A. & Ratti, O. (1977). *Aikido and the dynamic sphere* (p. 81). Rutland, VT: Charles E. Tuttle.

Wilber, K. (1982). The pre/trans fallacy. *Journal of Humanistic Psychology, 22*(2), 5–43.

Wilber, K. (1989). Two humanistic psychologies? *Journal of Humanistic Psychology, 29*(2), 230–243.

5

<hr />

Clarifying
Methodologies

As theoretical structures are the foundational framework of the professional home, *methodologies* are the working functions of the experiential and psychotherapeutic household. Methodologies are the specifically applied functions of theoretical structures. Observations confirm that many psychotherapists are remarkably unclear about their employed methodology and its influence on their clients. As often as not, psychotherapists are unaware of the methodological language they use to state opinions and requests for change to their clients.

Personal and professional expectations of psychotherapeutic results depend on the effective rendering of psychotherapeutic skills. Effectiveness demands that psychotherapists specifically know the feelings, thoughts, and behaviors they want from their clients. Later, it requires they communicate these suggestive implications or direct requests such that their clients can appropriately respond. At the very least, effective methodology is measured by a client's understanding of the psychotherapist.

Whether known or not, the specific language psychotherapists use with their clients ultimately defines their methodology as perceived by their clients. Language transfers explicit meaning as well as implied meaning. English and romance languages use nouns to designate objects and use verbs to designate actions that suggest the valuative orientation for nouns or objects. Verbs or predicates have the most subconscious (*implicit* meaning) power because they motivate behavior. Additionally, they have the most consciously recognized power (*explicit* meaning) because of immediate concrete imagery.

In psychotherapeutic dialogue, this mechanism is particularly obvious from the client's perception and understanding. As clients listen to their psychotherapists, they register dictated and implied messages primarily through action verbs. With intended compliance, clients then interpret requests and demands to change themselves according to the specific methodologies suggested by their psychotherapists.

Psychotherapeutic opinions, requests, or demands are either clear or vague in requesting desired responses from clients. The following vignette is an example of vague communication by a psychotherapist, which elicits equally vague responses from a client.

PSYCHOTHERAPIST: So, what's going on today?

CLIENT: Oh, not much. I guess I'm kind of tired.

PSYCHOTHERAPIST: Were you up late last night?

CLIENT: No, not any later than usual.

PSYCHOTHERAPIST: Well then, how is it that you're tired?

CLIENT: Maybe I'm kind of tired with the same old routine.

PSYCHOTHERAPIST: Yeah, I know what you mean.

CLIENT: You do? I don't! I'm confused.

PSYCHOTHERAPIST: So am I. I don't understand. Are you tired or are you confused?

CLIENT: I don't know. Maybe it's a little bit of both. You tell me. You're the doctor.

PSYCHOTHERAPIST: Now it sounds like you're angry.

CLIENT: That's strange. I'm not aware of that, and I certainly wasn't when I came in here today.

PSYCHOTHERAPIST: Well, what would you like to work on?

CLIENT: Not much of anything, I guess. I'm kind of tired.

Methodologies easily are divided by explicit and implicit language into three major messages as interpreted by psychotherapists and clients. The first methodology we are discussing is *behavioral*. It requires increasing effective actions that reinforce goals and are appropriate for symptom resolution. The second methodology, in order of presentation, is *cognitive*. It focuses on awareness of thoughts, beliefs, values, and logical and illogical reasoning. Cognitive methodology requires restructuring negative thoughts into positive affirmations and directing self-identity toward the present and the future. The third methodology is *affective* and includes awareness and acknowledgment of feelings and their expression.

Each methodology presumes different underlying curative beliefs. That is, each methodology assumes that it is the primary effect. As such, the other two methodologies are results. The behavioral methodology assumes effective behavior will elicit logical thoughts and appropriate emotional responses. The cognitive methodology assumes logical thoughts increase awareness, expression of feelings, and effective behavior. The affective methodology assumes that logical thoughts and effective behavior will follow increased awareness and expression of feelings.

Psychotherapeutic communications are either clear or vague. They also are either consistent or erratic in requesting desired responses from clients. This consistency or erratic quality is measurable and defined according to the verbs used to either give or request information. An example of inconsistency is an undefined mixture of behavioral, cognitive, and affective verbs. The following vignette is an example of inconsistent requests by a psychotherapist, which elicit confused responses from a client—methodologies are italicized and tagged by a notation in parentheses. Notice how the client becomes more confused in attempting to follow the variant methodologies of the psychotherapist.

PSYCHOTHERAPIST: How are you *feeling* (affective question) today?

CLIENT: I *feel* (affective response) better than usual. I mean there were the usual *ups* and *downs* (affective response) during the week.

PSYCHOTHERAPIST: What exactly *happened*? (behavioral question)

CLIENT: Oh, my boyfriend *left* (behavioral response) again after we *threw* (behavioral response) things at each other in a fight. He is *drinking* (behavioral response) again, but I don't *see* what I can *do* (behavioral response) about it.

PSYCHOTHERAPIST: Well, what *makes* (behavioral question) you *think* (cognitive question) it's your responsibility?

CLIENT: Actually, I don't *believe* (cognitive response) it is my responsibility. It's that I really am *angry* (affective response) this time.

PSYCHOTHERAPIST: What do you *mean* (cognitive question) by angry?

CLIENT: I can't *take* (behavioral response) it anymore, and I just want to *run* (behavioral response) away.

PSYCHOTHERAPIST: I don't *understand* (cognitive statement). Is that what you *feel* (affective question) like doing or is that what you are *going* (behavioral question) to do?

CLIENT: I don't *know* (cognitive response). I'm just saying that's how *angry* (affective response) I am, and I need the *situation to change* (behavioral response).

This over-simplified example illustrates a methodologically inconsistent, repetitive, and confusing dialogue that compromises psychotherapeutic ineffectiveness. It goes around and around and where it ends nobody knows. When this methodology is implemented, both client wellness and psychotherapeutic satisfaction are diminished, if not nullified.

Quite understandably, each of the trivariate methodologies has advantages and limitations from each of the perspectives of psychotherapeutic training, implementation, and effectiveness with different clients. These advantages and disadvantages will be discussed below within the parameters of a closer examination of the methodologies.

As an introductory remark, *expertise* is defined as psychotherapists knowing their belief systems, perceptual attitudes, and theoretical structures. Following through these paradigms, they can then implement a compatible and consistent methodology. However, limitations of a methodology can continue to compound when psychotherapists make erratic and confusing or conflicting opinions or requests of their clients.

When psychotherapists are clear and consistent with their methodological language, clients are more likely to learn, follow expectations, and achieve desired results. These are the results that yield increasingly effective psychotherapy for both client and psychotherapist. Although psychotherapists are not responsible for the success of their clients, they are explicitly responsible for making their expectations clear and consistent to their clients. Effectiveness with continued treatment is measured by both clarity and consistency of similar messages as perceived by the client.

The behavioral, cognitive, and affective methodologies are equally effective for specified purposes when intentionally and consistently employed. Of course, this implementation also depends on the limitations of the specific client receiving the targeted usage. Observation shows that, all too often, the obvious limitations of clients serve as a convenient rationalization by psychotherapists for ineffective results.

Subcategories of methodologies include *techniques* and *strategies*. Techniques are detailed implementations for achieving a desired goal. They are the tools of our craft and the specific skills we use to increase the effectiveness of our methodology. Techniques usually are identified or associated with psychotherapeutic models rather than with methodologies. A few examples of techniques include:

- Systematic desensitization and implosion (behavioral models)
- Reframing and thought-stopping (cognitive model)
- Role-playing and empty chair (affective model)
- Free association and dream interpretation (analytic model)
- Trance induction (hypnotic model)
- Sculpting (family model)
- Loosening muscular armor (bioenergetics model)

- Script analysis (transactional model)
- Meditation (transpersonal model)

Strategies are predetermined sequences of techniques designed for a specific purpose. Different from treatment plans, strategies may include a sequence of techniques from the same or varied methodologies or models for a predetermined specified goal. For example, Dr. Najera consistently employed a well-defined cognitive methodology although he was certified in a Gestalt therapy model. With a particular client, Dr. Najera discovered that his client was emotionally blocked from fulfilling well-intended conscious and rational decisions.

Strategically, Dr. Najera decided he would use a Gestalt therapy model during the next three sessions with his client to break through impasse resistances. He discussed with his client his reasons for this departure from the methodology and model. His client agreed with the circumscribed psychotherapeutic strategy. As the client experientially and affectively processed experiences of child abuse, he assumed responsibility for his projected anger at authority. After the three sessions using a Gestalt therapy model, Dr. Najera returned to his cognitive methodology. As a result of emotional awareness and resolution, the client successfully fulfilled his new conscious decisions.

Effective implementation is a result of methodological clarity of experiential parameters and explicit communication. Effectiveness also requires continuity and circumscribed methods that a client can follow. Clients need to be able to understand psychotherapeutic expectations. A closer look at different methodologies will help psychotherapists clarify their implementations and increase their effectiveness. Figure 5–1 illustrates all three psychotherapeutic methodologies, the four kinds of feelings with examples, and the corresponding levels of catharsis.

The Behavioral Methodology

Psychotherapists who implement a behavioral methodology use variations of the verb, *to do*. They communicate an interest in finding out what their clients *do* to change their situations from which they can offer suggestions for modifying specific behaviors. Examples of such questions and statements include:

- What did you do when she said that?
- Did you do the homework we talked about last week?
- What happened after the anger?
- How could you change the situation to act differently next time?
- Let's set up a plan where you can slowly pretend to be more assertive.
- How does anger run your life?
- What do you want to achieve?

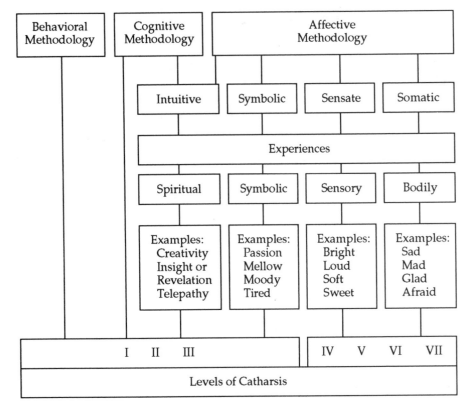

FIGURE 5–1   Psychotherapeutic Methodologies

- What are your accomplishments in this area?
- What will you do next time in the same situation?
- Does that performance work for you?
- What plan of action would make that happen for you?
- How can you act differently?
- Have you considered leaving the room?
- How will you handle leaving your job?
- What kind of conduct is right for you in those situations?
- How do you maintain your diet?
- Where will you go?

Example A: The following vignette illustrates a consistent *behavioral* method-ology (with an interpersonal perceptual attitude and productive theoretical structure) with a twenty-five-year-old, single, male client (Jamie) diagnosed with acute paranoid schizophrenia resulting from a drug reaction and currently on an inpatient service. This example also illustrates a psychotherapist who is willing to role-play through his client's resistance without focusing on emotional elicitation.

PSYCHOTHERAPIST: Good afternoon.

CLIENT: (no response)

PSYCHOTHERAPIST: (after long pause) Jamie, talk to me. What's happening in your world?

CLIENT: (no response)

PSYCHOTHERAPIST: (after long pause and in a monotone voice) Jamie, this is starship central command to satellite 386 in the cosmic galaxy. We have been transmitting for over five minutes without any response from you. We would appreciate a telegraphed message letting us know your location and bearing on your next orbit. Do you copy? Do you copy? Please indicate immediately by tapping your fingers on the chair three times and then talking to me. It is especially important that you tap your fingers three times on the chair, otherwise someone might hear our conversation.

CLIENT: (after tapping his fingers three times and now looking in the direction of the psychotherapist) I'm fairly spaced out today. It's all the medication they've got me on.

PSYCHOTHERAPIST: The medication just removes the static, Jamie. You can hear more clearly now because you are safe. By the way, how's your pool game?

CLIENT: (smile) No one in the organization can beat me. They try to fool me and use their powers to make me miss, but it doesn't work. I know who's in command.

PSYCHOTHERAPIST: Who's in command?

CLIENT: Jamie.

PSYCHOTHERAPIST: What's he doing now?

CLIENT: He's repairing the engine.

PSYCHOTHERAPIST: What's wrong with it?

CLIENT: I don't know. I'm still checking it out. Looks like some damaged parts.

PSYCHOTHERAPIST: Can you fix them?

CLIENT: I don't know. Can I get back to you?

PSYCHOTHERAPIST: No. I need to know now because our generator isn't working too well down here either, and we're afraid it's going to fail soon. You need to let me know whether you can fix your engine so we can depend on you. We need you Jamie.

CLIENT: (pause) I can fix it if I can find the right repair manual.

PSYCHOTHERAPIST: Good! Which one do you need? We've got a whole library down here. If you tell me which one and we find it, I can fax it to you.

CLIENT: It's Control Dictum, Volume VII. Do you have it?

PSYCHOTHERAPIST: Just a moment. I'm looking. (psychotherapist pretends to look for an imaginary manual all around his chair) Jamie, can you still hear me?

CLIENT: Yeah. I'm with you. Did you find it?

PSYCHOTHERAPIST: No! Somebody must have ripped it off. I saw it a couple of weeks ago [the time that Jamie was admitted] and I know it was here before. You've got to hurry up and fix it without the manual or we're all going to be in serious trouble. We're depending on your help now.

CLIENT: (long pause) Okay! I found the right manual, but some pages are missing.

PSYCHOTHERAPIST: I can barely hear you. Can you fix the engine without the missing pages?

CLIENT: (looking at the psychotherapist) Yeah. I can fix it. I just need a little more time.

PSYCHOTHERAPIST: Can I depend on you?

CLIENT: If you get your generator back in order, will you continue to monitor me?

PSYCHOTHERAPIST: Yes! That's a confirmation, Jamie. I'll see you tomorrow.

Example B: The following vignette illustrates a consistent behavioral methodology (with an interpersonal perceptual attitude and an innovative theoretical structure) with a twenty-two-year-old, male client:

PSYCHOTHERAPIST: Good morning. (pause) Well, how did you do on your homework last week?

CLIENT: I did a lot better this past week. I started reading the book you assigned me and learned how I let other people take advantage of me by not asserting myself.

PSYCHOTHERAPIST: That's great! How far did you get in the reading?

CLIENT: Uh, up to the part where the author starts talking about assertion being a perfect right and not unfit conduct. Reading that kind of changed the way I dealt with people during the week.

PSYCHOTHERAPIST: Tell me about that. Tell me how you handled people differently from the way you usually do.

CLIENT: Before, I've been afraid that if I ask people for what I wanted or even deserved, they would reject me. This has been actually happening in my job. I have been working there for three years and just found out I should have gotten a raise two years ago, but I was afraid to tell my boss. I do good work and I'm one of the senior people there, but I see that I've been putting my head in the sand because I didn't want to risk getting fired. (long pause)

PSYCHOTHERAPIST: So, tell me, what did you say?

CLIENT: (small chuckle) It was simple. I just walked up to her and showed her the last two years of my paycheck stubs and reminded her of the company policy of automatic raises every year. Then, she looked at me with this puzzled look on her face, said she was sorry, and that I was way overdue.

PSYCHOTHERAPIST: Exactly how did you tell her? Did you need to get angry, threatening, and intimidating to get what you wanted?

CLIENT: No! Not at all. I just told her as a matter of fact and that's when she looked at me and apologized.

PSYCHOTHERAPIST: Fantastic! So, you asserted yourself, were socially appropriate, got what you wanted, and didn't get rejected. It looks to me as if you were pretty successful.

CLIENT: Yeah!

The behavioral methodology focuses on changes of action and alterations of learned behavior. It focuses on plans of action and performances to change current ineffective behavior. One advantage of the behavioral methodology is there are not multiple *interpretations* of an act itself. Either we do something or we don't do it. In trying to do something, we have failed. Either we act differently or we don't. While there are endless ways of acting and doing, all methodologies suggesting change deal with concrete occurrences in the observable world rather than interpretations of meaning. Interpretations of meaning are within the cognitive methodology.

The Cognitive Methodology

The cognitive methodology includes variations of the verb *to think*. The cognitive psychotherapist focuses on discovering and restructuring how people think. The interest is in how people associate different thoughts, feelings, and behavior. The interest is in the sequence of thinking and illogical associations. On a conscious level, focus is on the client's values and beliefs. On the subconscious level, focus is on the circumstances surrounding the original formulation of values or beliefs. Psychotherapists implementing a cognitive methodology ask questions and make statements like:

- What was your interpretation of _____ ?
- What are you thinking right now?
- What went through your mind when that happened?
- What is your understanding of that now?
- From your experience, now as an adult, is that logical?
- What thoughts or ideas showed up for you when you heard that?
- How was that important to you?
- It sounds like you validate your self-worth through the opinions of others.
- How do you know?
- What do you mean by *love*?
- How do you value love in relation to your stated needs for freedom and independence?
- What are your considerations about money?
- How did you figure that out?
- I don't understand your reasons.
- How do you justify that in your mind?
- How do you compare _____ ?
- What is your belief about how you get sick?
- How do you connect what happened with your feelings of dissatisfaction?

Example A: The following vignette illustrates a consistent cognitive methodology (with an interpersonal perceptual attitude and innovative theoretical structure) with a thirty-year-old, divorced, female client:

PSYCHOTHERAPIST: Good afternoon.

CLIENT: Hi, how are you?

PSYCHOTHERAPIST: I'm fine, thank you. What would you like to work on today?

CLIENT: I had a really lousy week. My kids, age two and four, are driving me crazy. They don't seem to get along anymore. The babysitter can't control them and told me she wants to quit. When I get home from work, the older one complains and flops around on the floor like a fish out of water. The younger one just sits around and makes a mess when I'm trying to keep the house clean; it has been up for sale for over six months. The house isn't selling and I'm worried I'm going to have to let it go into foreclosure. And, I had to convince the lady a few houses down that I wasn't having an affair with her husband . . . which I am definitely not.

PSYCHOTHERAPIST: You left out your job. How's that working this week?

CLIENT: It's okay I guess. I mean, as always, I don't want to stay there forever, but I feel stuck, you know, because of the salary and benefits. I mean I need to keep the medical insurance for the sake of the kids alone.

PSYCHOTHERAPIST: So, among these many complaints, which one would you like to work on today?

CLIENT: I guess the one about my kids. They are driving me crazy.

PSYCHOTHERAPIST: So, it's their fault. I mean, they're the cause of your problem?

CLIENT: No, that doesn't make any sense, does it? Kids are just kids, but my kids seem to be terrible lately.

PSYCHOTHERAPIST: Are your children complaining?

CLIENT: No!

PSYCHOTHERAPIST: Then, who's problem is it?

CLIENT: It's mine I suppose, but I'm beginning to hate them.

PSYCHOTHERAPIST: What does that mean? What does *hate* mean to you?

CLIENT: It means that I can't take it anymore. I just feel like putting a gun to my head (overly dramatic as in previous sessions).

PSYCHOTHERAPIST: What's stopping you?

CLIENT: My kids! (pause)

PSYCHOTHERAPIST: I'm confused. Help me out here. I understand you to mean that your kids are both the cause of your distress and the source of your preservation.

CLIENT: What do you mean?

PSYCHOTHERAPIST: I mean that you're not making any sense. You are a living complaint. You give yourself and your children no way to both win and then justify the tragic results by your irrationality. And, now you additionally say your children are the cause of your problem, but you can't kill yourself because you love them so much.

CLIENT: You're right! That's what I'm saying.

PSYCHOTHERAPIST: I know! That's the problem. More accurately, the way you have your problem framed, you think it makes sense. The way you have it framed, if you satisfy your personal needs, you think you're a bad mother. If you're a good mother, then you're continually frustrated and angry that you're not satisfying your personal needs, even to the extent that you flirt with ideas of suicide. Is this an accurate assessment?

CLIENT: Yes! Yes, it is. I just don't know how to be a good mother and satisfy my own needs at the same time.

PSYCHOTHERAPIST: We can talk about ways to improve your parenting skills later, but right now, that won't work because when you would improve them you would continue to increase your personal burned-out frustration and dissatisfaction. You need to define a way to satisfy both your personal needs and your interpretation of your children's needs.

CLIENT: What do you mean?

PSYCHOTHERAPIST: What would happen to your children if you weren't around at all?

CLIENT: They would get into even more fights than they get into now. At their age, they just couldn't take care of themselves and would get into a lot of trouble.

PSYCHOTHERAPIST: So, your being there takes care of them. It prevents them from injuring themselves and each other, and prevents more bad things from happening to them. Is this correct?

CLIENT: Yes.

PSYCHOTHERAPIST: So, what you're saying is that your kids need you.

CLIENT: Yeah. I think they do.

PSYCHOTHERAPIST: Well, how do you like being needed?

CLIENT: I don't. All their demands are driving me crazy.

PSYCHOTHERAPIST: Well then, how would you like it if they didn't need you?

CLIENT: That would be a relief.

PSYCHOTHERAPIST: Then, why are you there? I mean, really, why are you putting up with all of this?

CLIENT: (pause with tears) Because, I'm needed. Ever since my husband left me, I don't feel very appreciated anymore and my children are there to fill in the blank space and keep my mind off of it.

PSYCHOTHERAPIST: Did you hear what you said? Tell me. I want you to say it again and listen to yourself.

CLIENT: I said, (pause) I said I need my kids.

PSYCHOTHERAPIST: If I understand you correctly, then, you are there because you need your kids and not because your kids need you. Is this correct?

CLIENT: Yeah, I suppose so, but I never thought about it that way before.

PSYCHOTHERAPIST: I know. That's been the problem. (long pause) So, with this new thought, you can meet your children's needs and your personal needs. In fact, with this new assumption, or belief, if you like, you are meeting your personal needs by meeting the children's needs. Does this make sense to you?

CLIENT: (small smile) Yes, it does.

PSYCHOTHERAPIST: This is a new thought for you and I want you to remind yourself of it all the time, particularly when you start your old pattern of complaining and dissatisfaction in response to your children. What do you think?

CLIENT: I think this is a change for me and . . .

PSYCHOTHERAPIST: (interrupting) You *think* it's a change for you?

CLIENT: I know it's a change for me.

PSYCHOTHERAPIST: How do you know?

CLIENT: I know its new because I never thought about it this way before. I never knew my kids were there for me.

Example B: The following vignette illustrates a consistent *cognitive* methodology (with an interpersonal perceptual attitude and creative theoretical structure) with a thirty-year-old, single, female client:

PSYCHOTHERAPIST: Good afternoon. How may I serve you today?

CLIENT: I've really been upset this past week. My boyfriend and I went hiking in the mountains last weekend. We backpacked about ten miles into a beautiful forest on top of a mountain. We had a great picnic and then started back because we wanted to return before sunset. On the way back, around a ravine, there was a beautiful field of wild flowers. Travis grabbed me and wanted to make love. No one was around for miles. I just wasn't in the mood. He continued to persist and tried to talk me into it. I got stubborn and we got into a fight . . . I mean, not a physical one, but angry words back and forth. Travis finally just walked away. I followed several yards behind, and we hiked back to the car in silence. I'm really upset about this. (tearful)

PSYCHOTHERAPIST: What are you upset about?

CLIENT: I don't know who whose fault it was. I wasn't really against making love. I love sex with Travis. It was that we were in different spaces that day, and he always turns everything into a sexual experience. (long pause) That might not bother me so much except sex seems to be the only way in which he shares his feelings. What do you think?

PSYCHOTHERAPIST: I'm not. I'm just listening.

CLIENT: We've been together almost three months, and he keeps telling me how much he cares for me. I really like that 'cause I like him a lot, too. The problem is that when we're together lately, he doesn't talk to me about his day. He listens well enough, but he doesn't share himself with me. (pause)

PSYCHOTHERAPIST: Okay, I've got that. So, what's the problem?

CLIENT: (becoming angry) The problem is that I don't know whose fault it is. I mean, I don't know whether I'm being too demanding or whether he should share more.

PSYCHOTHERAPIST: So you want him to share the way *you* want him to share? And he wants you to share the way *he* wants you to share?

CLIENT: (smile) Yes! And, I want to know which one of us or even if both of us need to change to make this relationship work.

PSYCHOTHERAPIST: Is that your goal, making the relationship work?

CLIENT: Well, it is for now.

PSYCHOTHERAPIST: Is that Travis's goal?

CLIENT: I think so. He says that he wants me.

PSYCHOTHERAPIST: You both sound pretty tentative to me . . . like both of you would like it to happen, but nobody wants to really commit.

CLIENT: I would commit if he shared more.

PSYCHOTHERAPIST: Yes, and he might be willing to commit if you were more sexually spontaneous. And that's not what's happening. What's happening is that both of you are not committed. What's happening is that both of you are waiting for the other to change. What's happening is that both of you are using that conveniently so neither of you have to risk and commit ahead of time.

CLIENT: Maybe.

PSYCHOTHERAPIST: No, there is no maybe about it. This is what's happening, and its really okay if that's what you want. You are already getting what you want but not what either of you say you want.

CLIENT: Say more. I mean explain this to me more.

PSYCHOTHERAPIST: Contrary to popular opinion, commitment isn't a two-way street or a fifty-fifty proposition. Personal commitment is a decision you affirm with yourself. Look! Bad stuff is always going to happen in life. It's especially going to happen in a relationship because relationships magnify the limitations of self. There is no such process as being a little committed. It's like pregnancy. Either you are committed or you're not. If you are committed, then when the bad stuff shows up, it merely serves as an opportunity to learn. If you're not committed, then when the bad stuff shows up, you use it as evidence to affirm your lack of commitment.

CLIENT: Okay. I understand that. I am responsible for my commitment, and Travis is responsible for his.

PSYCHOTHERAPIST: Good! So, what's the problem now?

CLIENT: Let's just say, for example, that we're both committed. I still don't understand who is more responsible for changing. I mean, do I need to be more sexually spontaneous, or does Travis need to learn to share his feelings more? If we knew what we were doing wrong, we could do something about it. Isn't that reasonable?

PSYCHOTHERAPIST: First, if you were both committed, according to the definition we have just discussed, you might be viewing the assumed conflict differently. In fact, it might not even show up as a conflict. Second, it's reasonable. It's not necessarily true.

CLIENT: I don't understand.

PSYCHOTHERAPIST: Have you ever had the experience of walking on a beach at sunset with the ocean breeze blowing your hair, and being completely absorbed in the experience such that there was no YOU present? I will bet there was no evaluation going on. Or, perhaps you have had this experience in making love to someone, Travis, or someone else.

CLIENT: (big smile) I know what you mean!

PSYCHOTHERAPIST: Now, during those times, was everything wonderful, perfect and right, without consideration of what's making this happen?

CLIENT: Yes.

PSYCHOTHERAPIST: So, notice then, that when events don't work out, you make the assumption something is wrong with somebody. Someone or something has to be at fault.

CLIENT: Okay. So, what's the point?

PSYCHOTHERAPIST: The point is that maybe, just maybe, nothing is wrong with anybody. Maybe Travis is just being Travis. Maybe you are just being you.

Maybe nobody has to change. Maybe, just maybe, this is the way things are. And, if they are the way you experienced them over the weekend, and no one has to change, what is your consideration?

CLIENT: Well, my first thought is that I don't want that.

PSYCHOTHERAPIST: Well, right now, you've got it. And you can choose to go with it or not. What you are not happy about is the acknowledgment that you cannot directly change someone else, no matter how much you love him or even commit to him.

CLIENT: (sad) Then, I'll end up alone.

PSYCHOTHERAPIST: By your story, you're already alone and there's certainly nothing wrong with that. However, if you don't want to be alone anymore, it's more a matter of acceptance and giving than attempts to change someone else and taking.

Cognitive psychotherapists focus on a client's understanding of limited past decisions and new alternatives. A working assumption is that all previous decisions were perfect solutions at the time they were made. However, as thoughts form and beliefs change in life, new alternatives emerge that may be more life-enhancing from an increasingly developmental perspective.

The Affective Methodology

The affective methodology uses language to inform, request, or demand feelings from clients, both in awareness and expression. Observation shows that most psychotherapists begin practice by believing their methodologies are affective or emotionally focused. This results from joining a profession that promotes itself as the healers and mental caretakers of humanity. Beginning psychotherapists frequently assume that pain and human conflict are the result of (1) a lack of awareness of feelings or (2) restricted expression and poor communication of feelings.

The affective methodology uses language that elicits, encourages, or requires feelings. Psychotherapists employing an affective methodology want clients to pay attention to and acknowledge their feelings. They want clients to express their feelings about themselves and others in a direct manner that demonstrates responsibility, rather than projection. They want them to share and communicate these feelings to themselves, family members (Brock and Barnard, 1988), or group members as required by self. Their method is to use the verb *to feel* and its familiar variations.

One difficulty in working with emotions is that specific requests for feelings are often vague. That is, the verb *to feel* has many meanings to define different kinds of feelings. Typically, psychotherapists are unaware of which kind of feeling they want to implement. The result is less effective psychotherapy, with psychotherapists blaming resistance on clients rather than their own lack of clarification.

Even when psychotherapists identify their methodology as affective, they need to further clarify the kind of feelings with which they want to work. There are four kinds of feelings. We label them by increasing levels of emotional involvement and attachment. Starting with the least and increasing to the most emotional involvement and attachment they are: *intuitive, symbolic, sensate,* and *somatic.* Psychotherapists committed to an affective methodology must know exactly what they are explicitly and implicitly verbalizing. This is so their clients can model effectively and heal according to prescription. Accurate prescription increases the probability for cure.

Intuitive Feelings

Intuitive feelings are spontaneous insights or revelations. They are global perceptions of answers, purpose, and direction in one's life. They include spiritual experiences of immediate cognition without evident rational thoughts as are often associated with spiritual experiences (James, 1958; Maslow, 1962; Bucke, 1961; Jung, 1966).[1] With this association, psychotherapeutic models that focus on intuitive feelings are usually within a transpersonal theoretical structure (Tart, 1975b) or are religiously or spiritually oriented. Psychotherapists employing other models, however, may claim methodological implementation of intuition. This occurs because, in actuality, intuitive feelings are not always feelings experienced with acknowledged or observable mood and affect as is usually ascribed to them.

Sometimes, intuitive feelings are like the initial *ah-ha* discovery experience in creativity. L. L. Thurstone (1952) made the claim, ". . . the creative act is characterized by the moment of insight that is often preceded by nonverbalized prefocal thinking." Clark Moustakas (1967) states, "the harmony and emergency of one's own life seem to come from the increasing capacity to find in the world that which also obtains within the depths of one's own being."

Intuitive feelings also include sixth-sense or extrasensory perception (ESP). More accurately, in scientific literature, extrasensory experiences are referred to as *psi* phenomena—telepathic, clairvoyant, precognitive, and psychokinetic experiences—as defined within the domain of parapsychology. Psi is a more accurate concept because extrasensory implies that some people are more genetically gifted than others. Our experience suggests that while certain predispositions exist, most people can learn to use these abilities with practice.

Regarding the acknowledgment of the existence of these abilities, and specifically telepathy, Charles Tart (1975a) states,

> . . . the reality of telepathy has been established beyond any reasonable
> doub. . . . when I say 'beyond any reasonable doubt' I imply that people who

disagree with me are unreasonable. Within the rules of scientific procedure, this has been the case in all of my experience. The people who disagree with me about the existence of telepathy have simply never bothered to read even a small fraction of the evidence for it, and I do not believe that a person who knows nothing about an area directly but nevertheless has strong opinions about it is being reasonable in any scientific sense.

Intuitive feelings and experiences defy common linear description or explanation. *Intuition* originates from Latin and means "immediate cognition . . . without evident rational thought." As such, intuitive feelings are in alignment with mystical experiences and their anecdotal reports. Intuitive feelings are experiences that include self, but without self as an object of focus. People highly value these experiences often because they occur outside of reason and intention. That is, the people who value these experiences trust them because they extend beyond rational thought, which they believe is contaminated with conventional limitations. By combining spiritual, creative, paranormal, shamanic, and religious experiences as representative of intuitive feelings, we are not implying that any of these are necessarily equivalent in facets outside the application of intuition. Indeed, the only reason to group these diverse experiences is that those persons who practice in these variant fields tend to refer to intuition as a methodology for awareness, discovery, creation, and a rationale for implementation.

Also, intuitive feelings are like visions that apprentices have in becoming a shaman (Eliade, 1964). For example, the psychotherapeutic (and physician) equivalent in Native American (Indian) tribes is a *holy person*, otherwise mistakenly interpreted by non-Indians as a *medicine man* (Lame Deer and Erodoes, 1972). The specific rites of passage for a holy person vary from tribe to tribe. For the Lakota Sioux, rites of passage include a *vision quest*. The traditional vision quest is a wilderness journey to the top of a mountain for four days and four nights without provisions. The culmination of this spiritual experience is a vision that is later intuitively interpreted by tribal elders and other spiritual leaders. Similarly, intuitive feelings are like a *calling* to which so many ministers, priests, and rabbis, whether of orthodox or mystical persuasion, refer to in choosing their careers. Notice that the concept of calling, from a nonintuitive perspective, may appear similar to auditory hallucinations or delusions.

Methodologically implementing intuitive feelings requires special training outside conventional psychotherapeutic training. It is possible for intuitive feelings to arise from personal experiences or in any psychotherapeutic session. However, the conventional psychotherapist would either typically diagnose them as delusional or need considerable advanced training to work with them effectively.

We include intuition in the affective methodology because a few psychotherapists, clergy, and many clients *believe* this class represents the way in which they become aware of their feelings that determine behavior and thoughts. Thus, we are following a conventional belief by including intuitive feelings in the affective methodology. Observations indicate that intuition often, but not always, begins with an immediate sensate feeling discussed later and is transferred to a thought or belief process within seconds. Sometimes, however, intuition appears to occur directly without sensate feeling. In either case, the only evidence for our beliefs are personal and professional experience and observations.

As a result of the ambiguity of referential locus for intuition, there is no predetermined or specified linguistic methodology. This is precisely because intuitive language is either embedded in the language and meaning of other kinds of affective feelings (see below) or is directly cognitive. Also, specific training required to effectively implement intuitive feelings either (1) is from extremely diversified systems of belief or (2) the metaphors for implementation originate from systems of belief outside the field of psychotherapy. The diverse range of systems that favor intuition outside the field of psychotherapy includes:

1. Exploratory creativity in fine arts or crafts
2. Psychic (psi) experiences
3. Shamanic or mystical experiences
4. Oracle casting and divination experiences
5. Martial arts experiences

The diversity of systems that favor intuitive feelings precludes including generic examples that could accurately represent or usefully illustrate the effective implementation of intuitive feelings in psychotherapy.[2]

Symbolic Feelings

Symbolic feelings are emotional attachments to values and beliefs. They are the emotional charge we hold *about* our values and beliefs. As such, they are feelings that have become intellectualized. Even as specific opinions, they are general feelings. Symbolic feelings are *about* something or someone rather than *of* something or someone. These are the kinds of feelings most people think of when asked for feelings. These are the feelings with which clients usually respond when a psychotherapist asks or states any of these:

- What are you feeling now?
- You look like you had a reaction when Mary said . . .
- How do you feel about John?
- What is your mood when you are around your mother?
- Do you like your job?
- How do you experience yourself when . . . ?

- What did it feel like when your father did that to you?
- What was your emotional response?
- Can you share that experience with me?
- Can you share that with your spouse?
- Are you comfortable with that alternative?
- How does that seem to you?
- Is that okay with you?

The following vignette illustrates a consistent *affective* methodology focused on symbolic feelings (with an interpersonal perceptual attitude and productive theoretical structure), with a thirty-year-old, single male client in conflict due to maternal incest.

PSYCHOTHERAPIST: Hi! How are you feeling today?

CLIENT: I'm still frustrated and having a difficult time with the events that happened.

PSYCHOTHERAPIST: You sound angry.

CLIENT: Well, I am, but actually I feel more guilty.

PSYCHOTHERAPIST: What do you feel guilty about?

CLIENT: Just that it happened to me. It's unfair.

PSYCHOTHERAPIST: Fair? Did you expect life to be fair?

CLIENT: Let me put it this way. If your house burned and you couldn't do anything about it, wouldn't you consider that unfair?

PSYCHOTHERAPIST: I would be upset and consider it unfortunate, but not necessarily unfair. By focusing on the event as unfair, I wonder whether that allows you to avoid your frustration and encourage your role as a victim.

CLIENT: I was a victim!

PSYCHOTHERAPIST: I know. I experience your pain right now. What I would like you to share with me, if you like, is what it is like to feel like a victim.

CLIENT: It was terrible and I don't like it. I wish it would go away. What I need from you is a way to dump these feelings in a safe environment so I can get on with my life.

PSYCHOTHERAPIST: Do you feel safe with me?

CLIENT: Yes.

PSYCHOTHERAPIST: Then why don't you dump them here in a garbage can? (Motions with both arms stretched out toward the middle of the floor, with palms up.)

CLIENT: (Proceeds to give a scenario *about* the entire molestation event at length and in detail, with intermittent withheld anger and sadness, all the while looking at the floor.)

PSYCHOTHERAPIST: So, how do you feel now?

CLIENT: I feel better. I feel *like* I've never told the whole story before. It feels good just to say it.

The answers to symbolic questions are usually general. Working with symbolic feelings, the psychotherpist has the goal of providing a safe opportunity for the client to share blocked feelings in an inexact and routine manner. This is particularly effective with children or mentally retarded clients who function more concretely than abstractly, as well as clients suffering from grief reactions.

However, symbolic feelings are frequently ineffective in working with emotions because of their lack of specificity. Actually, symbolic feelings are not biological or physical experiences. Like intuitive feelings, they are not actually feelings at all. They are symbolized beliefs *about* feelings. We include them as emotions within the affective methodology because most psychotherapists and clients *believe* this class represents feelings in general.

In practice, symbolic feelings are more successful with cognitive and behavioral methodologies, which acknowledge that symbolic feelings are vague and relatively safe to express because they represent opinions. Cognitive and behavioral psychotherapists inquire about symbolic feelings to establish rapport and gather diagnostic information. This information is useful later for cognitive or behavioral work. Cognitive and behavioral psychotherapists typically do not choose to work directly with somatic and sensate feelings. With this knowledge and purpose, the use of symbolic feelings contributes to an alternative methodology.

Most psychotherapists employ symbolic feelings, but using them as an exclusive methodology often limits psychotherapy to a superficial level of effectiveness. Using symbolic feelings lacks clarity for both the psychotherapist and the client. As communication and methodology become more specific, psychotherapy is more effective.

Sensate Feelings

Sensate feelings include all the perceived sensations a person has of his or her external environment, including and outside the organismic layer of skin. They include all the direct experiences of the environment through the five senses. Sensate feelings include experiences of touching a hot stove, sand paper, and ice. They include the external experiences of an opera, a carnival, a sunrise, and a thunder storm. They also include the external experiences of smelling, caressing, seeing a newborn infant, and tasting delicious food.

Sometimes people block experiencing parts of their environment because they are painful. They may not see or hear certain people or events anymore. They may become overly sensitive to being touched because they were physically or sexually abused, are afraid of intimacy, or are homophobic. They may not want to taste, touch, or smell objects in their environment that they associate with painful experiences.

A psychotherapeutic model that focuses almost exclusively on sensate feelings is sensitivity training (Appley and Winder, 1973). Sensitivity training is an interpersonal perceptual attitude of the National Training Laboratories, originally in Bethel, Maine. This orientation was responsible for starting the original T-groups. *T-group* refers to a training group. Group members are given structured tasks to increase their sensitivity and awareness of themselves, others, and their environment. Trainers[3] sequence structured tasks by the criteria of increasing risk, social disclosure, and responsibility. Psychotherapists who focus on sensate feelings ask questions like:

- Give me a word to describe your emotion.
- If you were to taste that experience, give me a word to describe it.
- How do you experience your surroundings?
- When you are touched by her, what does it feel like?
- Suppose you are in a white room without any furniture, describe your experience.
- Compare your feelings to an object that represents them.

The following vignette illustrates a consistent affective methodology focused on *sensate* feelings (with an interpersonal perceptual attitude and an innovative theoretical structure), with a thirty-seven-year-old male (Sam) and his wife (Gloria). Currently on leave, the husband was on active duty as a military officer and diagnosed as having Post-Traumatic Stress Disorder.

PSYCHOTHERAPIST: Good evening.

SAM: Good evening.

GLORIA: Hello.

PSYCHOTHERAPIST: (to Sam) So, after a week of vacation, how are you feeling?

SAM: I don't really know. I feel kind of emotionally shut down. My wife, I mean Gloria and I, drove up to the mountains and camped out for a few days. We hiked together, and I did some fishing. I kept thinking about some of my troops dying and wondering why I'm still here and they aren't. When these thoughts went away, no one was home. I've never felt this way before.

PSYCHOTHERAPIST: (to Gloria) How did you feel about the vacation?

GLORIA: I know Sam is having a tough time right now, but I feel he just needs some more time.

PSYCHOTHERAPIST: (to Gloria) What makes you feel that Sam is having a tough time right now? Did he share that with you verbally or nonverbally?

GLORIA: He won't talk about what happened over there with me, just that it was terrible. I've tried to encourage him a couple of times, but he just keeps telling me, "Maybe later." (pause) I know he's hurting though because . . . (pause, and looks at Sam) . . . Can I tell him about the other night?

SAM: (to Gloria) Sure. Go ahead. That's what we're here for.

GLORIA: Well, Sam's had difficulty performing in bed ever since he's returned. I completely understand, but he feels guilty and less of a man about the whole event. I told him to just relax and be with me, but it doesn't seem to comfort him much. He just becomes more frustrated. That's why we went on a vacation . . . to get away from it all, relax, and see if we could get back together. (pause, and then looking at Sam) I really love you. All of that macho stuff you feel is so important, doesn't matter to me just now. It'll come with time. Right now, I just want to be here for you in any way you need.

SAM: (wiping tears from his eyes and grabbing Gloria's hand) I love you too, honey.

PSYCHOTHERAPIST: (with intended humor) Gee, I almost feel like an intruder here. (pause after joint laughter from Sam and Gloria) Sam, did you ever get out of yourself during the vacation? Did you ever feel the earth, the weather, or glory in the fish tugging at your line? Did you physically connect with Gloria in bed at all or were you off in your rehearsals of past painful events?

SAM: No! I told you. I noticed all those events that you just mentioned, but no one was home. Nothing sunk through.

PSYCHOTHERAPIST: (with intended humor) That's what Gloria said.

SAM: (chuckle and with affection) You're funny, doc. Seriously, though, how can I break out of this?

PSYCHOTHERAPIST: I am being serious. Nothing is sinking through. Nothing is breaking out. You have no relationship with Gloria, hiking, the weather, or the passion of the fishing. You're absolutely right! No one is home . . . specifically, Sam is not home. So, where did you feel home was before, Sam?

SAM: It's back to the way I used to be when I enjoyed things like the outdoors, fishing, touching, and making love to Gloria.

PSYCHOTHERAPIST: Okay. I hear you. Gently, I want you to take both of Gloria's hands in yours and look in her eyes. I want you to feel her feelings through her hands. I am going to turn down the lights and give you both a few moments for this experience together.

PSYCHOTHERAPIST: (after five minutes) Now, tell me Sam, what feelings did you experience?

SAM: (glossy eyed) Good! Good ones!

PSYCHOTHERAPIST: Can you be more explicit and describe them to Gloria?

SAM: (looking at Gloria) I felt your warmth, and I feel your caring. I feel your devotion and your love for me.

PSYCHOTHERAPIST: Sam! (attempting to get Sam's attention away from Gloria) What I would like you to do next week is to touch, see, hear, feel, and taste all those feelings you have wanted to feel for the past seven months that you had to diminish for whatever reasons. You're on vacation, but you need to get out of your mind. During your normal routines, I want you to get out of your mind and come to your senses. I want you to taste your food. I want you to listen to the sounds in your surroundings. I want you not just to look at, but to see who you're looking at. I want you to smell your wife's perfume and feel her body without any goal of sexual performance. In fact, if you will both agree, I would like you to just sensually enjoy each other's bodies without the added pressure of penetration as a goal for next week. That is, I want you to make foreplay the entire experience, just for the next week. Would that be okay with both of you?

SAM: (smiling) Sure, I suppose so.

GLORIA: (looking at Sam) It's fine with me.

Working with sensate feelings, the psychotherapist has the goal of reorienting the client to the environmental world. This is particularly effective with schizoid disorders, obsessive-compulsive disorders, post-traumatic stress disorders, and some personality disorders. These disorders have similar defenses that make the client's world considerably smaller and encloses self-experience. Such self-enclosure diminishes opportunities to experience the outside world.

Somatic Feelings

Somatic feelings are organismic experiences of the body, usually a specific area. They are biological experiences. They are perceptions of sensations physically registered in the body and in awareness. The psychotherapeutic model of transactional analysis (Berne, 1961; Harris, 1967) differentiates and reduces somatic feelings to a manageable number of four.[4] Transactional analysis asserts that the four somatic feelings are sad, mad, glad, and afraid. Everett Shostrom (1967) reports similar research that substantiates four primary organismic feelings. These feelings are love, anger, strength, and vulnerability.

The psychotherapeutic model of bioenergetic analysis uses various techniques to enable the client to locate and experience somatic feelings (Reich, 1967; Lowen, 1958; Keleman, 1985). Bioenergetic analysis is not an esoteric model. Founded by Wilhelm Reich, it is a highly concrete model and validated by observable evidence. People register somatic feelings by the physical positions their bodies assume when they experience particular feelings, usually over extended periods. The body assumes constricted physical positions to block these feelings as they become painful.

One example is experiencing sadness, which includes the release of tears, deep breathing, and a vulnerable soft posture in the upper chest. As children, we learn to stop crying by assuming rigid postures to block tears; shoulders are raised into the neck region; there is an inhalation of air to stop breathing, thereby blocking tears and sadness. Bioenergetic therapists work to release suppressed somatic feelings and free constricted muscular structure. They usually are clear about their affective methodological implementation and techniques of releasing somatic pain and relaxing muscular armature.

Psychotherapeutic models that also work directly with somatic feelings include structural integration and the Feldenkrais method (Feldenkrais, 1972). Structural integration was founded by Ida Rolf (1962). It is a specialized technique of deep and often pain-releasing massage. Rolfing, as it also is called, is a direct manipulation of muscular tissue to release emotions. Similar to physical therapy, the Feldenkrais method is a model incorporating bodily movement. It focuses on somatic awareness of balance, alignment, and posture. The goal of both models is for the client to become a fully feeling-functioning human being.

Other psychotherapeutic models that work with somatic feelings, though with a less hands-on approach, include Gestalt psychotherapy (Hatcher and Himelstein, 1976), and psychodrama (Moreno, 1980). Gestalt psychotherapists work with people "getting in touch" with a particular somatic feeling. They orient their clients toward taking ownership of feelings in relationship to other parts of the body and self.

For example, clients with a grief reaction from loss or abandonment often report feeling a hole in the chest. They describe this feeling as an absence of feeling or an emptiness of air. They report experiencing air moving through this circular hole. Their description of this feeling even includes the size of the hole. Reports demonstrate some consistency between men and women. Men usually experience this hole as larger and slightly higher in the chest region. Women usually feel this sadness or loss as slightly smaller and lower in the upper abdomen. Gestalt therapy focuses on filling in the hole to complete the person. Gestalt psychotherapists might set up a dialogue between that part of the body that experiences loss and the rest of the body.

Psychodramatists work with an interpersonal perceptual attitude. They focus on the interpersonal object of loss. If the loss was of a loved one, directors[5] set up a spontaneous dramatic script. The protagonist[6] acts through this loss in relationship to someone role-playing the absent person. In psychodrama, if the loved one died, the director might even resurrect the loved one. The goal of this method is maximum catharsis.[7] Somatic methods encourage maximum exaggeration of emotional expression. They may use props—such as pillows, batacca bats, or body bags—for emotional release. Psychotherapists who use somatic feelings ask questions and make statements like:

- How do you experience your posture right now?
- What do you experience as you stand up and then sit back down? Where is there extra work going on?
- Can you tell me what your tears are saying? Let them go. Be your tearful sadness.
- Be your fist right now and tell me how you feel.
- What are you aware of inside your body right now?
- Say that louder. . . . Again, and louder. . . . Now say it with your whole body.
- Where are you experiencing sadness in your body right now?
- Tell me the way you really feel. Tell me what you really wanted to tell someone, but you never did.
- What is your *gut* reaction?

The following vignette illustrates a focused affective methodology focused on *somatic* feelings (with an organizational perceptual attitude and productive theoretical structure), with a thirty-five-year-old, married, male client in a group setting.

The psychotherapist follows a psychodramatic model[8] and employs a sociodrama. A sociodrama represents the emergent issue-theme representing most of the group members at the time. Sociodramas, as a subcategory of the psychodramatic model, require that the perceptual attitude be organizational because the problematic issue of the group becomes the protagonist (identified group conflict). In this organizational, perceptual attitude context, the "identified patient" or protagonist is drug abuse. It is dramatically represented by "the addictive and seductive substance" as a defined problem or disease in and of its context by definition.

Additionally, the vignette exemplifies a productive theoretical structure. It is important to note that the following example is *not creative* merely because it is dramatic in a presentational style. It is a productive theoretical structure because a problem is defined in the conventional sense as a disease created by previous patterns of ill-functioning as determined by the psychotherapist (and not necessarily the client in this case). Atypical of psychodrama, the group is seated in a circle.

PSYCHOTHERAPIST: So, what's going on with everybody today? [Note that initial questions and statements are intentionally not necessarily within the affective methodology.]

JAKE: (telephone operator) I'm feeling really depressed and guilty because I had a couple of drinks again last week. I was doing fine until my wife called me and told me she was going to try to get sole custody of my kids. I don't have any money to get an attorney and fight them in court. I'm scared, 'cause I feel she's serious this time, and I don't want to lose them. I've been doing really good for the past six and a half months, but, with this, it doesn't seem to matter anymore.

PSYCHOTHERAPIST: Sounds like it's pretty rough for you right now.

JAKE: (quietly) Yeah.

PSYCHOTHERAPIST: I also hear it is your wife who you feel is making you drink again.

JAKE: I know better than that. No way! She's just the bartender. I drank because emotionally I couldn't handle it anymore.

PSYCHOTHERAPIST: So, what would you like to work on?

JAKE: I'd like to work on the bottle being in control.

PSYCHOTHERAPIST: Thanks. I know this is difficult for you and we will come back to you. Now, what's happening with the rest of you since last week?

SARAH: (a marketing vice-president for a department store chain) Frankly, I'm embarrassed to say what I feel. I feel like I have it made compared to Jake, and I'm throwing it all away. I can't keep up with the competitive stress in my company. I haven't done any drugs (amphetamines) in a month, but I'm slowing down. I don't have what it takes to compete with what the company demands.

PSYCHOTHERAPIST: What would you like to work on today?

SARAH: I'd like to work on my increasing frustration with my job and depression, but I don't know where to start.

PSYCHOTHERAPIST: (intentionally blunt) Would you be willing to work on your amphetamine addiction?

SARAH: I guess you think that's where it started.

PSYCHOTHERAPIST: That's what I'm assuming and that's what you have to work with right now.

SARAH: Okay, I'll risk.

PSYCHOTHERAPIST: Sarah, you're already risking by living the way you are. I just want to know whether you're willing to work on this.

SARAH: Definitely!

PSYCHOTHERAPIST: Now what's everybody else feeling?

STEWART: (a stock broker) What Sarah's talking about is true. My pressure to perform is tremendous. We're all competing against one another for posted monthly quotas of performance. Some brokers conduct marginally unethical activities. I know who they are and that's their problem. Great world! I got to do drugs to keep up with the sociopaths.

PSYCHOTHERAPIST: If you're so concerned about the legality of the issue, why play the good Samaritan? If you're so angry about it, why don't you turn them in?

STEWART: That's not my act.

PSYCHOTHERAPIST: What is your act?

STEWART: (angrily) My act is speed. My game is winning. I can't keep up without using some lines (cocaine) in the morning. You got a problem with that?

PSYCHOTHERAPIST: No! I don't have a problem with that. You have a problem with it! You want to work on it or not?

STEWART: Sure.

PSYCHOTHERAPIST: Good. (looks around the group) Barb, I want you to help us out today.

BARB: What do you want?

PSYCHOTHERAPIST: (gets up and moves a swivel chair into the middle of the circle) I want you to be the addictive substance. To make it easy, each person will identify his/her addiction before confronting you. You will play either powder, pill, or bottle according to the designated addiction.

BARB: (gets up and sits in the chair and faces the group)

PSYCHOTHERAPIST: Barb, I want you to bring them into the action. I want you to be seductive and manipulative, anything that you can think of to make them use you. Got it?

BARB: Got it!

PSYCHOTHERAPIST: Okay, Jake, you start. What's your favorite drink?

JAKE: Oh, beer or bourbon. Fine.

PSYCHOTHERAPIST: Barb, as a reminder, here, you be a living bottle of fine bourbon. Go ahead, Jake, talk to it. You do all the time, anyway. This isn't any different, except that I want you to really get into your feelings that you shut down all the time.

JAKE: (looking at the floor and quietly stating) I'm angry at you. You got to me the other night again.

PSYCHOTHERAPIST: Jake, stand up. Look at the bottle. Raise your voice.

JAKE: (stands up, takes a deep breath, and in a much louder voice) I'm f____ angry at you. You're making me lose my kids and feel like a g____ damn failure.

THE BOTTLE (as played by Barb): Oh, come on. It's not my fault. I've been good to you and got you through some rough times, like the other night. Stop bad mouthin' me 'cause you can't do without me. You need me you weak son of a b____.

JAKE: Bullshit! I've done without you for over six months and done a lot better than when I used you the other night.

PSYCHOTHERAPIST: Good, Jake. Now stand up on top of the chair and be your anger and say the same thing again from your whole body.

JAKE: (stands on top of his chair)

PSYCHOTHERAPIST: Clench your fists!

JAKE: (very angry and thrashing his hands at the bottle) I've done without you for over six months, and I don't want you anymore. Get out of my life!

PSYCHOTHERAPIST: (to Jake) Good! Say the last part again, louder, and with your entire body.

JAKE: (in rage) Get out of my life! Get out of my life!! Get out of my life!!! Get out of my life!!!!

JAKE: (exhausted, shaking, crying, and wiping the tears from his face)

PSYCHOTHERAPIST: (goes over and embraces Jake's legs and braces him standing on the chair) Let the tears flow, Jake. Breathe! Breathe. Just let them flow.

JAKE: (crying and bodily crumbling)

PSYCHOTHERAPIST: Okay. Come off the chair and sit down and continue to feel the pain. (Complete silence in the group, with a couple of other members crying; psychotherapist motions to Barb to vacate the chair.)

JAKE: (crying and catching his breath in between the flood of tears)

PSYCHOTHERAPIST: (after a few minutes of silence) Jake. Look at the bottle.

JAKE: (Jake looks at the empty chair)

PSYCHOTHERAPIST: Jake, say good-by to the bottle in any way you want.

JAKE: (breathing calmly again and wiping a remainder of tears away from his cheeks—Jake quietly walks over to the empty chair, turns it upside down . . . as if emptying a bottle, and shakes it repeatedly.) F_ y_! (after a few minutes, sits down)

PSYCHOTHERAPIST: (directs Barb to sit in the chair again, and with intention of maintaining a high level of somatic expression, invites other members to participate) Next! Now, who's next?

[*Postscript:* (1) Sarah, Stewart, and others continue in similar affective expression of somatic feelings. (2) Following allotted time, a traditional closure is implemented.]

Delineating Levels of Catharsis

All methodologies use one or more levels of catharsis. Affective methodologies use higher levels of catharsis as their primary curative element. The word *catharsis* originates from the Greek language. Fundamentally, it means "to cleanse, purge, and purify the emotions." Catharsis refers to liberating emotionally charged memories and suppressed feelings that cause anxiety, depression, tension, stress, and undesired physical symptoms.

Long before drama became entertainment or an expressive art form, mentally disturbed people used stage productions for cathartic release. The mentally ill, as spectators in the audience, would moan, wail, and cry as they watched the drama unfolding on stage. Aristotle (McKeon, 1941), in his *Poetics*, expected catharsis to occur in the spectators rather than in the actors. Psychotherapists now use catharsis for clients who suffer personal tragedies.

While most psychotherapists encourage even minimal levels of catharsis in their clients, many are reluctant to admit it professionally. There are three reasons for this reluctance. First, most psychotherapists continue to associate catharsis with theatrics. For them, it signifies a lack of professionalism. Moreover, they believe that catharsis, as a curative factor, is merely histrionic, brash, or mundane. These psychotherapists often lack the knowledge and training to comprehend the healing power of catharsis.

Second, while mistakenly believing their methodology is affective, many psychotherapists prefer to keep the lid on their client's expression of feelings. Sometimes psychotherapists are afraid of their own safety and inability to deal with a client if they encourage emotional expression. Sometimes they are afraid of eliciting borderline behavior or psychosis in their clients. They believe full expression of feelings exemplifies decompensation and acting-out behavior. There certainly are many circumstances in which this reasoning is consistent with particular theoretical structures and methodology. There are also clients with whom, by any theoretical structural justification, catharsis should not be part of therapeutic work. At least, in these cases, it should be controlled at minimal levels.

However, psychodrama has been a psychotherapeutic model for more than half a century. It shows helpful results when used with chronic inpatients and severe psychotics. Until recently and since 1940, the federal government subsidized an entire Division of Psychodrama at St. Elizabeth's Hospital in Washington, DC. Moreover, R. D. Laing (1960) employed catharsis with age regression with severe schizophrenics at the Tavistock Clinic in London. For more than a decade, he reported curative results.

To disregard catharsis as an elicited decompensation is a prejudiced and misinformed belief. Many psychotherapists are poorly trained for the more expansive levels of cathartic techniques. They often resort to restraining client's feelings. When this is the case, they must acknowledge that their restraint is not for client's welfare. They restrict the client's affective expression because of their lack of knowledge and training with expansive levels of catharsis. Or, they prefer to work with lower levels of catharsis that are congruent with cognitive or behavioral methodologies.

The third reason that psychotherapists are reluctant to admit using catharsis is that the professional literature has not sufficiently delineated levels of catharsis and the requirements to elicit them. Josef Breuer (Freud, 1924), a colleague of Sigmund Freud, originated *abreaction*. Breuer used hypnosis to enable hysterical clients to recover suppressed experiences that caused physical symptoms. He encouraged clients to act out their conflicting events and alleviate contained emotions. In modern language, this model is known as hypnodrama.

Jacob Moreno (1980), the founder of psychodrama, detailed the use of catharsis. Psychodrama's goal is to increase spontaneity and full extension of role presentations. Moreno moved catharsis from the audience to the stage, from the spectator to the actor. He believed that for it to be curative, catharsis needed to be an interpersonal experience.

Alexander Lowen (1970) and Stanley Keleman (1982), who subscribe to a bioenergetics model, discuss catharsis as the basis for any psychotherapeutic healing. The goal of bioenergetics is to loosen muscular armor and rigidity and increase body fluidity. They believe, with Arthur Janov (1970)—the founder of primal scream therapy, that insights follow the discharge of feeling. When we reexperience and express originating pain, etiological memories cease to be unconscious and influential. Janov believes all emotions are positive. The only negative consequence of emotions is their constriction and lack of expression. Fritz Perls (1973) agrees that emotional restriction represents conflict and disharmony.

Volumes of literature describe affective orientations and discuss the value of and demand for catharsis. However, requirements for levels of catharsis remain vague and undifferentiated. A delineation of levels of catharsis and the requirements for each implementation starts below. The levels are arranged by increasing curative potential according to affective methodologies.

While each methodology and level of catharsis has its own strengths and weaknesses, they need clarification and consistent implementation. As psychotherapists, we must know the parameters of our science and art. We must take the responsibility to train clients to match our request by their desire to please and get well. We must become explicitly clear about our methodologies and how we ask for them to be understood and acted upon. When we do not achieve this clarity, we live with a mediocrity of client welfare and a depreciation of professional satisfaction.

Levels of Catharsis

Level I — Cleansing: The client actively engages in physical activity, exercise, or athletics to *drain* emotionally charged energy as a result of stress. Relief results from discharging muscular constriction and embodied stress as well as focusing on the activity itself. Relief is temporary physical relaxation and mental escape.

Requirements:
1. *Athletic activity involves maximum bodily participation, e.g., jogging, swimming, or yoga.*
2. *Conscious focus on the activity at the time of participation and avoidance of conflicts or situational stress.*

Level II — Sharing: The client talks about conscious feelings (usually symbolic) that have been or are emotionally disturbing.

Requirements:
1. *Clients must identify pain and conflicts with feelings rather than as a general expression of ideas or thoughts.*
2. *Self-disclosure to at least one other person of* pent-up *emotions, fears, or secrets.*

Level III — Absolution: The client talks to a chosen role model of authority—for example, priest or psychotherapist—*about* conscious feelings (usually symbolic). These feelings have been or are emotionally disturbing.

Requirements:
1. *The client must confess pain, guilt, or fear directly to an authority of choice and trust.*
2. *The client must believe that the chosen authority actually has the power to forgive and absolve.*
3. *The client must believe that the authority will forgive and absolve.*

Level IV — Awareness: The client expresses awareness of somatic or sensate feelings in the present moment. In the present moment, *aboutism* is the enemy of awareness.

Requirements:
1. *Expression must be stated in the first-person present tense.*
2. *Expression must stay in the present* awareness continuum *and not become a narrative, story, or fantasy of the future.*
3. *The client must take responsibility for the ownership of all feelings.*

Level V — Abreaction: The client brings to consciousness the originating events in the past that now elicit emotional pain. The client reexperiences and expresses feelings surrounding past painful events and conflicts.

Requirements:
1. *The client's experience must directly associate and relate to the original event or conflict. The experience must be specific.*
2. *The client must later acknowledge that current emotional conflict is a result of the best solution that could be made about the previous conflict at the time.*
3. *The psychotherapist controls active and overt display of emotions through hypnotic trance, guided fantasy, or relaxation techniques.*

Level VI — Purging: The client must extend and express somatic feelings of conflict through the exaggeration of these feelings and organismic expression.

Requirements:
1. *The client must engage in maximum extension of the currently experienced emotional conflict. Extension of emotional conflict may include shaking fists, biting, and yanking towels in the mouth to release anger, growling, screaming, and regurgitating. It does not usually include full action of the client's entire body.*
2. *The psychotherapist physically assists and takes responsibility for safety, management, and control.*
3. *The relation of emotion must be object, event, and person specific. That is, the emotional constriction experienced by the client must relate to the object of conflict.*

Level VII — Resolution: The client *acts through* rather than *acts out* emotional conflicts. When psychotherapists use interpersonal or organizational perceptual attitudes, other people (auxiliaries) role-play. When psychotherapists use intrapsychic perceptual filters (symbolic), they use empty chairs or objects to represent other people or objectified parts of self. Parts of self include sub-selves represented by emotional or public roles, organismic parts of the body, or concrete emotions.

Requirements:
1. The client must engage in full body animation and action, which can include walking, jumping, standing on chairs, hitting, and throwing pillows and body bags. The engagement of the specific emotional release must include the maximum extensive expression by the entire body in action.
2. Catharsis must be interpersonally experienced, with another person playing a public role or objective part of the conflict. Or, they must create a dialogue between two symbolized roles or parts of the organism or personality.
3. Maximum extension of the experienced emotion and role is required.
4. The psychotherapist assumes responsibility for safety, management, and control of the client.
5. The expression of emotion must be object, event, and person specific. The emotional trauma experienced by the client must relate to both the originating event and all the people involved.

Notes

1. William James referred to these experiences as *religious experiences*. Abraham Maslow referred to them as *peak-experiences*. R. Bucke referred to them as *cosmic*, and Carl Jung referred to them as *universal archetypes*.
2. Evidence indicative of a diagnostic differentiation between severe psychopathology and creative theoretical structures was presented in chapter 4 within the subheading Creative Theoretical Structures. Differentiations with less severe psychopathology are more difficult to determine objectively because of the variant interpretations from entirely different systems of beliefs. Spiritual or mystical experiences, that often include intuitive feelings, may encompass opposing interpretations as compared to coventional psychiatry and academic psychology. Moreover, methodological application does not necessarily follow or correlate with theoretical structure. Thus, any example presented likely would be more misleading than representative of intuitive feelings, the explanation of which is beyond the scope of our immediate intent.
3. Sensitivity training considers its function to be educational rather than psychotherapeutic. The authoritative person is called either a *leader* or *trainer*. Nonetheless, the training of such leaders is highly specific with years of supervision especially oriented to this model.
4. Our professional opinion is that transactional analysis is, in actuality, a cognitive methodology. Confusingly, it is nearer a psychodynamic model which does not directly work with somatic feelings. Regardless, our research supports that the respective founders of this model deserve the credit for differentiating somatic feelings.
5. In the model of psychodrama, psychotherapists are referred to as directors.
6. As a model of psychotherapy, psychodrama uses the concept of protagonist to replace client or patient, regardless of the severity of the pathology. Psychotherapists are redefined as *directors*.

7. Levels of catharsis are fully delineated in the next section of this chapter.
8. This example, particularly in the latter part, illustrates somatic feelings. It uses merely one style of a sociodramatic model and is not intended to represent psychodrama in general. That would be a task far beyond the scope of this book. For further details regarding the model of psychodrama, see Appendix C.

References

Appley, D., & Winder, A. (1973). *T-Groups and therapy groups in a changing society.* San Francisco: Jossey-Bass.

Berne, E. (1961). *Transactional analysis in psychology.* New York: Grove Press.

Brock, G., & Barnard, C. (1988). *Procedures in family therapy.* Boston: Allyn and Bacon.

Bucke, R. (1961). *Cosmic consciousness: A study in the evolution of the human mind.* New Hyde Park, NY: University Books.

Eliade, M. (1964). *Shamanism* (translated by W. Trask). Princeton, NJ: University Press.

Feldenkrais, M. (1972). *Awareness through movement.* New York: Harper & Row.

Freud, S. (1924). *Collected papers* (Vols. I, II). London: Hogarth Press.

Harris, T. (1967). *I'm Ok—You're Ok.* New York: Avon.

Hatcher, C., & Himelstein, P. (Eds.). (1976). *The handbook of Gestalt therapy.* New York: Jason Aronson.

James, W. (1958). *Varieties of religious experience.* New York: The American Library of World Literature.

Janov, A. (1970). *The primal scream.* New York: G. P. Putnam's Sons.

Jung, C. (1966). *The practice of psychotherapy.* New York: Random House.

Keleman, S. (1985). *Emotional anatomy.* Berkeley, CA: Center Press.

Keleman, S. (1982). *Somatic reality.* Berkeley, CA: Center Press.

Laing, R. D. (1960). *The divided self.* New York: Pantheon and Tavistock.

Lame Deer, J., & Erodoes, R. (1972). *Lame deer: Seeker of visions.* New York: Simon & Schuster.

Lowen, A. (1970). *Pleasure: A creative approach to life.* New York: Coward-McCann.

Lowen, A. (1958). *The language of the body.* New York: Collier-Macmillan.

McKeon, R. (Ed.). (1941). *The basic works of Aristotle.* New York: Random House.

Maslow, A. (1962). *Toward a psychology of being.* Princeton, NJ: Van Nostrand.

Moreno, J. (1980). *Psychodrama* (Vols. I–III). New York: Beacon House.

Moustakas, C. (1967). *Creativity and conformity* (p. 134). New York: Van Nostrand.

Perls, F. (1973). *The Gestalt approach and eye witness to therapy.* Palo Alto, CA: Science and Behavior Books.

Reich, W. (1967). *Character analysis.* New York: Noonday Press.

Rolf, I. (1962). *Structural integration: Gravity, an unexplored factor in a more human use of human beings.* Boulder, CO: Guild for Structural Integration.

Shostrom, E. (1967). *Man, the manipulator.* New York: Abingdon Press.

Tart, C. (1975a). The physical universe, the spiritual universe, and the paranormal. In C. Tart (Ed.) *Transpersonal psychologies* (p. 123). New York: Harper & Row.

Tart, C. (Ed.). (1975b). *Transpersonal psychologies* New York: Harper & Row.

Thurstone, L. L. (1952). The scientific study of inventive talent. In *Reports from the Psychometric Laboratory,* 81, 6. Chicago: University of Chicago Press.

6

<hr />

Understanding Relationship Dynamics

During childhood development, we learn numerous interactional methods to fulfill our needs from the immediate environment. The conglomerate of these methods forms a *dynamic*[1] of how we typically relate in adulthood. This includes our relationships in love, friendship, and business. We have found a polarization of how people relate to others and the world. There are three dynamic polarities. Each dynamic polarizes into a specific set of feelings, attitudes, thoughts, and beliefs about how relationships fill our basic needs.

The first dynamic polarity is *dependent*. The conventionally accepted definition of dependent is used here: to rely completely on someone else to fulfill needs and wants. For example, infants initially, are totally dependent on someone, usually their mother, for food, warmth, safety, and security. The second dynamic polarity is *counter-dependent*. The commonly accepted definition of counter-dependent is used here: to be completely free of reliance on anyone or anything for help or support. Counter-dependent is deliberately being nonsymbiotic[2] in a relationship.

The third dynamic is *intra-dependent*. This concept combines two word particles. The first originates from the Latin *intra*, meaning *assumed* or *within*; the second particle, *dependent*, means reliance on another for support. Intra-dependency means to assume or accept our dependency on others while retaining control and responsibility for the satisfaction of our dependency. Relationship dynamics are conceptually different from the popularized concepts of dependency/co-dependency. The concepts of dependency and co-dependency deal with the manipulation and interchange of emotions and their expression in relationships. In contrast, relationship dynamics deal with the responsibility for satisfaction of relational needs.

The Dependent Dynamic

Dependent dynamics are attitudes, feelings, and beliefs about relying on someone for need satisfaction. Dependent people believe that others must satisfy their needs, and do not realize that they have control or responsibility for the satisfaction. For the dependent person, satisfaction seems to occur by the wishes or desires of someone else.

For instance, the queen ant in her colony is part of a dependent dynamic. Although the ant does not ascend to the throne of queen by being entirely dependent, she quickly becomes dependent. As the only fertile member of the colony, the queen's role is to lay large quantities of eggs daily. She grows to many times the normal size of an ant, and because of her increased size, she becomes physically dependent on the nursery ants. She is so large that movement to search for and gather food and manage waste becomes virtually impossible for her. The nursery ants see to her every need, so much so that they determine her life schedule. They feed or withhold food from her to regulate the amount and timing of egg production, according to the seasons and availability of food outside the colony. When the queen gets too old to produce enough eggs, they starve her to death and a younger ant is nursed to become queen. The queen's wishes are of no consequence to those around her. She lives in a totally dependent dynamic.

Newborn infants are prime examples of dependency. They are born with several needs, though they lack immediate control or resources to satisfy them. Infants sense the powerlessness of meeting their needs; they completely rely on someone else to fulfill their needs just to survive. They are entirely dependent.

Adults in dependent relationships are similar in that they believe they lack control and responsibility for satisfying their needs. They behave as if they have little or no power. They assume minimal responsibility for personal need satisfaction and demonstrate disappointment when they are unsatisfied. They believe need satisfaction only occurs at the mercy or grace of someone or something else, like chance. Luck and fate are believed to be powerful determinants in their lives. Often, they feel they make sacrifices for their desires but believe the sacrifices are unrelated when they receive satisfaction.

People with dependent dynamics do not feel or believe they have control or responsibility for creating and maintaining relationships. They rely on hope and luck to satisfy their desires for a workable and loving relationship. Subconsciously, they expect others to recognize their needs. They have handicapped themselves by disclaiming the responsibility to satisfy their own needs. It is common for dependent people to change relationships often because they are "not satisfying." However, briefly into a new relationship, they feel helpless and hopeless once again. The cycle then repeats itself.

The dependent person is in a self-helpless relational dynamic and often will resort to various and unusual subconscious manipulations. They contrive "games" that indirectly manipulate others for attention and satisfaction of their needs. Manipulation provides a way to avoid responsibility of directly asking for what they need. Indirectly and unknowingly, they reinforce helpless, hopeless, submissive, and passive beliefs about themselves. They play a passively active role, but the relational dynamic remains dependent.

Dependent Relationship Dynamics: Case Study

Jean and Kevin M. live in a mid-western modern urban city. They reside in a single-family home, which they own and have lived in for about four years. They live with their two natural children—one son, age one, and one daughter, age three, from their current marriage, and two children—daughters ages nine and seven, from Jean's previous marriage.

History of Jean M.

Jean M. is a twenty-six-year-old, Caucasian-Hispanic, Baptist female. She is a homemaker who does not work outside the home. Jean is mother to four children. She has received previous outpatient mental health services for six months during her divorce. Currently, she is using a nonprescription medication to control her weight and a prescription drug to control her edema.

She reported her family-of-origin history in great detail. During childhood and adolescence, she was raised by her natural mother and father. Her parents never divorced and both are still living. She has one older brother, one younger brother, and one younger sister, all married. The mother reportedly had a nervous condition, suffered from depression, and occasionally drank. The father reportedly drank excessively and had respiratory problems. Jean reported her siblings suffered from depression, attempted suicides, drank excessively, and had problems that involved arguments and fighting.

When Jean was born, her mother was twenty-one years old. She described her mother as outgoing and gruff, and also moody, cold, and stingy. Her mother was viewed as responsible, pessimistic, and hardworking, while mostly unhappy and insecure. Jean felt her mother liked her but showed little love for her. Reportedly, the mother was not physically affectionate enough, which often made Jean feel neglected. She could not talk to her mother about problems. She is said to have criticized Jean about almost everything.

While her mother was viewed as having been interested in most of the Jean's activities, she never involved herself in Jean's interests. Reportedly she was very strict, although reasonable in some areas. She always wanted to know where Jean was going and with whom. When they disagreed, Jean could usually get her to give in. If Jean misbehaved, punishment was inevitable. To punish Jean psychologically, the mother would yell at her, tell her that she wished she never had had her, make her feel that she had been hurt, and take away privileges. Jean felt threatened with abandonment. Typical corporal punishments were hand spanking and ear or hair pulling. Jean reported that her mother slapped her and pushed her around.

Her father was twenty-two years old, when Jean was born. She described him as confident and energetic, yet also warm, impatient, and strict. He was viewed as hardworking, mostly unhappy, and short-tempered. Jean now perceives her father as having more affection for her than her mother. The father reportedly was rarely physically affectionate but made her feel loved because he often would buy things for her. Jean could not talk to him about problems. Her father was seen as having ignored most of Jean's activities and ignored her accomplishments. He is reported to have been an extremely strict disciplinarian who always wanted to know where Jean was going or what she would be doing. When they disagreed, Jean could not persuade him to change his mind. If Jean misbehaved, punishment was inevitable. To punish Jean psychologically, the father would yell at her, take away privileges, and hit her with an open hand. Typical corporal punishments were hand spanking.

Jean's developmental history follows. Before age fourteen, she considered herself to have been unhappy. She reported nail-biting after age seven until age eleven, enuresis after age six for one year duration, and insomnia from age eleven to thirteen. As a child and teenager, she reported never running away from home and denied sexual molestation, deliberate self-injury, suicidal preoccupations, or attempted suicide. As a teenager, she was as healthy as others. She had no unusual eating habits but considered herself too heavy and unattractive. Jean described herself as shy, awkward, and said she felt like she didn't fit in with others. Her parents were strict about rules and acted as if Jean's judgment could not be trusted at all.

Jean began to mature physically at about age fourteen, later than most of the girls she knew. She first learned about sex from a friend and several books—a somewhat correct explanation. Currently, she enjoys sex but says it's too infrequent. As to sexual intercourse, she complains that her husband does not last long enough to satisfy her sexual needs. She denies having had any homosexual experiences before age eighteen or afterwards.

Jean's current marriage began when she was twenty-two-years old; her spouse was twenty-four-years old. She was married previously. In her current relationship, she reported they both have problems with the amount of time spent together, religion, and relatives. She stated that her partner has problems talking about feelings, showing affection, and trust, with jealousy, sexual satisfaction, fidelity, and in-laws. They have strong arguments weekly. She is the primary caretaker of the children in the home. Childrearing has been problematic for Jean because of extreme nervousness or fear that her offspring will exhibit antisocial behavior.

At seventeen, she began drinking alcohol with her peers and now usually drinks wine daily. She reported a need to drink daily to "settle her down." Drinking has resulted, on occasion, in missed appointments and arguments with her husband about drinking. Jean reported no increase in her tolerance to alcohol over time, but upon discontinuation of drinking, she has experienced anxiety and tension. She used amphetamines and cannabis experimentally as a teenager—beginning at age eighteen—but does not use any now. She has not received treatment for drug or alcohol abuse.

She reported an episode of depressed mood accompanied by diminished energy level, anorexia, and sleep disturbance but no recent history of suicide attempts. Jean reported an episode of racing thoughts without elated mood, slightly increased energy level, and uncontrollable talkativeness after having drunk "too much." She admitted to having experienced persecutory beliefs, but there was no evidence of a thought disorder. She denied anxiety or panic attacks but reported unreasonable fears of confined spaces. Her current sleep pattern is characterized by waking up too early, feeling unrefreshed by sleep, and excessive daytime somnolence.

History of Kevin M.

Kevin M. is a twenty-eight-year old, Caucasian, Presbyterian male. He is employed full-time, working forty hours per week as an assembly-line foreman and taking home $2,000 per month. He has had no psychiatric hospitalizations but reported receiving outpatient mental health services during his high school years. Currently, he is using prescription medication for a sinus condition.

Kevin reported his family-of-origin history with fair detail. During childhood and adolescence, he was raised by his natural mother and father. The parents were divorced when he was ten years old. After the divorce, he lived first with the mother, then moved his father's at age thirteen. The move occurred mainly because his mother felt she could no longer control him and wanted him out. Both natural parents still are living.

He has one older brother and an older sister, one younger brother, and one younger stepsister. Kevin's natural mother is reported to have had a nervous condition, and suffered from depression, headaches, and gastrointestinal problems. The natural father is reported to have drunk excessively. His siblings are reported to have suffered from depression, attempted suicide, drunk excessively, and had problems with headaches. When Kevin was born, his mother was twenty-four-years old.

He described his mother as outgoing and gentle, yet also quiet, cold, and stingy. She was viewed as responsible, realistic, and hardworking but mostly unhappy and insecure. Kevin perceived his mother as having liked, but not loved, him. The mother reportedly was not physically affectionate enough and made him feel neglected. He could not talk to her about problems, and she is said to have criticized Kevin about almost everything. His mother is seen as having been disinterested in most of Kevin's activities and ignored his accomplishments.

Kevin's mother is reported to have been very strict, although reasonable in some areas. She always wanted to know where he was going or what he would be doing. When they disagreed, Kevin usually could get her to give in. If he misbehaved, punishment was inevitable. To punish Kevin psychologically, the mother would yell at him, tell him that she was ashamed of him, make him feel she had been hurt, and take away privileges. Kevin sometimes also was locked in a room for more than one hour and threatened with abandonment. Typical corporal punishments were hand spanking, ear pulling, and arm twisting. Kevin reported that his mother punched him and hit him with solid objects such as a flyswatter, cords, belts, and a broom handle.

When Kevin was born, his father was twenty-five-years old. He described his father as confident and energetic, yet also cold, impatient, and hard. He was viewed as hardworking but irresponsible, mostly unhappy, and short-tempered. Kevin perceived his father as having only tolerated him; the father was never physically affectionate and made Kevin feel he would have been better off without his son. Kevin could not talk to him about problems. He is said to have been overly faultfinding, but sometimes accepting. His father is seen as having ignored most of Kevin's activities and his accomplishments.

His father is reported to have been an extremely strict disciplinarian who always wanted to know where Kevin was going or what he would be doing. When they disagreed, Kevin could not persuade him to change his mind. If Kevin misbehaved, punishment was inevitable. To punish Kevin psychologically, the father would yell at him, take away privileges, and hit him with an open hand; Kevin also somtimes got threats to his safety and well-being. Typical corporal punishments were hand spanking and shoving. Kevin reported his father had punched him and hit him with a belt or strap.

Kevin's developmental history follows. Before age twelve, he considers himself to have been very unhappy. He reported nail-biting from age five to seven, enuresis after age four for about six months, insomnia, and frequent nightmares for about one year after his father left the home. He recalled being a roughneck—repetitive stealing, frequent lying, and getting in many fights. He was ill no more often than his peers.

As a child and teenager, he reported running away from home, however, he denied sexual molestation, deliberate self-injury, suicidal preoccupations, and attempted suicide. He first ran away from home at age eight, repeated this once but never stayed away overnight. As a teenager, Kevin was as healthy as others, had no unusual eating habits and did not consider himself too thin or unattractive. He described himself as shy, awkward, a rebel, and feeling like he didn't fit with others. His parents were strict about rules and acted as if Kevin's judgment could not be trusted at all.

He began to mature physically at about age sixteen, later than most of the boys he knew. Currently, he usually enjoys sex. As to sexual intercourse, he complained of premature ejaculation. Further investigation showed it was his wife's complaint that he "came too soon." It was her wish that they have longer sexual intercourse rather than his premature ejaculation as he reported it. He denied homosexual experiences. Before age eighteen he claimed to have had two close friends with whom he could discuss almost anything but has no such friends now.

Kevin attended several schools or workshops operated by his employer to improve his managing skills. He completed his elementary education in one public school and reported his performance was average. He reported difficulty learning to read but took no special classes for learning problems. Kevin admitted to repeated trouble with school authorities and provoking fights but took no special classes for this behavioral problem. Socially, he described himself as neither shy nor outgoing, not liked or disliked by most schoolmates, and having one or two close friends. In general, he disliked elementary school much of the time.

Kevin's current marriage began when he was twenty-four years old, and Jean was twenty-two-years old. He was not married previously. He describes his partner as shy, quiet, impatient, and stingy. He also reported her as realistic, hardworking, mature, sometimes happy, but sometimes irresponsible. In their relationship, he said they both have problems with the amount of time spent together, religion, and relatives. He stated that his partner has problems with talking about problems, showing affection, having trust in him, jealous feelings, the sexual relationship, fidelity, managing money, household chores, and in-laws. Arguments occur at least weekly. The primary caretaker of the children in the home is his partner. Childrearing has been problematic because of extreme nervousness or fear about antisocial behavior by his children.

Kevin currently works for an hourly wage and is a union member. He has had this job for seven years, is somewhat satisfied with it, and is not thinking about changing jobs. The positive aspects of the job are the compensation, good future, security, and relationships with coworkers. The negative aspects of the job are the lack of stimulating work and conflict with upper management. He has been promoted regularly on this job.

Complaints have been made about him regarding violation of policy, and he was placed on probation pending investigation. He believes these complaints are due to a misunderstanding, politics, and deliberate attempts to create problems for him. He had two previous jobs in the same occupation. He has never quit a job, but he was laid off one time due to an economic slowdown. His income supports six people, and through it has increased somewhat over the past year, is barely sufficient to pay for basic necessities. Primary responsibility for money management resides with Kevin.

He began drinking alcohol at age seventeen and now drinks beer daily. He reported a need to drink daily and attempts to control his intake. Drinking resulted, on occasion, in missed work, arguments about drinking with his wife, and tickets for DUI (Driving Under the Influence). He reports no increase in tolerance to alcohol over time. On discontinuation of drinking, he experienced anxiety, tension, and insomnia. He used amphetamines, cannabis, and inhalants experimentally as a teenager—beginning at age thirteen—but does not use any now. He has not received treatment for drug abuse.

Kevin reported an episode of depressed mood accompanied by diminished energy level, loss of appetite, sleep disturbance, or suicidal ideation but no recent history of suicide attempts. He reported an episode of racing thoughts without elated mood, increased energy level, or uncontrollable talkativeness after having drunk "too much." He admitted to having experienced persecutory beliefs but without evidence for a thought disorder. He reported no anxiety or panic attacks but did report unreasonable fears of confined spaces. His current sleep pattern is characterized by waking up too early and having trouble falling back to sleep, feeling unrefreshed by sleep, and excessive daytime somnolence.

During the first psychotherapeutic session, Jean's chief complaints were that she was very unhappy and depressed and was home all the time and never got to go anywhere. The kids were making her crazy (too demanding). Her husband never wanted to be with her and did not take her to romantic places anymore. Kevin's chief complaints were that Jean didn't do anything around the house, like cleaning or cooking, and didn't take care of herself or her appearance. She was not affectionate before or during "love making," and complained all the time.

Case Script

The following partial script from the initial session with Kevin and Jean M is nearly verbatim, with minimal editing. This presentation method has been chosen to convey the inflections and client mental processes as verbally presented. The psychotherapist intentionally remained inactive and neutral for the purpose of obtaining an accurate script to demonstrate dependent dynamics. The comments were added during editing to help identify the dependent dynamics.

PSYCHOTHERAPIST: Come in and please sit where you will be most comfortable. (pause while they're selecting a seat) I have read each of your histories and understand you are both here because of a number of complaints about each other and your relationship. While in session I would like, when you talk, that you address each other rather than me. Okay! Who would like to start first?

Comment: *There was a long pause during which no one spoke.*

PSYCHOTHERAPIST: (speaking toward Jean) You mentioned on the phone that you were upset or had some complaints that Kevin never took you out.

JEAN: Yeah, we never go anywhere. He seems so reclusive. I'm beginning to take it personally. I feel shut in at home. I'm bored.

PSYCHOTHERAPIST: (toward Kevin) What do you have to say about that?

KEVIN: Well I . . . actually . . . I work so hard, and a lot, that I come home tired. . . . I just don't want to go out. I just don't like crowds or people, you know. You got to worry about parking and all that stuff. Anyway I don't understand why she always wants to go out? What's the big deal about going out? I don't know what she wants anyway.

JEAN: I just like to go out. I need to go out, get out of this house.

PSYCHOTHERAPIST: (motioning to Kevin to respond to Jean) What would you like to say to Jean about that?

KEVIN: (shifting his attention to Jean) For what?

JEAN: (speaking to the psychotherapist) I like to meet people and socialize. It's a good experience.

PSYCHOTHERAPIST: (motioning that she should talk to Kevin) Talk to Kevin.

KEVIN: Well, is going out going to do that?

JEAN: Sure! I like to socialize and meet people.

KEVIN: Well, why don't you get a job or something? Why don't you do that, or . . . ? Well, you want to go out, but you don't take care of the house or . . . either. . . .

JEAN: (interrupting him) I don't know what you mean by that.

KEVIN: (interrupting her) What? Do you want your cake and eat it, too?

JEAN: We don't even go out for dinner. Just because I'm not working doesn't mean you can't take me out. I'm home all day with four kids. I have a big job taking care of those kids, and I just want to go out. . . . Once a week would be fine.

KEVIN: Well you don't work hard at the factory like I do. . . .

JEAN: (interrupting him) Right! . . . I work hard in the home!

KEVIN: (interrupting her) . . . and I'm just beat. Well, you get time to watch the soap operas. You can sit down when you need it. And you sit and talk to your girl friends on the phone for an hour or so. It's rough down at the factory. You can't talk. You can't do anything but go, go, go. You got to meet these deadlines and stuff. . . . You know . . . Give me a break!

JEAN: I just want you to pay attention to me.

> Comment: *This is the first instance that Jean actually mentioned what she wanted. Up to this point they had both concentrated on telling each other what the other should do in order to "even up" the perceived imbalance in their contribution to the relationship.*

KEVIN: Well I do!

JEAN: Not enough though!

KEVIN: Well . . . I seem like I do. . . . When I come home, I have my beer and I always feel like making love. I mean that's the most important. That proves love!

JEAN: No, that proves horniness. Besides I'm too tired after chasing the kids all day. . . . And, I don't want to make love after you've been drinking beer. Besides, I'm fat, I really don't feel very loving.

KEVIN: Well . . . you know . . . the kids get in the way but . . . besides you don't have to work in order to make love. Just take it easy. You know? . . . Enjoy it! And, speaking of your weight. Why don't you do something about it? I mean I don't take you out sometimes because, frankly, I'm a little embarrassed. You look frumpy.

JEAN: (she starts crying, with her head in her hands)

Comment: *Jean assumes a defensive position about her needs, and when attacked, employs the defenseless position of crying.*

KEVIN: Here we go again! . . . . You're always crying. Ha, give me a break here. You know it doesn't work. You know . . . do something about it. Just don't cry about it. (says under his breath) Lousy marriage. Do something about it!

JEAN: Well . . . Would you go on a diet with me? We're both overweight you know . . . I feel the same way. You're kind of unattractive and sloppy, too.

KEVIN: Well . . . Me . . . I . . . Ok . . . Why don't you start it off?

JEAN: (talking at the same time) No way!

KEVIN: And that way I can see how it goes. You know I work hard; I need that extra energy and weight.

JEAN: Well, what about you? Look at you.

KEVIN: Well . . . It's not the same.

JEAN: It is the same.

KEVIN: I mean . . . I mean . . .

JEAN: Yes it is very much the same.

Comment: *Both partners defer their ability to change to the other, reflecting their mutual and reciprocal dependency on each other.*

KEVIN: But you don't have to go through what I have to go through.

JEAN: Sure I do. It's very much the same.

KEVIN: Well look at the house . . . Well, still . . . The house is a mess . . . Look at yourself. Do your hair a little bit. You know, it's not a big deal.

JEAN: (crying now in sobs) But . . . But . . . I want you to love me anyway.

KEVIN: Well, I do, I do! Of course I do!

JEAN: (reduced sobbing now) You know, I work hard, and so, the only pleasure I have is to eat. And I really want you to love me anyway.

KEVIN: I do love you, but if you're going to be fat. Well . . . It's not really for sexual reasons. I want you to look sharp. I would probably go out more if you wore something besides pants.

JEAN: (crying again)

KEVIN: So what's the big deal, can't you just lose some weight and look better, wear a dress? Other women can do it.

JEAN: Sure . . . I suppose . . . I could . . . I'll try.

KEVIN: It's not just a matter of your weight, and I really do love you. It's just that . . . and I love you with your weight, but your weight and the fact I don't feel I get very much affection from you. It's just really turning me off.

JEAN: But you don't give me much affection, either.

Comment: *Jean states what she doesn't receive from Kevin but is unable to directly ask him for it.*

KEVIN: Well . . . It's because you don't start it. It's that, I come home and I'm tired, and everything, and you know, like I want to do it but, I feel like you don't want to . . . or something like that. I want you to really let me know you love me. I would just like it sometime if when I come home you would be more affectionate, more appealing, sexy. It would be nice if when I came home, you would be dressed up and met me at the door, had dinner ready, and looked sexy. You know that kind of thing. And then that would go with a nice bottle of beer. (Jean starts crying again) What's wrong?

JEAN: The kids are just too much. I try.

KEVIN: The kids?

JEAN: Yeah, they're always after me.

KEVIN: Well?

JEAN: I need help!

KEVIN: Well, just shut them up, send them to bed, or something. You just cater to those kids all the time. Come on . . . You know . . .

JEAN: Well, why don't you give me some money for babysitting and then I'll feel better? Then I'll feel better when you come home.

KEVIN: It's always money. You always want money. What do you think? I'm down there working all the time now. I'm working hard, and I got to pay the rent. The car is broken all the time. . . . And, what do you think??? Money doesn't grow on trees. . . .

JEAN: I know, but you want me to be nice and loving when you come home, and I just need some money for babysitting. I need help. It's just too much! I need some help with the housework and . . .

KEVIN: No way! . . .

JEAN: I need some help if you want me to have time to be . . .

KEVIN: (interrupting her) No way . . . look at the payments we have to make on the boat and rent . . .

JEAN: If I had some time, then I could take some aerobics and go on a diet, and clean the house . . .

KEVIN: I mean we have to have the boat. Remember we agreed. So we can't afford a housekeeper, and sitter, and all those things. You know, it doesn't have to be a perfect house, just, you know . . . clean it up.

JEAN: Well, I do the best I can, but if you're asking me to lose weight, then I just have to get more exercise. I need someone to watch the kids and clean the house and . . .

KEVIN: (interrupting her) Whoa, whoa . . . Maybe you could get your exercise by doing the housework. Well, you know, if you could do just a little more work, you could build your aerobics into it. Couldn't you?

JEAN: I'm doing that already, it's not good enough.

KEVIN: Well . . .

JEAN: No . . . I need Jenny Craig or NutriSystem.

KEVIN: Well, its not just this weight thing you know. You know there are other things. I think you just want to get out of the house for other reasons. I mean, is there some other reason you want to get out of the house for? Like you just don't like me. You want to go out on your own? Like that. What is it?

JEAN: No, I'm asking you to take me out. I want to be with you. I love you, and I just want you to take me out more often. But when you don't take me out . . . yeah, that's what happens . . . sure I want to go out.

KEVIN: Yeah, but you're talking about classes and you know. There were other things you mentioned before, that you wanted to get out of the house and have some time to yourself.

JEAN: Well, that too, in addition to spending more time with you. I also want more time for myself, away from the children and . . .

KEVIN: Yeah, and for what reason, I mean I don't understand that?

JEAN: (long pause) I think there's more to life than just this house and this family. I think it becomes a prison. I think there is nothing wrong with getting away outside the home.

KEVIN: Well, I don't know. I just . . .

JEAN: I just want to have fun. I want you to take me out so we can have fun.

KEVIN: Well, we have fun. We go out on the weekends and Sunday. We go out and do some stuff. Besides I get tired . . .

JEAN: Would you go to church on Sunday?

KEVIN: Well, I . . . No . . . You know I don't like to go to church. You can go to church. That's ok, you can go. And . . . I'll stay home and do . . . something.

JEAN: Why can't you do something with me? That's what I want to do.

KEVIN: I do. I do some things. You know . . . Or, we could figure out some stuff. You know . . . things are pretty good. Can't you just be happy with the way things are?

> Comment: *Both Jean and Kevin are unwilling to change anything on their own or take responsibility to initiate changes. Neither takes the responsibility to make an open request for a need satisfaction. Each wants the other to change and thinks those changes will automatically satisfy their needs, assuming everything would be okay after that.*

The Counter-dependent Dynamic

Counter-dependent dynamics are attitudes, feelings, and beliefs about being completely free of relying on someone else for satisfaction else of needs. People relating counter-dependently believe they don't need help or support from anyone. This is commonly because they are unaware of their basic needs. They believe they are in control of everything or at least everything that is controllable. Their sacrifice is the denial of direct need satisfaction. However, basic needs must be satisfied. For the counter-dependent person, need satisfaction occurs by indirect manipulation of others.

An example of a counter-dependent relationship is that of the Dodder plant, genus *Cuscuta*, to its host plant. In the California chaparral there grows a parasitic plant. Dodder, unlike other plants, has no chlorophyll to convert raw materials into nutrients with sunlight. Seedlings sprout from the ground and quickly twine onto the branches of neighboring plants. It soon roots itself into the cambium layer of the host plant. With modified roots embedded in the host, it draws nutrients and spreads like golden threads over the host's crown of branches. Its rapid and dense growth consumes large quantities of the host's nutrients. By doing so, it soon kills the host on which it is living. In killing the host so quickly, the Dodder often dies along with it before producing its own seed and then loses its ability to reproduce.

Counter-dependent dynamic people harbor the assumption that they are completely separate and autonomous. They believe they are detached from their environment, society, and other people for need satisfaction. The counter-dependent dynamic exemplifies an attitude similar to, "I can do it myself. I don't need to rely on anyone." People with counter-dependent dynamics are more aggressive. They feel as if others consistently demand too much of them. They remain emotionally unattached and are usually loners.

Relationships for counter-dependents create several problems. They still must satisfy their basic needs with their relationships. Counter-dependents cannot ask directly for basic need satisfaction. They subconsciously command specific performances by their partners that indirectly satisfy basic needs. This becomes a way to avoid direct recognition of needs and direct requests.

For example, they cannot ask directly for someone to caress or touch them to satisfy the need for belonging. They indirectly fulfill this need by selecting a relationship in which the partner is a kinesthetic person. They subconsciously seek and attach to relationships that satisfy their needs without their having to specifically ask for basic need satisfaction. Their selection of relationships temporarily satisfies their needs. The cost is either a "merry-go-round" or serial pattern of relationships.

Directly requesting need satisfaction appears to them as weak, passive, and dependent. In addition, they have difficulty expressing their emotions when they receive satisfaction. They view emotional expression as an inability to take care of themselves. Their mistaken perception of independence is not actually independent at all. Rather, it is a response directly counter to dependency. It is an exaggerated reaction and overcompensation from the fear of becoming dependent.

The result is that their partners do not get reinforced for need satisfaction. The need satisfying behavior diminishes. Soon, the rewards and attraction of the relationship deteriorate, as does the relationship. The consequence of the counter-dependent dynamic is that it inhibits mutually satisfactory and beneficial relationships. The positive qualities at the beginning of the relationship define the relationship's short-term benefits.

Contracts and agreements about need satisfaction improve relationships. Lack of open discussion prevents contracts and agreements from being made. Counter-dependent dynamic persons appear unemotional, restricting spontaneity and emotional expression. Often, they become hostile or avoidant when feelings surface in their relationships.

Counter-dependent people may become addicted to a behavior or substance in order to desensitize themselves to feelings that arise in a relationship. An addiction serves to disassociate counter-dependents from their feelings—the same feelings that arise when other people satisfy their needs. When counter-dependent people are addicted, they reason they are independent. They use the addiction as an excuse for need satisfaction. Their belief is that they are not really doing the asking. The need satisfaction arises from the addictive behavior. After all, they cannot help what they do in their addictive state.

Counter-dependent Relationship Dynamics: Case Study

Sabrina and Aaron S. live in a northwestern rural area near a small town. They reside in a single-family home on a large orchard, which they own, and have lived there for about eight years. They live with their four natural children: three sons, ages four, seven, and eleven, and one daughter, age nine, all from their current marriage.

History of Sabrina S.

Sabrina S. is a thirty-four-year old Caucasian, Lutheran female. She is a homemaker and does not work outside the home. Sabrina is mother to five children. She has had no psychiatric hospitalizations. However, she had outpatient mental health services for six months following the birth of her first child. Currently, she is using a nonprescription medication to control her sinus allergies.

She cooperatively reported her family-of-origin history. During childhood and adolescence, she was raised by her natural mother and stepfather. Her natural parents divorced when she was six months old; both parents are still living. She has one older brother and one older sister, and both are married. The mother had a serious allergy condition, suffered from depression, respiratory, and gastrointestinal problems. The father drank excessively, and had respiratory problems. She reported her siblings as having suffered from depression, and attempted suicides. When Sabrina was born, her mother was twenty-four years old. She described her mother as quiet, shy, gruff, moody, cold, and stingy. She viewed her mother as responsible, pessimistic, and hardworking, while mostly unhappy and depressed.

Sabrina felt her mother loved her and often showed her love for her in her "own special way." She reported that her mother was not physically affectionate and occasionally made her feel neglected. If Sabrina misbehaved, punishment was inevitable. However, the mother always manipulated the stepfather into enforcing punishment. Emotionally, the mother would yell at her, tell her that she wished she had never had her, and make her feel she was hurt. Sabrina was sometimes threatened with abandonment. Typical corporal punishments were hand spanking and arm and ear pulling. She reported that the mother slapped her and pushed her around.

When Sabrina was born, her father was twenty-five-years old. She was unable to describe her natural father because of his departure when Sabrina was very young. She viewed her stepfather as hardworking, mostly happy, and short-tempered, and Sabrina perceived her stepfather as having less affection for her than her mother had. The stepfather rarely was physically affectionate but when alone with Sabrina would be very physical. However, she reported she was never physically or sexually molested and would not comment further. Sabrina could not talk to him about problems.

Her stepfather was reported as an extremely strict disciplinarian who always wanted to know where Sabrina was going and whom she was going with. When they disagreed, Sabrina could not persuade him to change his mind. If Sabrina misbehaved, punishment was inevitable. To punish Sabrina, her stepfather would yell at her, take away privileges, and hit her with an open hand. Typical corporal punishments were hand spanking.

Sabrina's developmental history was as follows. As a child and teenager, she reported never running away from home. She denied sexual molestation, deliberate self-injury, suicidal preoccupations, or attempted suicide. As a teenager, she was as healthy as others. She had no unusual eating habits but considered herself overweight and unattractive and described herself as shy and awkward. Her parents were strict about rules and acted as if Sabrina's judgment could not be trusted. She began to mature physically at thirteen, about the same as most of the girls she knew.

She first learned about sex from a friend and magazines and received a somewhat correct explanation. She began dating at age fifteen. Currently, she enjoys sex but complains of its quality; that her spouse does not use enough foreplay for her satisfaction. She denied any homosexual experiences.

Sabrina's current marriage began when she was twenty years old; her spouse was twenty-two-years old. She was married once before. In this relationship, she reported problems with the amount of time spent with her husband and relatives. She stated her husband had problems with sharing feelings, showing affection, trusting her, and feeling jealous. Arguments occur at least weekly. She is the primary caregiver for the children. Childrearing has been problematic because of her extreme nervousness or fear about the affect isolation may be having on her children.

She reported an episode of depressed mood accompanied by diminished energy level and sleep disturbance. She reported a brief episode of racing thoughts without elated mood, slightly increased energy level, and uncontrollable talkativeness afterwards. Sabrina admitted having experienced persecutory beliefs but without substantial evidence to support a thought disorder. She reported fears of confined spaces. Her current sleep pattern is characterized by waking up too early, feeling unrefreshed by sleep, and excessive daytime somnolence.

History of Aaron S.

Aaron S. is a thirty-six-year old Caucasian, Catholic male. He is employed part-time, working twenty to thirty hours per week, as a warehouseman and takes home approximately $2,800 a month. He has no previous psychiatric hospitalizations or outpatient mental health services. Currently, he is using prescription medication for a spasmatic shoulder muscle.

Aaron reported his family-of-origin history in some detail. During childhood and adolescence, he was raised by his natural mother and father; his parents have remained married and are still living. They moved to a northwest rural area when he was thirteen. Aaron has one older brother and one younger sister. The mother had a nervous condition, problems with headaches and suffered from minor depression. The father drank excessively, had back and neck pain, and gastrointestinal problems.

When Aaron was born, his mother was twenty-one-years old. He described her as quiet, gentle, and yet also faultfinding and unforgiving. She was viewed as responsible, realistic, and hardworking, but mostly unhappy and insecure. Aaron perceived his mother as not physically affectionate which made him feel unloved. He could not talk to her about problems. She is said to have criticized Aaron about almost everything. His mother was seen as disinterested in most of Aaron's activities and ignored his accomplishments. She was permissive and seldom wanted to know where he was going or what he would be doing until age fourteen. When Aaron misbehaved, punishment was inevitable. To punish Aaron, the mother would yell at him, tell him she was ashamed of him, and take away privileges. Typical corporal punishments were hand spanking, ear pulling, and arm twisting. Aaron reported his mother punched him but never hit him with solid objects.

When Aaron was born, his father was twenty-three years old. He described his father as confident, self-assured, cold, impatient, and hard. He was viewed as hardworking, irresponsible, unhappy, and short-tempered. Aaron perceived his father as having only put up with him. The father reportedly was never physically affectionate and made Aaron feel he would have been better off without him. Aaron could not talk to him about problems. His father ignored most of Aaron's activities and accomplishments. He was an extremely strict disciplinarian who always wanted to know where Aaron was going. When they disagreed, Aaron could never persuade him to change his mind. If he misbehaved, punishment was inevitable. To punish Aaron, his father would yell at him, take away privileges, and hit him with an open hand. Aaron also was given threats to his safety and well-being. Typical corporal punishments were hand spanking and arm twisting. Aaron reported his father never punched him but hit him with a belt or strap.

Aaron's developmental history follows. As a child and teenager, he reported running away from home. He first ran away from home at age eleven, repeated this once, but stayed away only overnight, returning the next morning.

He began to mature physically at about age fifteen, later than most of the boys he knew. He first learned about sex from a friend and received a somewhat incorrect explanation. He first had heterosexual intercourse at age sixteen and reported feeling anxious and excited. Currently, he always enjoys sex, however, he complains his wife is not active enough. He denied homosexual experiences.

Aaron's current marriage began when he was twenty-two-years old, and his spouse was twenty years old. He was not married prior to this marriage. He described his partner as shy, quiet, impatient, stingy, realistic, hardworking, and mature. In their relationship, he reported they both have problems with the amount of time spent together, religion, and relatives. He stated his partner has problems with talking about problems, showing affection, maintaining trust, feeling jealous, managing money, and taking care of housework. Arguments occur at least weekly. The primary caregiver for the children in the home is his wife. Childrearing has been problematic because of their nervousness or fear about the affect isolation may be having on their children.

Aaron is employed and is paid hourly wages, and he is not a union member. He has had this job for seven years, is dissatisfied with it, and is thinking about changing jobs. The positive aspects of the job are the compensation and relationships with coworkers. The negative aspects of the job are the lack of stimulating work, no hope of promotions, and the attitude of upper management. Complaints have been made about him regarding violation of policy. He has been placed on probation and been investigated. He believes these complaints are due to a misunderstanding and deliberate attempts to create problems for him. Aaron has had two previous jobs in the same occupation but has never quit a job. He was laid off one time due to an economic slowdown. His income has not increased in more than three years and is barely sufficient to pay for basic necessities. Primary responsibility for money management resides with Aaron, including what is made from the yearly harvest of his orchard.

He began drinking alcohol at age seventeen and now usually drinks beer daily. He reported a need to drink daily and attempts to control his intake. Drinking has resulted in missed work and arguments about drinking with his wife. Aaron reported no increase in tolerance of alcohol. On discontinuation of drinking, he has experienced anxiety, tension, and insomnia. He has not taken drugs and does not use any now.

Aaron denied suicidal ideations or attempts. He reported an episode of racing thoughts without elated mood, increased energy level, and uncontrollable talkativeness after having drunk "too much." He admits to having experienced persecutory beliefs. There was no evidence for a thought disorder. His current sleep pattern is characterized by waking up too early and having trouble falling back to sleep, feeling unrefreshed by sleep, and excessive daytime somnolence.

During the first psychotherapeutic session, Sabrina's chief complaints were that she was unhappy and sometimes depressed. She complained of being home most of the time and never going anywhere—Aaron never took her to romantic places anymore. She stated that the orchard took too much of her time, and they were isolated. Aaron's chief complaints were that Sabrina didn't do enough work around the house or orchard, was a poor money manager, didn't take care of her appearance, was not affectionate enough before or during "love making," and complained too frequently.

Case Script
The following script is nearly verbatim, with minimal editing, from the first session with Aaron and Sabrina S. This presentation method has been chosen in order to convey the inflections and mental processes as the clients presented them. The psychotherapist intentionally remained inactive and neutral to obtain an accurate script demonstrating counter-dependent dynamics. The comments were added during editing to help identify the relational dynamics.

PSYCHOTHERAPIST: Come in and please sit where you will be most comfortable. (pause while they're selecting a seat) I have read each of your histories and understand you are here because of a number of complaints about each other. While in session, I will ask, when you talk, that you address each other, rather than me. Okay! Who would like to start first?

SABRINA: I would. (short pause) I'm here because I got . . . We've got some problems at home. I'm not very happy with it. It's not . . . I'm concerned about the kids. They're very isolated out there on the farm and Aaron hardly ever comes home. They probably need their father around, nobody else is around. They are out there on the farm with nobody else around, working hard. I think the family needs a little more time as a family, and doing things together, and you coming home and being with us.

AARON: Well. (short pause) I think the kids are doing fine. Living out there on the farm is good for them. It creates independence. They learn how to take care of themselves. Self-sufficiency is important these days. Too many people these days are on welfare and having the country take care of them. My kids won't be that way. My kids will be independent.

SABRINA: Yeah. Well, you know what I think, they should be very independent too but, they are just starting to show signs. They're getting whiny. They're not doing all the chores they are supposed to. I have to keep after them all the time. You don't help with that. I mean you're not around to help with that. You need to help us out. What you're doing is all fine for you, but what if I want to go out? What if I want to do something? I don't need these kids particularly hanging on me all day.

AARON: That's fine. The kids can take care of themselves.

SABRINA: (interrupting him) Where are you, what are you doing when you're out?

AARON: Well, I'm . . . I'm . . . Well, you know I work, and then I see the guys down at the bar, and have a couple of beers now and then.

SABRINA: Oh!, right, while we're home working . . .

AARON: (interpreting) We get to talking and talking, about ah, where there might be some better work. I'm tired of this part-time stuff, and ah, I'd like a better job.

SABRINA: Admit it, you're drinking a lot! Everyday you go to that bar.

AARON: Well, that's where the guys are. That's where we talk. That's where I find out what's going on.

SABRINA: Right, yeah . . . We're home here working hard, and you should be here with us working, too. Instead, you're out there drinking the paycheck.

AARON: Couple of beers!

SABRINA: We need that money.

AARON: Hey, look! I'm not drinking the paycheck. Come on. Get off of it.

SABRINA: A family should work hard together. You play after you work. I want you to come home and then you play after family time. That's how families should be.

AARON: No, I'm around enough. The kids know that I work. I take care of things here. I'm doing fine.

SABRINA: No, no! You're not doing fine. You're not working.

AARON: And besides, you bitch all the time. You're a nag. You're nagging all the time. You think I want to be around here with all your nagging?

SABRINA: Well, be around here, and it will be all right!

AARON: You know. I work hard. What's your problem?

SABRINA: Just get your ass home!

AARON: You just get more of a nag all the time.

SABRINA: You haven't seen anything yet. Stop drinking and grow up!

AARON: I'm leaving! I need a beer!

SABRINA: Oh no you don't. You promised to come here and work on our relationship. Besides it's the middle of the day, it's not time for drinking.

Comment: *Aaron and Sabrina have shown their unwillingness to assume any part of the problem. Both blame the other for what they are not doing. They assume that if the other followed their expectations, everything would work out.*

AARON: Well it's your nagging. That's why I have to go down to the bar all the time. Besides that, you don't make love very good anymore either. It's the same old thing all the time. If you were a little more exciting . . . (pause) Wear some nice things.

SABRINA: Look, I'm too tired. I'm tired because I'm carrying your extra weight. I do more than my share of the work around here.

AARON: Give me a break. I work, too.

SABRINA: Well, come home and we will work together.

AARON: No, I mean trying to find work, and everything with the guys. Beside I deserve a break after work that's with the guys. You know what I mean?

SABRINA: Yeah! I know what you mean! My dad did that and look what happened to our family.

AARON: Oh! That's your problem. And, what's all this stuff about work anyway? You're always nagging about work. You're constantly pushing work this, work that. You know, I like to have a little fun and take it easy. Lighten up! Besides I don't see where you're doing all that much work. When we moved here, it was your idea to take care of the orchards. It was your idea to make extra income instead of taking a real job. I don't see where you manage the money for it.

SABRINA: I know you don't! That's because I'm too busy keeping the chickens, bringing in the corn, wiping asses, and chasing kids.

AARON: Oh, sh__. I just don't know what you want anymore.

SABRINA: I just want to have an honest, hardworking, good family here.

AARON: That doesn't sound like any fun.

SABRINA: Well, maybe if you were home more often, things wouldn't be so stressful. Maybe we could have sex more often. Maybe, then, there wouldn't be so much stress. Then I wouldn't be so angry at you for being gone all day and leaving me to tend the kids all the time. Maybe if you were here more often, things might smooth out by themselves.

AARON: Yeah . . . Maybe, maybe, maybe! What? Are you trying to tease me?

SABRINA: No. It was just a suggestion to give you a little outlet, motivation, something to try.

AARON: Promises, promises . . . Yeah . . . You know, I'm not going to buy that stuff. You've said stuff like that before. You know, you're the one who wanted to move to this farm and be out here. That's okay, but I thought we moved out here to be back to nature. You're the one who wanted to be the farmer, take care of the kids, and have chickens and cows. Oh, what the h__. You can take care of the farm. You're here all day long. I mean I work hard. One of us has got to bring in some money.

SABRINA: Sure, but you're doing a lousy job of that. You're drinking most of the money.

AARON: (interrupting her) Whoa! Now wait a minute. Don't go kicking me in the balls. You know what things are like here in the northwest. This damn depression has got everything in the toilet. I'm lucky to have the job I've got. You're lucky to have the money I give you to keep the milk on the table.

SABRINA: Oh, come on, Aaron.

AARON: (interrupting) You want to trade places with me? You go down to the fu__g warehouse and try it. Yeah, you'd bust a gut the first time you try to move anything.

SABRINA: I want a divorce!

AARON: Go for it!

Comment: *Conflict is presented as complaints. However, the complaints are about each other, not about taking responsibility for her or his own situation. Neither person directly asks for what they want from the other. Their need-requests are disguised within accusation, blaming, and faultfinding. No one listens; no one hears. Each person remains with self-justified beliefs.*

The Intra-dependent Dynamic

Intra-dependent dynamics include attitudes, feelings, and beliefs of recognizing and accepting our symbiotic dependency on others. When we relate intra-dependently, we accept that we must have outside sources to satisfy our needs. Satisfaction occurs as a result of serving other's needs, and others serving our needs. Mutual satisfaction leads to mutually beneficial and symbiotic relationships.

The African rhinoceros has seemingly odd companions, Buffalo Birds. However, a symbiotic relationship exists. At first sight, the birds appear to be just "getting a free ride" above the high grasses on the backs of the rhinoceros. With detailed inspection, a much closer relationship is found. The bird's main diet is insects it removes from the eyes, ears, and heavily folded skin of the rhinoceros. The rhinoceros benefits from the bird's keeping his skin and wounds clean of unhealthy lice, insects, and worms. What is a free meal for the bird, is a benefit for the rhinoceros.

However, this symbiotic relationship extends beyond the food chain. The keen eyesight of the Buffalo Bird makes it an excellent sentinel. This compensates for the African rhinoceros's eyesight and hearing, which is relatively poor and makes it difficult to detect long-range dangers. The bird's alertness serves to warn the rhinoceros. In return, the height of the rhinoceros's back makes a safe platform for the bird; it is well above the dangerous savanna floor. This mutually beneficial relationship serves each and harms neither. After hours of observation, researchers found that no individual bird belonged to any one rhinoceros. The birds move from rhinoceros to rhinoceros, yet no rhinoceros was long without its companions. This is an example of a mutually beneficial, symbiotic, and intra-dependent relationship.

An example of a mutually beneficial relationship in modern society is how we satisfy our need for food. We routinely purchase food at the neighborhood store or supermarket. Because we only purchased the food—we have not raised, cultivated, or preprocessed the food—we depend on someone else to perform these functions. Typically, we assume we have a choice of whether or not to allow someone else to do this processing.

Functioning with an intra-dependent dynamic about food includes knowing we can acquire our own food, if not at our usual supermarket, then at another. Or, under the worst possible circumstance, we could search for food in many places. We could find, harvest, process, and prepare it ourselves. With a little more knowledge, if it became necessary, we could even plant and cultivate it. The intra-dependent dynamic is knowing and accepting that we could do all of these processes ourselves if need be. Our choice, however, is to allocate the responsibility to others. Being intra-dependent means that we accept that we have needs and that other people satisfy those needs. At specific times, we select specific people and circumstances to satisfy certain needs. Additionally, we know that if a source of a need-satisfaction stops, we can establish a new supplier of that need, or we can temporarily take care of it ourselves.

Intra-dependency provides responsibility *and* control. We delegate and selectively relinquish, temporarily, our control of providing for a specific need satisfaction. However, we retain control to redelegate the services to someone else. While allowing others to satisfy a need, we retain responsibility and control of who, when and how it occurs.

Intra-dependent people accept that they selectively rely on people to fulfill their needs. They readily seek and encourage relationships to satisfy these needs. Contrary to either dependent or counter-dependent people, intra-dependent people know they are ultimately responsible. They control how, when, and with whom their relationships occur. The multiplicity of their relationships affords them comfort in the knowledge that if one of their relationships ceases to fulfill a need, they can select a new source or relationship. This knowledge provides self-confidence and self-assurance. There are minimal feelings of loss and loneliness. Loss is redefined as a temporary inconvenience or interruption of need satisfaction.

Intra-dependent people have additional options to delegate numerous sources or relationships for their higher-rated needs. They can determine which needs demand more attention or are at greater risk of loss. Then, they create additional relationships or resources to satisfy particular needs.

Intra-dependent people feel comfortable with their emotions, which are less likely to be classified as bad or good feelings. Feelings either make them pleased or happy, or they don't. What others know as bad feelings are quickly changed by their actions to redelegate their need satisfactions. They acknowledge their needs and express their feelings. Intra-dependent people continually explore the varying aspects of their needs and assume the responsibility to create self-identity. They examine areas of their basic needs that may not be completely fulfilled. With this knowledge, they are open to explore options until they satisfy these unfulfilled needs. The more adept we are at looking, the more apt we are to find. The more we find, the more adept we become at self-exploration. In the cycle of looking and finding, we continually satisfy those newly discovered needs with new-found and delegated relationships.

Intra-dependent people experience power, stability, understanding, and feel themselves and their environment—they sense their own stabilizing ability. They assert themselves readily because they relate from a dynamic of self-control and responsibility. They are confident, self-assured, self-responsible, and have high self-esteem.

Intra-dependent Relationship Dynamics: Case Study

Rebecca and James B. live in a suburb of a large East Coast city. They reside in a single-family home, which they rent, and have lived there for about two years. They live with their two natural children: one daughter, age two, and one son, age five, from their current marriage.

History of Rebecca B.

Rebecca B. is a twenty-four-year-old black, Fundamentalist female. She is a homemaker with part-time employment. Rebecca is mother to two children. She has had no psychiatric hospitalizations. However, she has used outpatient mental health services for six months during her first year of college.

She reported her family-of-origin history with fair detail. During childhood and adolescence, she was raised by her natural mother and father. The parents have since divorced and both are still living. She has one younger brother and one younger sister, both of whom are married. The mother was reported to have drunk occasionally. The father was reported to have had fair health and worked excessively. She reported her siblings as having suffered from depression.

When Rebecca was born, her mother was nineteen years old. She described her mother as warm, outgoing, affectionate, moody, and argumentative. She also was viewed as responsible, optimistic, and hardworking. Rebecca felt her mother loved her; reportedly, the mother was physically affectionate and made her feel loved. Her mother was seen as having been interested in most of Rebecca's activities and supportive of Rebecca's interests. She was reported as reasonable and always wanted to know where Rebecca was going. When they disagreed, Rebecca could usually reason with her. If Rebecca misbehaved, punishment was negotiable. One time, however, she was threatened with a whipping. Typical corporal punishment was hand spanking.

When Rebecca was born, her father was twenty-one years old. She described her father as confident, energetic, warm, and strict. He was viewed as hardworking, happy, and even-tempered. Rebecca perceived her father as having as much affection for her as her mother had. The father, reportedly, was often physically affectionate and made her feel loved. As much as possible, he would take the family places and often bought her what she wanted. Rebecca could easily talk to him about problems. Her father was seen as attentive to most of Rebecca's activities and accomplishments but rarely became involved in them. He was reported to have been a strict disciplinarian who always wanted to know where Rebecca was going. When they disagreed, she could sometimes persuade him to change his opinion. If Rebecca misbehaved, punishment was inevitable. To punish Rebecca the father would yell at her and threaten to take away privileges. Typical corporal punishment was time alone in her room.

Rebecca's developmental history follows. As a child and teenager, she reported never running away from home. She denied sexual molestation, deliberate self-injury, or suicidal ideations or gestures. As a teenager, she was as healthy as others. She began to mature physically at about age twelve, earlier than most of the girls she knew which, she claims, caused some of her social awkwardness. Rebecca learned about sex from her friends and magazines and received a somewhat correct explanation. She began dating at age fourteen. Currently, she enjoys sex, but complains of its infrequency. She denied homosexual experiences.

Rebecca's current marriage began when she was twenty years old, and her spouse was twenty-two years old. She was not married prior to this. In their relationship, she reported they both have problems with the amount of time spent together and relatives. She stated that her partner has problems with talking about feelings, jealousy, the sexual relationship, and fidelity. Arguments occur monthly. She is the primary caregiver for the children in the home. Childrearing has not been problematic.

She began drinking alcohol at age seventeen with her peers but does not drink now. She used amphetamines, marijuana, and cocaine experimentally as a teenager, beginning at age nineteen but does not use any now.

She has not received treatment for drug or alcohol abuse. She reported an episode of depressed mood accompanied by diminished energy level and sleep disturbance. She reported no history of suicide ideations or gestures.

History of James M.

James M. is a twenty-eight-year-old black, Christian male. He is employed full-time as a salaried executive office manager, taking home $3,500 per month. He has no previous psychiatric hospitalizations or outpatient mental health services. Currently, he is not using prescription medication.

James reported his family-of-origin history with good detail. During childhood and adolescence, he was raised by his natural mother and father. His parents were divorced when he was six years old. After the divorce, he lived first with the mother, then moved to his father's at age twelve. The move occurred by agreement for shared custody. Both parents are still living. He has one younger sister, two younger stepbrothers, and one younger stepsister. The mother was reported to have suffered from depression and had problems with headaches. The father is reported to have drunk somewhat and had back and neck problems.

When James was born, his mother was eighteen years old. He described his mother as outgoing, caring, faultfinding, and temperamental. She was viewed as responsible, realistic, and hardworking. James perceived his mother as having loved him. The mother reportedly was physically affectionate and made him feel loved. James could talk to her about most of his problems. His mother was seen as having been interested in most of James's activities and acknowledged his accomplishments. She was reported to have been very strict, although reasonable in some areas. When they disagreed, James could usually get her to give in. If he misbehaved, punishment was inevitable. To punish James, the mother would yell at him and take away privileges. There was no corporal punishment.

When James was born, his father was twenty years old. He described his father as stubborn, serious, friendly, and outgoing. He was viewed as hardworking, responsible, and mostly happy. The father reportedly was physically affectionate and made him feel loved. James could talk to him about most problems. His father was seen as having been interested in James's activities and recognized his accomplishments. He was reported to have been an extremely strict disciplinarian who always wanted to know where James was going. When they disagreed, James could not persuade him to change his mind. If he misbehaved, punishment was inevitable. To punish James, the father would yell at him, and hit him with an open hand. James was sometimes given threats to his safety and well-being. Typical corporal punishments were hand spanking and shoving. James reported that his father never punched him or hit him with a belt or strap.

James's developmental history follows. He reported enuresis after age four for about six months. He also reported insomnia and frequent nightmares for about one year after his parents divorced. As a child and teenager, he reported running away from home only once, at age eight, but never stayed away overnight. As a teenager, he was as healthy as others, had no unusual eating habits, did not or consider himself unattractive. He described himself as shy, awkward, and felt like he didn't fit in with others. He began to mature physically at about age fifteen, later than most of the boys he knew.

He first learned about sex from a friend and received a somewhat incorrect explanation. He began dating and first had heterosexual intercourse at age fifteen and reported feeling anxious and confused. Currently, he enjoys sex. He remembers having a homosexual experience before age eighteen but none afterwards.

James's current marriage began when he was twenty-five years old, and his spouse was twenty-one years old. He was not married prior to this marriage. In their relationship, he reports that they both have problems with the amount of time spent together, religion, and relatives. He stated that his partner has problems with talking about problems, showing affection, trust, managing money, and his parents. Mild arguments occur at least monthly. The primary caregiver of the children in the home is his wife.

James is employed as an executive and is paid by salary. He has had this job for six years, is satisfied with it, and is not thinking about changing jobs. The positive aspects of the job are the compensation, good future, security, challenge, and relationships with coworkers. The negative aspects of the job are the long hours and required traveling. He has been regularly promoted on this job. His income supports four people and has increased over the past year. It is sufficient to pay for all necessities. Primary responsibility for money management resides with James.

James began drinking alcohol at age seventeen and now drinks socially, usually mixed drinks. He reported no need to drink daily. Drinking has never resulted in missed work, arguments with his wife about drinking or trouble with the law. He reported no increase in tolerance to alcohol over time. He used amphetamines and marijuana experimentally as a teenager, starting at thirteen, but does not use any now. He has not received treatment for drug abuse.

He reported a teenage episode of depressed mood unaccompanied by diminished energy level, loss of appetite, and sleep disturbance. He denied any history of suicide ideations or gestures and admitted to having experienced persecutory beliefs. There is no evidence of a thought disorder.

During the initial phone conversation, Rebecca's chief complaints were that she was unhappy about not seeing James enough and not doing things together. She complained that he traveled on too many business trips and she worked at home too much. She would rather work more outside the home. James's chief complaints were that Rebecca wasn't organized enough around the house. She was not affectionate enough, especially when he returned from his business trips. He complained that she frequently complained about the housework and his hours.

Case Script

The following partial script is nearly verbatim, with minimal editing, from the initial session with James and Rebecca B. This method of presentation has been chosen to convey the inflections and mental processes as clients presented them. The psychotherapist intentionally remained inactive and neutral for the purpose of obtaining an accurate script to demonstrate intra-dependent dynamics. The comments were added during editing to help identify the relational dynamics.

PSYCHOTHERAPIST: Come in and please sit where you will be most comfortable. (pause while they're selecting a seat) I have read each of your histories and understand you are here because of a number of complaints about each other and your relationship. While in session, I will ask, when you talk, that you address each other, rather than me. Okay! Who would like to start first?

REBECCA: (speaking to the psychotherapist) I would. I asked James to come with me today because I've been noticing . . .

JAMES: (interrupting) Talk to me, would you please, honey.

REBECCA: (turning to face James) Okay . . . because I've been noticing this behavior and these feelings I've been having lately, and I want to do something about them right away. I've been feeling depressed the last few days. These are things I don't normally experience in my life. I think something is not working, but I want to know what it is. I want to do something about it.

JAMES: What is it?

REBECCA: Well, what I'm feeling is that . . . Ah, with all the traveling you've been doing lately . . . Ah, is that it's just not working for me. (pause) I really feel that I need more time with you at home. I need help with the kids, and I need you to give me emotional support.

JAMES: Why is this showing up for you right now? Why hasn't this come up for you before?

REBECCA: Well, for a while it seemed that it was okay. I enjoy our time together. When you're away, I have things that I'm doing, but this is going on for a longer time than I expected when you started traveling.

JAMES: I still don't think that I understand. I don't know why it's getting worse for you now.

REBECCA: Basically, it's just not working for me. I don't know why, but I just feel overwhelmed. I miss you and your support.

JAMES: What would you like?

REBECCA: I would like you to talk to your boss, and see if you can work something out where you're home more often. I understand your situation. I know that you need to work, but I think there are options where we could make compromises. I mean, how do you feel about it?

JAMES: Well, I don't like you unhappy, and I don't want you to feel lonely.

REBECCA: Yes, but, I am. You know I really like the time we spend together, and I miss that. Lately, we've been kind of like ships passing in the night.

JAMES: I miss you, too. I don't like being gone on these trips either, but I enjoy being important. I like being paid, being in demand, and having a successful career. That's important to me. Although, I wish I didn't have to travel so much. But, it's the dues I have to pay for this kind of a position. And, I would like us not to . . . I would like us to not have it be a big deal that I'm gone, and then when I'm home, it's just great. In other words, I don't want to have to do a lot of relationship repair work when I get back home. I would like to be greeted with open arms. I want to be given a hero's welcome, and we just have a great time while I am here.

REBECCA: Well, are you saying you really don't want to do anything about this, like talk to your boss, or make more time for us to be together?

JAMES: No! I would like to be home more. I would, but I feel like it's a price I have to pay, right now. And, I can't say exactly how long right now is, but I have a good thing going for me, for us, and I would like, ah . . . (pause) I'll tell you what. I will talk to my boss, and see if I can reduce the amount of traveling. However, the more successful I am, the more they are going to want me to travel. The better at the job I am, the more in demand I am. And I don't want to change jobs. I'm not sure that's what you would want. Look, my understanding when I selected this job was that, when we discussed it then, you were completely supportive of this new opportunity for me.

REBECCA: Yeah . . . And, it did seem okay, but it's been, like you said, the more successful you are the more time they want you, and it's getting a little less time at home, less and less as it goes on. And, I'm . . . Maybe we could work out a limit. You know, a limit where you won't let it go any further than . . . Can you do that? You know, I really don't want you to travel anymore than you do right now. In fact I'm wanting it to revert a little bit. We need to define some boundaries here together, and I'm just letting you know that for me the boundary is here and now.

JAMES: Well, that's hard. That's hard to do because when you're an executive, if the computer system goes down, everything's going to grind to a halt unless you're there to take care of it. You know, I have to be there to see to it that it's fixed. I can't always predict when that's going to be, or how much time it's going to take.

REBECCA: So you're saying you can't have any boundaries for that?

JAMES: I'm saying it's kind of hard for me to know. I would like to have boundaries, but it's kind of hard for me to see how I'm going to do it.

PSYCHOTHERAPIST: What do you see as the priority in your life, right now, James?

JAMES: Ah . . . Well, Rebecca is!

PSYCHOTHERAPIST: Can you direct that to Rebecca?

JAMES: Yes. (turning to Rebecca) Well, you are, honey! You're my priority. It's just that right now work is at a critical point. It's going great, and I don't think we should rock the boat. So, for a while, work is top priority, but you know you are my real priority.

REBECCA: Well, that's okay, but can we have a timer on that temporary priority? Like, tell me how long it will last. You know, I just don't like the situation, and I'm just not happy with it.

JAMES: Well, ok, I'll consider that. But, before I do that I've been thinking of other possibilities. How would you feel about coming with me sometimes?

REBECCA: Oh! . . . I'd like that! (pause) I could make that work out.

JAMES: But, as we discussed before, the difficulty I have is that frequently I'm busy during the day, and I'm afraid I would not be around to be with you or entertain you. I might have some evenings or part of an afternoon that I could get away.

REBECCA: You're talking about when you're traveling?

JAMES: Right. But I'm saying that you would pretty much be on your own, most of the time, and I'm not sure. Maybe you could go shopping or whatever you want to do, but I'm not sure that this would satisfy your needs. I mean we would be together on the plane and, of course, at nights, but I'm not sure that will satisfy you. See, I really don't have much control over scheduling. You see, these trips are not vacations. They're business trips. I'm busy all the time. Frequently, in the evenings I'm busy. Some of that is socializing, but even the socialization is business oriented.

REBECCA: Well, don't you know at the beginning of the trip how much time you're going to be involved in business, so we can decide before we go how much time we would have together?

JAMES: I usually do, and most of the time I already know that I don't have much time. I'm just letting you know. Perhaps I haven't let you know before, that I would be open to considering that if it would solve how you are feeling. I'm not sure that it would.

REBECCA: James, talk to me! Would you like it if I came along?

JAMES: Not particularly. I mean that would be okay, but it's a mixed blessing for me. In other words, I would like you to come along with me. I would like your company, but I would not feel good about you going with me if you were bored or lonely all day while I had to go to work.

REBECCA: Right . . .

JAMES: See? That would be a trap for me. If you're expecting . . .

REBECCA: (interrupting) Yeah, yeah. I understand that. Well, you know I like to travel, too. I can find plenty of things to do, but I would like to spend some time with you, either in the day or evening.

JAMES: Yes, I would, too. And I think that as long as you weren't expecting too much of my time, then we could have a good time in the time allotted.

REBECCA: Okay, but we also need to discuss the children.

JAMES: Well, taking the children along would be very distracting for me. Maybe we could have them stay with my parents, or we could get a sitter to come in. What do you think? That may not be the complete solution, but that can be part of it. But, it's also really important to me when I come home from these trips, that I don't have to do a lot of damage repair. I want you to be okay with me being gone and be happy when I'm back. And, that way we can pick up where we left off. Well, I mean, is that something possible?

REBECCA: Well, I'm not feeling very happy about it right now. I'm not sure that's going to be enough.

JAMES: What do you need for that to happen?

REBECCA: I really need for us to spend more time together. I really think we need to talk about some boundaries on how much longer this kind of travel is going to go on. And we need to have a plan about how we are going to deal with this.

JAMES: That sounds like a good idea. I'm willing to think about it. I agree I don't what this to go on. I love you, and I enjoy being with you and the kids; that is my ultimate priority.

REBECCA: So, maybe you could think about this, and we could talk about this some more a week from now.

JAMES: Yes, I would be happy to do that. In the meantime, I could check my office and see what the demands are going to be on me in the future, at least as the travel requirements are concerned. I would like to continue progressing in this job because our ultimate goal is to have enough money so we can retire comfortably. I don't want to limit ourselves in that respect. So, there is that to consider also. There seems to be a proportion between the salary I make and the amount of travel I'm required to make. There is going to have to be some compromises. So, in the next week I'll see what that demand is going to be.

REBECCA: Okay. Sometime next week we'll talk again. And, I'll check on sitters who are able to stay full-time with the kids.

Comment: *Both James and Rebecca voiced their need in this particular conflict and were able to move quickly to problem solving. They were willing to discuss their needs with each other and express the concerns they had about satisfying the other's needs. Although it may appear these people are devoid of expressive feelings and emotions, they, in fact, later clearly demonstrated they were not. In this situation, they recognize that displaying emotions does not solve this problem, or help the other person to know what they want or need. In actuality, this couple was very loving and affectionate with each other and appropriately sad when grieving was needed.*

When psychotherapists understand the relationship dynamics between their clients, and between their clients and the psychotherapist, the application of our orientations and methods becomes more clearly defined. Then, this clarity can be applied to the interpretation of what we observe in session about clients' reality. Next, we must attend to the policies governing the application of knowledge in the healing profession. Finally, there are a number of important considerations about how and when to apply this knowledge to establish policies of imposition.

Notes

1. *Dynamic* means the functional approach of our subconscious drives, processes, and their interactions.
2. *Symbiosis* is defined first as "the living together in more or less intimate association or close union of two dissimilasr organisms," and second as "the intimate living together of two dissimilar organisms in a mutually beneficial relationship."

7

Establishing
Policies
of Imposition

Psychotherapists are in an authoritative role by cultural and social definition. Authoritative roles are socially and judicially assigned positions of responsibility. Tribes and governments[1] ordain and license psychotherapists to perform rites and rituals of emotional and mental healing (Torry, 1987; Kiev, 1964). This privilege carries the responsibility of serving the community's well-being and that of the clients whom they serve. Other professions that contain similar, socially authoritative roles are teachers, ministers, police officers, attorneys, judges, physicians, and politicians, to name a few.

Because authoritative roles are a result of the historical development of cultural roles, most people are aware of and sensitive to their stereotypes. While modern society slowly changes these stereotypes, the myths that support them remain embedded in peoples' subconscious belief systems.[2] Before they establish their psychotherapeutic policies of imposition, psychotherapists must understand their polarity dynamics and the authoritative influences present in stereotypical beliefs.

This reminds us of a story told by a colleague about two children in a swimming pool. The first child, Tom, was an experienced swimmer. He was instructing another younger child, Barry, how to swim. After about twenty minutes of lessons, Barry said to Tom, "I hope that someday I will be able to swim as well as you."

To the compliment, Tom replied, "Well thank you. I'm sure that with practice you will. After all, you're learning really fast."

"Well yes, but you're not teaching me what you're doing." said Barry.

Tom, feeling rather puzzled, questioned, "What are you talking about?"

Barry answered, "I don't mean swimming like you're teaching me. I mean staying afloat like you have been doing for so long while you're teaching me."

Tom quickly replied, "Oh, you mean treading water?"

"Yes." answered Barry.

Tom replied, "Oh well, that's easy! Just put your feet down and stand on the bottom."

The moral of the story is test the depth of the water to figure out how much we will have to swim. Applied to the present context, it means that we need to know the mythological influences and transcultural norms of the stereotypical authoritative roles before taking responsibility to shift them beyond the norm.

Throughout history, and crossculturally, people have learned to seek their mothers for food, comfort, nurturance, and emotional support. Sam Keen (1991), a renowned theologian, states,

> *Mother represents food, everlasting arms, teacher of language and philosophy, the horizon within which we live and move and have our being. . . . Within the warp of her womb our bodies are woven—flesh of her flesh. Within the woof of her arms our minds, spirits, and visions of the world are braided together. She is the teacher of categories by which we will understand ourselves. Her face was our first mirror.*

In polarity, people have learned to seek their fathers for hunting, farming, practical advice, power, efficacy, and survival skills. The poet and mythologist, Robert Bly (1990), speaks to the father role when he writes,

> *The father gives with his sperm a black overcoat around the soul . . . made of intensity, shrewdness, desire to penetrate, liveliness, impulse, daring. The father's birth gift cannot be quantified. His gift contributes to the love of knowledge, love of action, and ways to honor the world of objects.*

Robert Bly (1990, p. 234) also has stated,

> *Some say, "Well, let's just be human, and not talk about masculine or feminine at all." People who say that imagine they are occupying the moral high ground. I say that we have to be a little gentle here, and allow the* masculine *and the word* feminine *to be spoken, and not be afraid that some moral carpenter will make boxes of those words and imprison us in them.*

We say, know the stereotypical expectations. A knowledge of stereotypical expectations permits increased degrees of freedom for enhancing psychotherapeutic effectiveness.

Defining Authoritative Dynamics

For more than three thousand years, Chinese thought has viewed nature as composed of *yin* and *yang* principles. Yin represents soft, yielding, and feminine characteristics. Yang represents hard, rigid, and masculine characteristics. Although these natures are opposing, they are rooted in underlying harmony. In Chinese philosophy, there is no competition between light and darkness, moss and granite, and summer and winter. Chinese thought considers people, regardless of sex, as exemplifying both feminine and masculine characteristics.

Carl Jung (1957) also investigated the internalized (introjected) and external (projected) roles of male and female, and their balance for the wholeness of the individual. According to Jung, people retain and are influenced by an opposing sexual personification of themselves. For the man, there exists the *anima*, for the woman the *animus*. Jung claims that the anima is the latent feminine principle in man and is one of the major archetypes in the collective unconscious (Jung, C., 1957). For the woman, the equivalent polarity is the animus, representing the latent masculine archetype (Jung, C., 1957).

According to the principle of polarities, the anima in man influences his attitudes, choices, and relationships with women. It originates from the man's relationship with his mother and the internalized resolution of the Oedipus complex. The woman's animus originates in the same fashion except that it emanates from her relationship with her father (Jung, C. 1957). The anima can be negative or positive toward the man's psychic wholeness, as can the animus in the woman. Jung (Jung, C., 1933, 1964) claims that the important aspect of psychotherapy is to recognize and fully integrate the contrasexual tendencies of the anima or animus into the subconscious.

The assumed styles of authoritative roles originate from these embedded myths and culturally learned patterns of development. Most psychotherapists naturally gravitate toward one stylistic authoritative role or another when practicing psychotherapy. By gaining clarity and learning the advantages and disadvantages of each of these roles, psychotherapists have a greater chance of conveying their messages to clients.

Cultural and social expectations differentiate authoritative roles into accepting and directive influences. Erik Fromm (1956) differentiated two ways in which mothers and fathers express their acceptance or love. *Mother love* is freely given. *Father love* must be earned. Accepting and directive roles are more fundamental than those defined by the stereotypically performed tasks of either sex. Neither changing diapers nor fixing appliances adequately represents distinguishing characteristics of accepting and directive roles. Conventionally viewed macho male truck drivers have been known to bake in the kitchen, wash dishes, and write poetry. Maiden seamstresses have plowed fields, fixed tractors, and shoveled dung.

People do not exemplify these polarities simultaneously. The figure of the yin-yang represents perfect balance (see Figure 7–1). Carl Jung's concepts of the anima and animus represent a similar coordinated and complete whole. Eric Fromm's concepts of mother love and father love extend the above polarized and complimentary dynamics into a stereotypical social expression. When functioning socially, people predominantly experience only one side of the polarity at any given moment. Therefore, at any single moment, psychotherapists present authoritative expectations of one role more than another, particularly as perceived by the expectations of their clients.

Many authoritative roles have undertones of polarized expectations that we have come to depend on with convenient predictability. For example, there is the lenient and hanging judge, the good policeman and bad cop. There is the easy and hard teacher, the liberal versus the orthodox priest. There is the Hasidic versus orthodox rabbi, the Unitarian minister versus the fundamentalist preacher. The advantage of these socialized polarizations is that they provide a handy reference with which people can easily relate. These authoritative social role models allow an easy identification of their expectations. Without readily identifiable roles, people would have to constantly evaluate role predictability to meet their basic needs of autonomy and belonging.

The effects of these myths on the polarity of authoritative roles are implicitly present in every psychotherapeutic relationship. The effects are present not only in the client's mind, but also in the psychotherapist's. Accepting roles are nurturing, supportive, and favor emotional expression (Rogers, 1961, pp. 60–63). Psychotherapists who use unconditional positive regard[3] (Rogers, 1961, p. 283) favor the accepting role (Rogers, 1942). Psychotherapists who willingly or unknowingly favor manipulation and confrontational statements toward their clients favor the directive role (Rosen, 1953; Greenwald, 1973, 1974; Bach, 1974; Ellis and Grieger, 1977; Glasser and Zunin, 1979). Directive authority is

FIGURE 7–1   The Figure of Yin-Yang Represents Perfect Balance

active and demanding with an expectation of compliance and operative results. When psychotherapists clarify their presentational roles, it provides them an awareness of their dominant role and its effect. Psychotherapists can then use authoritative roles to their most effective advantage, and later, if they choose, to shift the balance according to a client's circumstances.

Shifting Authoritative Roles

Psychotherapists increase their psychotherapeutic effectiveness by clarifying the authoritarian role. Knowing the exact percentile mix of authoritative roles is less important than an awareness of the primary authoritative role as presented and experienced by their clients. Some psychotherapists might prefer to get closer to an even split of their accepting and directive role presentations. Others might want to extend their role presentation to nearer one hundred percent of either the accepting or directive styles. Discovering *previously* assumed authoritative roles in psychotherapy permits psychotherapists to determine whether the authoritative role is congruent with their preferred perceptual attitudes, theoretical structures, and methodologies.

Although it would be convenient for psychotherapists to employ simultaneously all characteristics of accepting and directive authoritative roles, the ability to effectively present both roles equally and simultaneously is rare.[4] Role expectations and presentations are polarities by definition. Trying to be both accepting and directive is like trying to be both a defending and a prosecuting attorney with the same client. While the underlying polarities of yin and yang are always present, when they are manifested socially, people favor an identifiable role presentation polarity. However, like the yin-yang, people can choose to *shift* from one authoritative role polarity to another at different times and for different purposes. As psychotherapists, we can learn to vary the mix of authoritative roles according to clients' circumstances.

Shifting parental roles is like switch-hitting in baseball. Most baseball players favor their right or left hand for batting. A few exceptional players cultivate ambidexterity and bat both right- and left-handed. Although, switch-hitting players are not equally successful at right- and left-handed batting, they have an advantage—these batters have a choice. They base this choice primarily on the skill and pitching tendencies of the pitcher they face. Switch-hitters determine their choice to take advantage of the pitcher's weakest style.

Similarly, psychotherapists can learn to cultivate shifting their authoritative roles. Shifting allows them to choose their authoritative role according to their perceptions of individual clients' circumstances. Jacob Moreno (1980) viewed health and healing as the ability to choose easily among a variety of roles, and then extend them to any desired level of intensity. Ideally, psychotherapists can choose to assume an accepting or directive role at any particular time, as required for the effective healing of any client's situation.

Many effective psychotherapists already shift, perhaps without being aware of it. Shifting authoritative roles increases the ability to resolve clients' pain and counter their resistance. When clients cry or become angry, they may need unconditional acceptance and support. This is accomplished by attending behavior and effective listening (Ivey, Gluckstern, and Ivey, 1982) that is more available when the psychotherapist portrays the accepting role. Clients' tears and anger, however, may be manipulative and enhanced for secondary gain or avoidance. In these circumstances, it may be more therapeutically effective to shift to the directive role with the objective of confronting defenses and examining fundamental issues (Ivey and Gluckstern, 1984). Shifting authoritative roles increases flexibility to a wider variety of clients' situations. By defining authoritative roles and learning how to shift, psychotherapists can effectively both support and confront. The timing and use of authoritative roles are then integrated into a global psychotherapeutic orientation.

Encroachment of Values and Judgments

Psychotherapists of all orientations need to consider carefully the values and judgments they impose in the psychotherapeutic relationship and process. *Valuing* is a process of ascribing positive or negative opinion inward. An example is the way one feels about an object or person he or she holds either as cherished or offensive to oneself. *Judging* is a process of ascribing positive or negative opinion outward. An example is the way one views another person's behavior in relation to how he or she would personally behave.

Judgments occur in all relationships. However, they become especially crucial within psychotherapeutic relationships. Clients expect psychotherapists to solve their problems. Society expects psychotherapists to serve their clients' needs. Consequently, they experience expectations from society, clients, and even themselves to apply their judgments to heal.

Blindly applying psychotherapeutically trained judgments can result in serious consequences. We consider this similar to learning how to drive a car, but then driving with your eyes closed. Firm boundaries of imposition must be known and practiced. Psychotherapists must firmly establish these boundaries so that the context of sessions cannot alter them. In establishing these boundaries, psychotherapists must conscientiously respect the context of *raw* experience within which clients actually live.

Clients do not live in a psychotherapeutic bubble. To dismiss a client's personal values is to violate their identities and personal integrity. Often, acting on the basis of a genuine and professional concern, some psychotherapists inadvertently advise clients to *conform* to their judgments (Halleck, 1971). These psychotherapists genuinely may believe their advice will foster healthful living. Advice, spawned by judgments, is a protective manipulation that often serves only the psychotherapist's expectations. Psychotherapeutic impositions, in the form of either advice or intercessions,[5] are hidden judgments. Impositions complicate and diminish clients' psychotherapeutic healing. Impositions also compromise and deteriorate clients' self-sufficiency, self-esteem, and self-responsibility.

Other psychotherapists claim an obligation and desire to change their clients' values and behaviors. They are eager to label, diagnose, and repair. One esteemed psychiatrist, giving a Grand Rounds Lecture, strongly proposed that psychotherapists take full responsibility for their sick patients. "Like surgeons," he said, "we need to cut out the mental pathogens." Many psychotherapists believe that rescuing is their professional responsibility. They cite evidence to prove people are healthier when they subscribe to the typically endorsed values of the mental health profession.

This is the same profession that generally counsels against manipulation and offers the ostensibly *obvious advantages* of the psychotherapeutically or-dained values of emotional openness and expression, trust, interdependence, reason, socialization, productive independence, and caring. These imposing psychotherapists use their professional judgments and corresponding behav-iors of imposition to replace those they believe contribute to the client's present disorder, disease, conflict, or suffering. Intended to promote a lifestyle of increased alternatives, freedom, and joy, professionally imposed judgments risk achieving the opposite result. Psychotherapists must be explicitly aware of their judgments and the possible consequences of their authoritative imposition.

Judgment Considerations

Psychotherapists make observations that are implicit within their psychothera-peutic orientation. Regardless of orientation, their primary skill is observation. As they observe, they also interpret and judge of their beliefs. As a result of this inherent tendency, they automatically contaminate what should be solely the client's process. Therefore, reduction of this inherent contamination must be their constant vigil. This demands that psychotherapists increase their aware-ness of personal and professional judgments and interpretations. By increasing awareness and understanding of their observation skills and subsequent judg-ment processes, they gain clarity of both the client's self and the client's reality.

Imposition Boundaries

Once aware of psychotherapeutic judgment and interpretation processes, we can become clearer about the differences between our observations and judg-ments. With this clarity, we are able to consider our application of these observations in the psychotherapeutic session. As stated before, we know observation is the primary and most essential skill in psychotherapy. Second is evaluating and judging the client's thoughts, feelings, and actions by these observations.[6] The third essential skill of psychotherapy is the ability to apply these observations, interpretations, and judgments—the content and process of implementing psychotherapeutic observations, interpretations, and judgments. Application is most productive when we follow a few simple rules, and when our therapeutic orientation is congruent with our goals. The three policies of application of psychotherapeutic observations and judgments—*required imposition*, *requested imposition*, and *applied observations*—apply to **all** orientations.

Required Imposition

Psychotherapists are ethically, morally, and in many states, legally obligated to protect clients from physically and psychologically injuring themselves and others.[7] Observations and judgments that indicate imminent danger automatically assume priority. Assuming that this priority exists, psychotherapists then use professionally required methods to restrain the client from acting out in dangerous ways. Under these circumstances, their judgments and values are clearly defined. At first glance, it may seem that the deciding factor to *impose* their judgments is the imminent danger, as defined by legal and professional associations. In actuality, both the professional judgment and the imminent danger must exist for the psychotherapist to intervene.

Numerous humanists/existentialists consider that under no circumstance should values and judgments be imposed on a client. People subscribe to values by being a member of society, thereby acknowledging commitment to societal values. Psychotherapists, regardless of theoretical orientation, assume the values imposed by the society on their profession; these values can be avoided only by choosing a different society. Even shamans of tribal cultures assume the values of life and reduction of pain—they commit to the tribal social values.

Most psychotherapeutic observations and judgments do not, however, fall into the above category. Clients more frequently seek their services because life is not working well or is too painful. This latter category is where impositions are less delineated.

Requested Imposition

Psychotherapeutic settings begin with the clients' expectations of help. Clients seek psychotherapeutic counsel with hopes that the psychotherapist will resolve their psychological conflict or pain. They request the psychotherapist's imposition because of their social reputation as healers. However, imposition, as either advice or intercession at any stage of psychotherapy, hinders the client's psychological development. The only exception is when the imposition fits the category of required imposition.

Decades ago, during the Peace Corps' fledgling years, its founders studied the failures of many third-world helping agencies. They learned that openly giving away needed commodities did not have a positive, long-term effect. What they found was that as the commodities became depleted, the people soon were back in the same plight. The Peace Corps learned that providing methods by which people could take care of themselves and solve their own plight was most effective. Today, the Peace Corps operates under the same philosophy—they teach people how to individually and socially contribute to themselves.

In psychotherapy, *advice* and *intercession* lead to temporary solutions. Advice fixes a problem for a client by directly telling him or her to do something. Intercession directly or indirectly acts to fix or reconcile the client's problem. Neither of these impositions creates methods by which clients solve their problems outside the session. Advice and intercession hinder the process of creating self-sufficiency and thwart clients' self-esteem. Although both can be useful for *Band-Aid* remedies, developing self-sufficiency, self-esteem, and self-responsibility are essential for long-term health and life-enhancing beliefs. When the psychotherapist's judgments arise during requested imposition, but are presented as observations, they enhance clients' development.

Applied Observations

Clients confused by a proliferation of symptoms are unable to perceive and understand the cause of their problems. Therefore, clients often are unaware of their problems. Psychotherapists use their trained skills of observation and knowledge to discern these disguised problems. They make judgments they think will help, though a client has not requested advice or intercession (Ivey, Gluckstern, and Ivey, 1982). However, psychotherapists have a professionally vested obligation to make observations of what may be painful for the client. Yet, they must withhold advice and intercession resulting from these observations.

Psychotherapists must hold judgments confidential. They must use their interpretations to help clients understand their situations and make their own decisions. Effective psychotherapists present observations by the combination of their perceptual attitudes, theoretical structures, and methodologies. Employing this process will help clients discover alternatives. It teaches them to self-evaluate and become self-sufficient. Orientations provide both structure and allowances for variations within a defined methodology. The structure and function of orientations also predetermines how to help clients discover answers for themselves. Only in this way can clients build self-esteem and responsibility for their changes.

Regardless of orientation, applying observations requires psychotherapists to make clients aware of past and potential consequences resulting from their problems. Observations are applied to guide them in solving their problems themselves (Pelletier, 1977). By helping them increase their awareness, they learn about the consequences of their problems. Additionally, helping them become aware of consequences affords them the opportunity to discover their responsibility toward their symptoms, providing them with more control over their life situation.

Psychotherapists apply their observations when clients resources fail to perceive the results of their actions, or thoughts, or when they lack other options. They apply observations, not judgments. They can formulate a cause and diagnostic classification. However, psychotherapists really do not *know* their clients' problems. They only know their formulated beliefs and professional interpretations of *their* problems. By applying observations, they help clients discover their problems within the clients' own reference of experience and understanding. The psychotherapeutic goal is to have clients discover the conflicts within their own belief systems.

As clients discover their problems and consequences, formulating solutions can begin. If directly applied observations are unsuccessful, psychotherapists can employ numerous indirect methods, such as *secretive, narrative, paradoxical, expressive, metaphorical,* or *explorative.* The objective for each of these applied psychotherapeutic observations is to increase client awareness, not directive resolution. With this awareness, clients can then decide on, with their own judgments, their preferred actions.

Applying observations allows clients the choice to discontinue, change, or continue the problem. The final responsibility for change always is the client's anyway. Psychotherapists' responsibility is only to increase awareness of problems and its consequences. In this mode, it is not the therapist's responsibility to change them. Awareness helps clients discover the nature of their problems, so they can formulate options and alternatives. Clients reap the rewards of increased self-esteem and self-responsibility, in addition to resolving the initial problems.

Techniques for Applying Observations

The following techniques—secretive, narrative, paradoxical, expressive, metaphorical, and explorative—are used for applying psychotherapeutic observations. Some are excluded from certain theoretical structures but are included here for breadth of exposure. Space permits only a cursory explanation of each technique. Further study of books listed in the references is recommended to attain a sufficient level of skill for implementation.

Secretive
Often, clients are unaware of the full range of alternatives and options available for them, alternatives that may alleviate or solve their conflicts. They become so frustrated by their perceived lack of alternatives that they become disheartened with the search for solutions. They succumb to their frustration, and their

search ends. This may be observed in the psychotherapy session in the despair contained in various phrases. Examples of despair heard in client sessions include:

- "I just don't know what to do."
- "I give up."
- "I don't care anymore."
- "He's just so stubborn, that I give up trying to change him."

An indirectly motivating technique for applying these observations is the secretive technique. With this method the psychotherapist, after hearing about the client's situation or conflict, implies hidden knowledge of a solution. It is neither necessary nor important that the psychotherapist actually knows a solution. The implication of a solution is the curative quality sought with this technique.

The psychotherapeutic objective is to pique the client's interest in discovering what he or she needs to know. Messages are used toward directing the client to search for solutions again. Using the secretive method, motivation can be accomplished without the client knowing the specific goal of the search. The crucial objective is to motivate the client to search. The success of this method is indicated when the client realizes that quitting the search for a solution is an ineffective way to resolve conflict or pain. After all, the psychotherapist said so!

After initially hearing the secretive technique, the client often asks for the secretive solution. The reply must be that it is essential that the client find the solution him/herself for it to work correctly. The psychotherapist must keep the secret, while assuring the client it is definitely an effective solution. The psychotherapist's evidence is that it has worked for others. Once motivation is achieved and assumed by the client, other techniques are employed to facilitate the client's search and tests for the effectiveness of newly discovered alternatives.

Narrative
A narrative is a psychotherapeutic story told by the psychotherapist about a person or event. The curative impact of the story is in the client knowing it solved a problem similar to the client's. Often the narrative is a description of a similar circumstance and resolution that includes options or additional responsibilities for solving the problem. A psychotherapeutic narrative must exclude the details of how the person in the story actually solved the problem. However, it also must include describing the result. When the client asks how the problem was solved, the psychotherapist should employ the secretive method. For example, "Well, I really don't know, he never told me how that came about."

The objective of the narrative, when used in psychotherapy, is to suggest that a solution exists and to offer a direct invitation to search for it—the narrative suggests there is a solution. The proof is the description of the result in the story. The power of the narrative is:

1. The psychotherapist has directly experienced the resolution.
2. That the psychotherapist, as a respected authority, believes the results in the story apply to the client and can occur again.

The final step of the narrative technique requires reviewing the story, using key elements as guidelines for the client to explore further options and apply them to his or her own circumstances.

The psychotherapist chooses a narrative using the following criteria:

1. The narrative must be closely related to the client's presented problem in as much detail as possible.
2. The person in the narrative must be described with enough details that the client can identify with the situational person.
3. The story must finish with a well-defined description of the resultant change without defining the resolving process.

These criteria lend the narrative credibility for the client and increase beliefs that the client can achieve the same solution. This, then, motivates the search for alternative solutions.

Paradoxical

Paradoxical intention is a technique of applied observations used to indirectly encourage or motivate the client to confront objects or events that are feared or avoided (Frankl, 1969). The technique uses anticipatory anxiety and the power of self-fulfilling prophecy. An understanding of these concepts is essential for the proper application of paradoxes in psychotherapy. As with the behavioral techniques of implosion, the goal of paradoxical intention is to break the self-defeating cycle of the client's feared object or event caused by the anticipatory anxiety. For example, when clients are told to do deliberately what they believe to be occurring involuntarily, they demonstrate that the fear of it being involuntary is untrue. This technique is known as symptom prescription or joining the resistance.

While practicing at the Mental Research Institute, Palo Alto, California, George Bateson and Paul Watzlawick (Watzlawick, Beaven, and Jackson, 1968) successfully developed an understanding and application of paradox in psychotherapy. They defined paradox as a logical contradiction following consistent deductions from correct premises. They delineated three types:

1. *Paradoxical definitions*: These are statements that are inherently paradoxical because of their language. An example is the statement, "Everything that I say

is false." If this statement is believed to be true, it must be false according to the statement. If the statement is believed to be false, then "everything I say is true." This assertion also is false because of the first hypothesis. To avoid a paradoxical definition, we must view language as having both a detonable (information) level and a metacommunicative level. Use of paradoxical definitions allows comments on the detonable level to be made from a meta position.

2. *Logical mathematical paradoxes*: This includes definitions of items that cannot, at the same time, be members of the same collection. For example, the term "dog" cannot itself be described as a dog in the same way a German shepherd is a dog. The word or term *yellow* cannot be used to describe what the color yellow looks like.

3. *Pragmatic paradoxes*: These paradoxes state injunctions or predictions by an authoritative person, someone who is in a position superior to that of the receiver. The situation requires that the injunction or prediction be obeyed only by disobeying it, and where it is impossible for the subordinate to step beyond the authority's sphere of reference. The classical example of paradoxical injunction is the command "to be spontaneous." In order for the subordinate comply with the command, it must be done by not complying. The subordinate cannot, by definition, be spontaneous to a command to be spontaneous.

Paradoxical definitions and mathematically logical paradoxes are difficult to construct so as not to be detected by the client. Therefore, we recommend they seldom be used in psychotherapy. Pragmatic paradoxes, however, are commonly employed. The most familiar occurrence of this kind is when it operates in interpersonal relationships as double binds. Pragmatic paradoxes create a double bind for the subordinate member of the relationship. Strategic psychotherapists have used pragmatic paradoxes effectively in treatment (Bateson, 1972; Cade, 1980; Haley, 1963). George Bateson (Bateson, et al., 1956) has developed the use of paradox as a therapeutic technique. Paul Watzlawick (1978) described several examples of paradoxical interventions—symptom prescription, double binds, the Devil's pact, and reframing. His intent was to confuse the rational and logical areas of the brain.

Confusion techniques of paradox remove the client's problem from the authority's sphere of reference. Milton Erikson (Haley, 1973) was particularly creative with the technique of paradox. He created an illusion of alternatives, where the client was forced to choose between only two possibilities. No other choice was available. For example, he gave a client the choice of admitting himself or having the psychotherapist admit him to a drug treatment clinic. Either choice accomplishes the psychotherapist's goal and the goal of the paradox. The paradoxical intent is that the client does not consider the third, not offered, choice of not being admitted to a treatment clinic.

Another of Milton Erickson's techniques was *rehearsing a relapse*. Relapse rehearsal is prescribing a symptomatic behavioral relapse after the client has achieved a psychotherapeutic change. Prescribing a relapse to the old behavior is a confirmation that the change is successful.

A third paradoxical technique that Milton Erickson used was *symptom substitution*—temporarily substituting other situations that are less restrictive. For example, a client who compulsively honked his car horn at each red traffic control light reasoned that honking the horn would cause the red light to change to green more quickly. The symptom substitution was that tapping one foot lightly on the floor would make the light turn green even quicker than honking the horn. Tapping the foot was far less annoying to those near the client than honking the horn. However, after several of these symptom substitutions, the client concluded that none of them really had any effect. Consequently, he stopped foot tapping and honking the horn.

Rohrbaugh, et al. (1977) subdivided paradoxes into three types: *positioning, prescribing,* and *restraining strategies.* In the positioning type, the psychotherapist takes the position of accepting the client's view, which is designed to counter the client's original view. For example, a client presents her compulsive pattern of constantly needing to clean her house. The psychotherapist presents the position that this may actually be helping her solve some other problem, and she should continue to clean so that this other problem does not occur.

A prescribing strategy is a paradox that has a remedy built into it. If countered, it will solve the client's conflict. Using the same compulsive client as in the previous example, a prescribing paradox would be to tell her to clean more often and get her family to help. In following this prescription, the client would receive needed recognition from her family and their involvement in her healing.

A restraining paradox inhibits the symptomatic behavior in a greater fashion than the original presenting conflict. The client is forced to choose either the paradox or the original conflict. With neither choice as acceptable, the client will choose a third alternative containing less symptomatic behavior. An example of this type of paradox, with the above compulsive client, is to tell her to send her family away and then compulsively clean for days.

Jay Haley (1976) outlined these five methods of paradoxical intervention:

1. *Encouraging resistance*: In this method, the client is caught in a situation where continued resistance is cooperative.

2. *Providing a worse alternative*: In this method the object is to get the client to make his/her own choices while changing within the framework of psychotherapeutic growth. This is accomplished by directing the client to choose one direction while provoking him/her to choose another more healthy direction. For example, Erickson (1980) writes of a client who became anxious each time he drove his car beyond the city limits. He directed the client to stop the car and lie in the roadside ditch each time he felt the anxiety coming on as he drove himself out of town. The prescribed action of lying in the ditch became viewed

Imposition Boundaries   189

as worse than the original anxiety, although it replaced the anxiety attack. The client stopped lying in the ditch because it messed his clothing. Since lying in the ditch controlled the anxiety and he was controlling lying in the ditch, he knew he could control the anxiety.

3. *Encouraging a relapse*: In this method, when improvement is rapid, the client often assigns the responsibility for this change to the psychotherapist. Encouraging a relapse offers a challenge. This challenge, if taken, fosters making his/her own choices and self-responsibility.

4. *Encouraging a response*: In this method, frustrating a client's pseudowillingness to respond with a change can be enhanced by allowing the beginning of the change to occur, but then quickly frustrating it. Then, at a later time, the psychotherapist can return to the directive, and the client will be prepared to respond without the previous resistance. For example, a client in a family session was reluctant to speak after several opportunities. The psychotherapist patiently encouraged the client to speak. As the first few words were spoken, the psychotherapist cut the conversation by saying, "It's okay not to speak," and quickly moved to another family member. Later, in the session, the psychotherapist again gave the quiet client an opportunity to speak. The client quickly took advantage of the opportunity.

5. *Amplifying a deviation*: In this method, the psychotherapist chooses a small deviated response from the symptom pattern to build a larger or more pervasive response and eventual change. The concept is that small changes can lead to larger changes of symptomatic behavior. For example, a small hole in a dam can have disastrous effects on the structure of the dam; plugging the leak can save the dam.

Jay Haley (1976) also outlined seven steps for the implementation of paradoxical intervention:

1. Define the client–psychotherapist relationship in terms of bringing about change.
2. Define the client's problem as presented.
3. Help the client establish the psychotherapeutic goals.
4. Develop a plan or rationale.
5. Disqualify other authorities on the problem, such as a relative, spouse, or friend.
6. Encourage the standard behavior while reinforcing a no-change position.
7. Refute credit for the client's changes.

Paradoxes are powerful therapeutic techniques used to help the client. However, they also are known to cause pathological dysfunction. If the client is cooperative and motivated, paradoxical interventions are not recommended and should be avoided. The strength of paradoxes is their ability to break down highly resistant and complex defenses and logic (Haley, 1963).

Expressive

Several techniques exist for expressive application of observations. For ease of understanding, we subdivide them into three types:

1. Techniques performed by the client and directed by the psychotherapist, where the psychotherapist does not actively participate.
2. Techniques genuinely performed and demonstrated by the psychotherapist.
3. Techniques contrived and performed by the psychotherapist.

Techniques that are directed by the psychotherapist include those found in the practice of emotive therapy—requesting the client to scream, beat pillows, pound on chairs, and hit couches with battaca bats. Other expressive applications include play therapy, sand-tray play, age regression, rebirthing, and Riechian bodywork.

In each of these applications, psychotherapists direct clients to perform to facilitate the release of emotions. The goal is for clients to become aware that their emotions are only symptoms of their problems. Staging the opportunity for the client's emotional expression is the technique. Deciding how to use the technique is determined by the psychotherapist's observations and interpretations of the client's conflict. The psychotherapist observes the harbored emotions and then uses the technique of expression to release these emotions in the safe environment of the session. Objective observation may be that the client has directed emotional energies to an object. However, the object is used as only a projective prop when applying the expressive technique. An example of the expressive technique with a prop is the following case study of Vince.

Vince, a twenty-four-year-old male, during the first session, repeatedly stated his anger at his wife. He reported that he was afraid he might hurt her. His every attempt at quieting or controlling explosive situations at home only led him to greater frustration and anger. Often, his wife or someone at work would make rather minor mistakes that caused exaggerated responses of anger. Recently, this had occurred as many as four or five times a day. His focus was so concentrated on controlling his anger that he seldom addressed the actual problems being presented him. To control his anger, he became reclusive, talked less, avoided challenges and people, took long walks, smoked a lot, and drank heavily.

Midway into the first session, Vince and his wife had a serious argument in which he became enraged. Vince was given a battaca bat and the psychotherapist told him to pretend the pillow sitting on the couch was his wife. With increased coaching, he began to strike the pillow relatively gently. As the enactment took on a more real situation for him, he struck with more force and uttered loud and angry words. As he poured his emotional energy into striking the pillow, his anger built to a rage and then his rage converted to sadness. Within ten minutes, he fell to the floor on his knees, dropped the battaca bat, and grasped the pillow to his chest. Clutching the pillow, he sobbed into the couch. After several minutes his sobbing slowly subsided. As he looked up from the pillow he said, "I really don't want to hurt anyone. I only want someone to care about me."

From this insight, the psychotherapist proceeded to help him find options for solving the problems he is faced with each day and ways to ask for the caring he wants. In this example of the expressive technique, the pillow was a prop for the object of Vince's anger. In this particular incident the object of his anger was his wife. The psychotherapist had observed that he was angry with her currently by his outburst in the argument. With a little coaching to enhance the role play, the safety of the session was the only remaining component necessary for his expressive enactment.

The second type of expressive method is an exaggerated expression or acted-out emotional reaction to clients' descriptions of their situations or conflicts. Acting-out is a psychotherapeutically safe process in which to demonstrate the consequences of clients' conflicts. In this second type of expressive technique, the psychotherapist genuinely expresses the feelings elicited by what is heard from a client.

For example, a psychotherapist says with harsh overtones, "I'm really upset you missed the last appointment, and you didn't even give me the courtesy of a call!" Another psychotherapist says with a sincere tone, "I was very worried when you missed your appointment and didn't call to let me know what happened!" Both of these were genuine expressive responses to clients' behavior and are intended to make clients aware of the consequences of their actions.

The third type of expressive method is an exaggerated expression or an acted-out emotional reaction to clients' descriptions of their situations or conflicts. Again, this acting-out is a psychotherapeutically safe situation in which to demonstrate the consequences of a client's situation or conflict. In this third type of expressive technique, however, the psychotherapist contrives an expressive response to what is heard from the client. Stated another way, the psychotherapist contrives an emotionally expressive response similar to what the psychotherapist thinks would be someone else's expressive response to the client's presenting information.

In the previous examples, the two psychotherapists may have actually felt the emotions they were expressing. In those cases, they were sincere statements. However, if they did not feel that way, they could have acted as if they felt them. They could have contrived believable expressions. The client's results, gaining insight into the consequences, would be similar. The essential difference is that the psychotherapist would not be genuine. Of course, this lack of authenticity is important only in the context that the psychotherapist believes that it was significant for personal expression rather than client circumstances. The following role-play is an example of a contrived expression.

After many weeks of soul-searching and intense psychotherapy, Beth, a twenty-two-year-old married female, had concluded she wanted to have a child. However, she decided that impregnation should be solely her decision. Her plan was to wait a few months until she could no longer hide the pregnancy, and then tell her spouse. Reasoning that she was determined to have a child regardless of her spouse's concerns, her plan was to force the decision until after it was too late to consider having an abortion. Her idea was to confront her spouse when she was about three months pregnant.

The psychotherapist burst forth with anger and accusations of mistrust and betrayal. As these subsided, accusations of infidelity started with more anger and threats of terminating the psychotherapeutic relationship. The client countered with amazement, and then began to realize she would have reacted in much the same way if she were in the psychotherapist's position. The psychotherapist proceeded to help the client review her options with this new insight.

In actuality, the psychotherapist was not experiencing the feelings being expressed; nor, was it necessary. The objective was to provide the client with another perspective, to gain awareness of the likely consequences of her planned actions. Then, with this new awareness, she could review alternative ways to satisfy multiple desires.

Metaphorical
This technique of applied observations involves using two discrete ideas or elements of meaning. These two elements or previously separate ideas are interplayed in a story by comparison, which then serves to create new meaning for the client. This is accomplished by making one of the elements or ideas in the metaphor familiar or relevant to the client. By comparing the new element or idea to the client's familiar element or idea, new information is brought to the client. The interactions between the two ideas, that previously were considered disconnected, are connected by the psychotherapist's metaphoric story. This connection creates a new perspective for a client to interpret his or her situation or conflict.

Metaphors are very similar to narratives in that they directly address the same situation or problem presented by the client. The difference is that narratives are a direct, reality-based story, whereas metaphors have no requirement for a reality base. Metaphors can, and often are, fictional and imaginary.

There are two kinds of metaphors—those that originate from the client and those that arise from the psychotherapist. Referring to those that originate from the client, Black (1962) describes the use of metaphors as a distinctive technique for activating insight into the client's situation. For the psychotherapist, such insight from the client's metaphoric content is used to interpret the client's situation. Much information given by the client is in the form of stories that contain meaningful information, but proper interpretation is essential. The second kind of metaphor occurs when the psychotherapist consciously uses metaphors to enable the client's insight and change.

Client Metaphors. Studies of psychotherapeutic language has found most to be a metaphorical expression of clients' inner experience or interpretation of their external reality (Haley, 1976). The metaphor is a means of connecting the two. Therefore, the psychotherapist and client always will be interpreting the hidden meaning of each other's metaphors. Language requires us to compare metaphors and symbols, and then differentiate between what is conveyed by the metaphor and what is meant by using the metaphor (Bandler and Grinder, 1982).

A symbol is used to mean something else. For example, the symbol "$" means dollar—a unit of currency in the United States. A metaphor is used to be something else (Cade, 1982). In the practice of House-Tree-Man drawings, the house universally is equated to the self-body of the person doing the drawing. For metaphors to be effective, the psychotherapist must interpret the client's metaphors, and then work within the client's system of meaning.

Psychotherapists electing to work with the client's metaphor must first interpret the metaphor correctly. For example, the psychotherapist can interpret a person's story about the condition of her or his car as the state of her or his marriage. After a few confirming and probing questions, the psychotherapist can then indirectly elicit changes in the marriage by telling stories about how others fix their cars. Working within the metaphor, rather than outwardly interpreting a marital situation, is especially useful with resistant clients.

Psychotherapist Metaphors. The second kind of metaphoric technique requires the psychotherapist to construct an original metaphor that contains embedded information with which clients can identify, and thereby apply to solve their conflict (Bandler and Grinder, 1975). A number of techniques—fictional storytelling, retelling true stories, guided imagery, and guided fantasy—exist to accomplish this process (Wallas, 1985; Mills and Crowley, 1986).

Fictional storytelling entails creatively constructing a story that contains elements similar to the client's life and situation (Mills and Crowley, 1986). Within the story are elements of solutions and multiple options for viewing the client's conflict or situation (Minuchin, 1974). Retelling a true story, by the psychotherapist, allows the message of the metaphor to be removed from the client's ownership. This permits easier acceptance of the embedded solution.

Milton Erikson (Erikson and Rossi, 1979) suggested the importance of metaphors with highly resistant patients. The reason is that the metaphor is related to the client's subconscious conflict, while appearing to be completely removed from it. Since the suggestion is embedded in the metaphor and seemingly unrelated, the client will have no defensive barriers to its acceptance (Gordon, 1978).

Explorative

The use of explorative techniques of applied observations establishes alternatives when clients are prompted to explore other options to their current dilemmas. The first step is to let clients know they have other options, and the second is to provide them methods of discovering these alternatives. Minuchin (1974), Haley (1976), and other structural family psychotherapists make use of small activities—tasks, directed communications, enacting transactional patterns, recreating communication channels, manipulating space, moderated negotiations, or homework assignments presented as problem-solving techniques. Each of these techniques is designed to explore the area of the dysfunction. The objective is to increase alternatives for clients to deal with the dysfunction.

Some examples of small activities or tasks are:

1. Playing, while in session;
2. An explorative therapeutic board game;
3. Having parents interact with their children through craft activities, like modeling clay, finger painting, drawing with crayons or colored pens, or making collages with magazine cutouts;
4. Taking turns acting through an emotion or drama;
5. Building a sand-tray scene and telling a story about the scene;
6. Taking turns telling about an object or event they like and then, after a few rounds, talking about one object or event they don't like.

Each of these activities is performed in the session by one or more clients and may or may not include the psychotherapist. If the psychotherapist is involved, keeping input to a minimum is essential. The psychotherapeutic objective is to keep the clients involved in the activity. It is to help them understand the information being presented in the course of the activity.

The psychotherapist can direct communication during the session to help clients explore causes of conflict rather than symptoms. This is an especially useful technique when dealing with a group, couple, or family. Clients are prompted to question or respond to other clients. Feelings and thoughts are equally open for prompting.

Opening and directing communication also can be accomplished by a technique called enacting transactional patterns. Minuchin (1974) and Satir (1983) clarified the use of transactional patterns to mobilize the family or group to enact the dysfunction rather than to describe the conflict. In the process of having them transact in the session, additional information is exposed to both the psychotherapist and clients. This added information allows a greater chance for self-interpretation and clients' sought-after insight.

Recreating communication channels is somewhat similar to enacting transactional patterns. The difference is that, when a client is talking about someone in the group setting, he or she is requested to communicate directly to that person. The tendency is for group members to talk about each other to the psychotherapist. They reason that they have already tried talking to each other with no results. With this member-to-member communication in process, it allows the psychotherapist to observe transactional patterns, which provides valuable information for further interventions.

Manipulating physical space in the session is another method of exploring alternatives. Whether in individual or group sessions, the arrangement of furniture and people creates different feelings for the clients. These feelings can be questioned and explored for content and cause. For example, the psychotherapist may sit far from the client or turned away and then ask for the client's feelings or thoughts. Minuchin (1974) writes how boundaries were enacted around the parental subsystems of a particular family, such that a child could not enter. In a session, that boundary was broken by rearranging the seating so the alienated child was closer to the mother while investigating an issue between them.

Moderating negotiations is another technique for controlling communication while increasing opportunities for clients to learn new alternatives. This technique involves controlling the transactional patterns between clients such that each has the chance to participate. Psychotherapists can take on a top-dog to under-dog role (Perls, 1969), or parent to child communication pattern (Berne, 1964, 1961), in which the roles attempt to manipulate one another. The psychotherapist's goal is to balance the roles so each can contribute to solving the conflict or problem.

Homework assignments provide practical ways to extend psychotherapy beyond the allotted session time. They also can involve people, who are not in the session in the healing process. This gives the principles of psychotherapy an opportunity for practical application within the client's world. The following are a few examples of homework assignments available to the psychotherapist:

1. Assign shared work projects. For instance, a mother and daughter could redecorate the daughter's room or plan the daughter's slumber party. A father and son plant a garden or fix the family car together.
2. Have a couple go to the local shopping mall to observe couples and note how they behave toward each other, with special attention as to how they resolve their differences and gain cooperation.
3. Have clients make lists of likes and dislikes, wants and needs, or requirements for relationships.

4. Assign or give reading materials that provide information about clients' particular situations or conflicts.

It is essential to follow through whenever homework is assigned. The most important reasons for this are to confirm the assignment is being done correctly and to process the learning achieved by the homework.

Dynamic and influential psychotherapeutic forces lay at our beck and call. The psychotherapist's responsibility is to use these with knowledgeable adeptness. Telling people what to do with their lives, when that specific knowledge is uninvited, serves only to make them more dependent. Like the lesson of the Peace Corps, establish boundaries, policies, and techniques that provide clients the tools for self-sufficiency. The ultimate psychotherapeutic goal is for the client to no longer require our professional services.

Notes

1. Similar authority is granted the psychotherapist, shaman, medicine man, and witch doctor. For a complete comparison and explanation of cultural healing roles, see E. Fuller Torry and A. Kiev cited in the references.
2. The concept of belief systems was thoroughly covered earlier in this book.
3. Carl Rogers originally used this term. He believed unconditional positive regard to be essential for permitting a safe atmosphere in which clients are willing to risk.
4. This presumption is, first, a difficulty with psychoanalytic models that postulate analysts should be a neutral mirror for the mechanism of transference. Our position is that counter-transference is somewhat inevitable and psychotherapists need to take responsibility for effective implementation of their authoritative role. Second, the expression of a neutral role would, nevertheless, exemplify an authoritative accepting role.
5. Intercession is the act of interceding; to act between parties for the purpose of reconciliation.
6. Every theoretical structure and model of psychotherapy implies criteria by which to interpret observations. Choosing a theoretical structure affords us a criterion by which to interpret and judge our observations.
7. In the state of California, psychotherapists also are obligated, by legal precedence, (1) to notify judicial authorities and potential victims of homicidal intent, and (2) to timely notify appropriate agencies regarding child and senior abuse. In many other states, such notification may violate confidentiality.

References

Bach, G. (1974). *Creative aggression.* New York: Doubleday.
Bandler, R., & Grinder, J. (1975). *The structure of magic I.* Palo Alto, CA: Science and Behavior Books.
Bandler, R., & Grinder, J. (1982). *Reframing.* Moab, UT: Real People Press.
Bateson, G. (1972). *Steps to an ecology of mind.* New York: Granada.

Bateson, G., Jackson, D., Haley, J., & Weakland, J. (1956), Toward a theory of schizophrenia. *Behavioral Science, 1,* 251–264.

Berne, E. (1964). *Games people play.* New York: Grove Press.

Berne, E. (1961). *Transactional analysis in psychotherapy.* New York: Grove Press.

Black, M. (1962). *Models and metaphors.* Ithaca, NY: Cornell University Press.

Bly, R. (1990). *Iron John.* Reading, MA: Addison-Wesley.

Cade B. (1982). Some uses of metaphor. *Australian Journal of Family Therapy. 3,* 135–140.

Cade, B. (1980). Strategic therapy. *Journal of Family Therapy, 2,* 89–99.

Ellis, A., & Grieger, R. (1977). *Handbook of rational-emotive therapy.* New York: Springer.

Erikson, M. (1980). *The nature of hypnosis and suggestion* (Ernest L. Rossi, Ed.). New York: Irvington.

Erikson, M., & Rossi, E. (1979). *Hypnotherapy: An explanatory casebook.* New York: Irvington.

Frankl, V. (1969). *The will to meaning.* New York: New American Library

Fromm, E. (1956). *The art of loving.* New York: Bantam Books.

Glasser, W., & Zunin, L. (1979) Reality therapy. In R. Corsini (Ed.), *Current psychotherapies* (2d ed.). Itasca, IL: F. E. Peacock.

Gordon, D. (1978). *Therapeutic metaphors.* Cupertino, CA: Meta.

Greenwald, H. (Ed.). (1974). *Active psychotherapy.* New York: J. Aronson.

Greenwald, H. (1973). *Direct decision therapy.* San Diego, CA: Edits.

Haley, J. (1976). *Problem solving therapy.* New York: Harper & Row.

Haley, J. (1973). *Uncommon therapy.* New York: W. W. Norton.

Haley, J. (1963). *Strategies of psychotherapy.* New York: Grune & Stratton.

Halleck, S. (1971). *The politics of therapy.* New York: Science House.

Ivey, A., & Gluckstern, N. (1984). *Basic influencing skills* (2d ed.). North Amherst, MA: Microtraining Assc.

Ivey, A., Gluckstern, N., & Ivey, M. (1982). *Basic attending skills* (2d ed.). North Amherst, MA: Microtraining Assc.

Jung, C. (1964). *Man and his symbols.* Garden City, NY: Doubleday

Jung, C. (1957). *Animus and anima.* New York: Spring.

Jung, C. (1933). *Psychological types.* New York: Harcourt.

Keen, S. (1991). *Fire in the belly* (p. 18). New York: Bantam Books.

Kiev, A. (1964). (Ed.) *Magic, faith, and healing.* New York: The Free Press.

Mills, J., & Crowley, R. (1986). *Therapeutic metaphors for children and the child within* (pp. xv–xxi). New York: Brunner/Mazel.

Minuchin, S. (1974). *Families and family therapy.* London: Tavistock.

Moreno, J. (1980). *Psychodrama: Vols. I, II, III.* New York: Beacon House.

Pelletier, K. (1977). *Mind as healer, mind as slayer.* New York: Dell.

Perls, F. (1969). *Gestalt therapy verbatim.* Moab, UT: Real People Press.

Rogers, C. (1961). *On becoming a person.* Boston: Houghton Mifflin.

Rogers, C. (1942). *Client-centered therapy.* Boston: Houghton Mifflin.

Rohrbaugh, M. (1977). Paradoxical strategies in psychotherapy. Quoted from Gruman, A. S. and Kniskern, D. P. *Handbook of family therapy.* New York: Brunner/Mazel.

Rosen, J. (1953). *Direct psychoanalytic psychiatry.* New York: Grune & Stratton.

Satir, V. (1983). *Conjoint family therapy.* Palo Alto, CA: Science and Behavior Books.

Torry, E. F. (1987). *Witchdoctors and psychiatrists: The common roots of psychotherapy and its future.* Northvale, NJ: Avonson.

Wallas, L. (1985). *Stories for the third ear.* New York: W. W. Norton.

Watzlawick, P. (1978). *The languages of change.* New York: W. W. Norton.

Watzlawick, P., Weakland, J., & Fisch, R. (1974). *Change: Principles of problem formation and problem resolution.* New York: W. W. Norton.

Watzlawick, P., Beaven, J., & Jackson, D. (1968). *Pragmatics of human communication.* New York: W. W. Norton.

Appendix A

*Psychotherapeutic
Orientation
Worksheets*

1. Perceptual Attitudes

☐ Intrapsychic
☐ Interpersonal
☐ Organizational
☐ Universal

2. Theoretical Structures

☐ Productive
☐ Innovative
☐ Creative

3. Methodologies

	Forbid	Discourage	Permit	Encourage	Require
Behavioral					
Cognitive					
Affective					
Intuitive					
Symbolic					
Sensate					
Somatic					
Catharsis level (circle one)				I, II, III, IV	V, VI, VII

4. Techniques from Psychotherapeutic Models

Check all that apply.[1]

- ☐ Active Dream Therapy
- ☐ Assertiveness Training
- ☐ Bibliotherapy
- ☐ Cognitive Structuring
- ☐ Communication Skills
- ☐ Confrontation
- ☐ Didactic Teaching
- ☐ Dream Analysis
- ☐ Empty Chair
- ☐ Free Association
- ☐ Homework Assignments
- ☐ Hypnosis
- ☐ Implosion
- ☐ Increasing Insight
- ☐ Joining
- ☐ Loosening Muscular Armor
- ☐ Meditation

- ☐ Modeling Behavior
- ☐ Paradoxical Intent
- ☐ Psychodynamic Interpretation
- ☐ Relaxation Training
- ☐ Role-playing
- ☐ Rule Making
- ☐ Script Analysis
- ☐ Sculpting
- ☐ Sensitivity Training
- ☐ Socialization
- ☐ Structural Integration
- ☐ Systematic Desensitization
- ☐ Systematic Training
- ☐ Use of Metaphor and Myths
- ☐ Use of Contracts
- ☐ Use of Humor
- ☐ Other _____

---

1. For definitions of these, see Walrond-Skinner, S. (1986). *Dictionary of psychotherapy*. New York: Routledge & Kegan Paul.

202 _Psychotherapeutic Orientation Worksheets_

5. Primary Psychotherapeutic Model: _____
(Fill in name from list below)

By founder, e.g., Adler, Beck, Berne, Bion, Bowen, Ellis, Erickson, Freud, Glasser, Greenwald, Jung, Minuchin, Moreno, Perls, Reich, Rogers, Satir, Sullivan, Whitaker, Wolpe, or another.[2]

6. Policies of Imposition

Authoritative Role (Total = 100%)

[__ %]   Accepting

[__ %]   Directive

Policies

☐ Required Imposition

☐ Requested Imposition

☐ Applied Observations

Techniques of Applying Observations

☐ Secretive   ☐ Expressive

☐ Narrative   ☐ Metaphoric

☐ Paradoxical   ☐ Explorative

2. For further information on these, see Corey, G. (1982). _Theory and practice of counseling and psychology._ Monterey, CA: Brooks/Cole.

Appendix B

Hypnotic Scripts for Disengaging Beliefs

Investigation of Belief Systems

The following methods access beliefs, gain insight, and effect change; they afford us an opportunity to further develop our belief systems or modify selected beliefs and behaviors. Minimally, we could use these methods to know about belief systems that create problems or limit our personal life functions. As adults, we can access and change limiting beliefs. Access, in this context, means to bring to conscious awareness. Our primary area of focus is on life-limiting beliefs. Because these beliefs are less accessible, defended, and subconscious, we initially are aware of only their emotional effects, physical, or behavioral symptoms. To access limiting beliefs, we need to first define the problems or conflicts we have. Problems are uncomfortable events or situations in life. Conflicts signal that we are failing to achieve satisfaction of basic needs. We accomplish this with a method called *belief investigation.*[1]

Belief investigation is a method for accessing problematic or conflict-creating belief systems. The first step requires clearly defining the problem by answering the following questions:

- What problem exists in your life at the present time?
- How is your life not working for you?
- What is it that you don't feel good about?

With attention to detail, specifically define the problem as you experience it.

Answering the following questions will help uncover specific problematic dynamics.

- How does this problem affect you?
- What does this problem make you think about?
- What does this problem make you do or act like?
- How does this problem make you feel?

After you finish answering these, list how the problem affects others around you. Answer each of the following questions.

- How does this problem influence others to think about you and your situation?
- How does this problem influence others to act?
- How does this problem make others around you feel?

Complete this belief investigation list thoroughly before continuing.

With the completed list, place yourself in a comfortable position, sitting or lying down where it's quiet and you will not be distracted or disturbed. Remember back as far into your own past, as possible. Remember when you first experienced this problem or one similar. Think back to when you first became aware of a similar problem. Recall your earliest memory. Recollect the scene, thought, or event. Accept the first memory that comes into your mind. It does not matter how silly or disconnected it may seem at first.

On paper or using a tape recorder, describe what you remember was happening at that time. Answering the following questions will help you picture the event.

- What was taking place around you?
- What were people doing?
- Who was there?
- What was the effect of this problem?
- What was this problem causing you to think at that time?
- Describe what your problem was causing you to do.
- Describe how you felt at that time.
- How did your problem affect others, make them feel?
- What did it cause others to think?
- What did your problem make other people do?

After you thoroughly investigate this memory, search even farther back into your memory. Find an event that occurred at an earlier time. Remember an event similar to the one you just described. This will be the next earlier memory, relative to the problem. Accept the first memory that arrives. Ask the previous questions again. Begin with, "What was taking place around you?" Answer as many questions about this memory as you can.

The next step is looking for similarities or patterns. Answer the following questions about this entire memory-recall experience. Answer them as quickly and accurately as possible. Accept whatever answer first arrives in your mind, regardless of how ridiculous or childlike it may seem at first. The earlier the experience the more childlike the answers are likely to be. Write the answers down or record them at first awareness. Avoid questioning, judging, or analyzing your answers as they come to you. You will have an opportunity to do that later. For now, it is important to get the first, uncontaminated responses. Every question will have at least one answer. Answer the questions consecutively; do not skip questions.

- What patterns do you notice in your thinking?
- What patterns do you notice in your feelings?
- What patterns are there to other people's thoughts, behaviors, reactions, and feelings about your problem?

With the information or insight provided by the above questions, answer the following.

- What reasons are there for you to have this pattern of thinking, acting, or feeling?
- What advantages does this pattern provide you?
- How does this pattern solve the situation of your memories which you just recalled from your childhood?
- How is the present-day problem a solution for the situation in your memories, your childhood?

Belief investigation is a method to understand and improve our life-enhancing beliefs. Obviously, we don't want to decrease life-enhancing beliefs. Life-enhancing beliefs are, by definition, beneficial. However, this access methodology also is useful to check the quality of their functioning and possibly of improving them. Naturally, most of us prefer to keep our life-enhancing beliefs operating at their maximum potential.

Accessing Belief Systems with Trance

Trance, developed in hypnosis, is a method commonly used in psychotherapy sessions to access more repressed mental processes. Trance increases the exploration of beliefs and belief systems equally. Stanley Krippner (1972) defines trance as one of numerous forms of altered states of consciousness (ASC). There are many methods that can produce an altered state. Any method that you, or if you are working with a client you both, agree on will suffice. Once you or the client has achieved a light trance, questioning can proceed as outlined in belief investigation previously described.

A symbol,[2] created by the client to represent the problem or conflict, is useful during trance. Symbols are especially useful as clients work closer to protected core beliefs. For example, a client raised by an angry and abusive mother, who now feels intimidated by her boss, might use a symbol of a fire-breathing dragon cornering her in a shallow cave. This quickly references her thoughts and feelings while confronted by her boss.

Clients also benefit by creating an additional symbol representing life without the problem or conflict. This second symbol represents their healthy state. It provides an easily recognizable goal. The above client might visualize her healthy symbol as her riding a white stead. Proudly she views a cheering crowd, with the dragon's head draped over the saddle. This symbolized goal allows the client thought patterns of the healthy state without thoughts about the problem condition. The clients' wishes move away from the problem or condition by concentration on the healthy symbol. This is a transcendent rather than reparative or restorative theoretical framework.

Deep trances assist in discovering strongly protected and defended belief systems. However, lighter trance states allow the client to consciously create new solutions. Clients need these new solutions to replace old limiting beliefs. Once solutions are formulated, replacement is accomplished by integrating rational solutions. This integration allows the subconscious acceptance of the new solution. Deep trances are most useful to start the belief investigation process but should be lightened for the creative conclusion of the process. Following are several sample scripts[3] and processes that are useful for the psychotherapist's or client's belief investigation and belief system changes.

Use of the belief investigation process as outlined for a well-defined description of the problem and behavior patterns is essential. Repeat the entire memory regression process, if necessary, from the beginning until all available information is brought to light. Each time, reach farther and farther back into your memory. This method locates the patterns (solutions) of how you solved your childhood problems. Notice how patterns solved the problem at the time of their formation. More important, notice the original problem and that, possibly, the original problem no longer exists. If the original problem still exists, might there be a more effective solution?

Hypnotic Scripts

Belief Modification

Use the belief investigation method to define:

1. The problem.
2. How your life would be without the problem.

In the following belief modification script, replace the parenthesized word with the text of your definition. For example, if the problem was, "Yell at friends to make them more distant," use, "Yell at friends to make them more distant" in the script in place of "(problem)."

First, record on audio tape a light hypnotic induction script of your choosing. Second, record the belief modification script and then the Awakening

Script (see page 213 of this Appendix). Play back the entire tape while in a relaxed position and light trance.

The scripts are written for their subconscious and literal meanings. The goal is to elicit subconscious processes. **Use the wording exactly as written, even though it appears improperly written.** Repeated words, use of commas for short pauses, and the requested longer-than-usual pauses are necessary. Great care was taken to use the correct wording and tense. Please do not substitute other words or phrases. Proper English usage is the least important objective in hypnotic scripts.

Belief Modification Script

Allow yourself, to become, more comfortably relaxed. Take three, slow, deep breaths. Pause between each breath. Everything working, more calmly, more efficiently, more relaxed.

[pause ten seconds]

If you wish, allow yourself to relax, even more relaxed, and wishing, allowing, yourself to understand that your (problem), is the result of beliefs, and belief systems, that you had, as a child. Because long ago, the situation was different, and caused you to have (problem) the way you do.

Long ago, the solution seemed to be helpful, but today such (problems) may only be holding you back. It is these beliefs and belief systems that cause you to have (problem), the way you do.

Realize, and believe if you wish, that long ago, such beliefs and belief systems were accepted as solutions, to the position you were in during childhood. Later on, you encountered situations and other experiences, that proved these life-limiting beliefs.

The (problem) is actually, your successful following of such beliefs and belief systems as solutions of what existed long ago.

[pause three seconds]

Long ago, others may have teased you, because of your (problem), or the way you behaved because of your (problem). Or perhaps the (problem) helped you avoid your job, activity, or chore.

[pause five seconds]

As you look into the memory, of those events, you may have used them to support, those life-limiting beliefs. These (problems) may have helped, you avoid certain fears, doubts, or guilts. Or, to get others to behave a certain way. Or, to get others to feel or stop feeling something.

[pause three seconds]

As you become more aware, of the causes of the (problem), you may notice that the problem is less, in some areas than others. And in some areas (without problem). People commonly report that sometimes their problem completely disappears.

[pause three seconds]

I want you to acknowledge, if you wish, relaxation combined with changes in your beliefs, enables you, to be the way you want to be (without problem). I want you to allow yourself, if you wish, set aside all interfering beliefs, at least for now, allowing you, yourself to recall all the many, many times you were (without problem). Allowing yourself to daydream, fantasize, imagine a situation, seeing yourself (without problem).

[pause five seconds]

And in that image, see you, yourself being rewarded for being (without problem).

[pause three seconds]

Those around you, complimenting you (without problem). Allowing yourself to feel, to feel all those compliments, and recognition, and the wonderful feelings they bring. Bask in this wonderful feeling, feelings of accomplishment and success.

[pause five seconds]

Right now, you enhance these wonderful feelings. And these feelings set in motion, a new belief that enables you to be (without problem).

[pause three seconds]

As you practice now, such images, in your dreams or awake, realize that soon, you are allowing yourself, for some time now, to be (without problem). Allowing yourself day by day, hour by hour, to strengthen this, your new positive belief, to become your strong and deep belief system. Truly your benefit.

Eliciting Symbols

Use the belief investigation method to define:

1. The problem area.
2. The result of having your problem.

In the following Elicit Symbol Script, replace the parenthesized word with the text of your definition. For example, if the problem area is, "Yelling at friends" use, "Yell at friends" in the script in place of "(problem area)."

First, record on audio tape a light induction script of your choosing. Second, record the Elicit Symbol Script and then the Awakening Script (see page 213 of this Appendix). Play back the entire tape while in a light trance and relaxed position.

Elicit Symbol Script

As you relax back, I want you to see, imagine, or in some way sense, in your mind's eye, a screen, much like a movie screen, or TV screen, and on that screen, an image, object, or action.

I want you to see or in some way sense, in your mind's eye, a screen, much like a movie screen, or TV screen, and on that screen, an image, object, or action. That best represents or best symbolizes that which, or the way your subconscious mind perceives, your (problem area) concepts ideas, or thoughts, your (problem area) symbol.

[pause three seconds]

That image that best symbolizes your (problem area), your attitude about (result of problem) thoughts, ideas, and beliefs about your (problem area). Now, that best symbolizes your (problem area) concepts and ideas, that represent the real subconscious thoughts and feelings you have.

[pause four seconds]

Notice the way your subconscious mind sees your (problem area) symbol, studying that object, noting all the object's characteristics, and properties. Studying that subconscious symbol closely, what it looks like, its size, its shape, its color, all its physical properties just the way it looks to you.

[pause three seconds]

It may be in motion or still, it may have color or no color, it may be three-dimensional or not three-dimensional. Studying that (problem area) symbol carefully.

[pause two seconds between each question]

What does it resemble? What does it seem like? What does it look like? What does it actually make you think of?

Fix in your mind's eye, memory, the symbol as you come to full awakening. Bring the symbol, as you awaken, to full consciousness.

Changing Belief Symbol

Record the Change Symbol Script on audio tape after recording your own induction script. Play this second tape to reprogram your old life-limiting belief symbol with the new life enhancing symbol of your choice. Play this tape several times during the next week for maximum benefit. Periodically, replay the Elicit Symbol Script. Watch for changing symbols and changes in your life.

Change Symbol Script

I want you to see if you would become more closely, more in contact, with that image, that symbol. Take a look at the possibility you notice the many and varied details of this memory, this picture, this symbol.

[pause two seconds]

Allowing yourself to more closely contact this symbol. And you do, and doing, ask your nonconscious mind, what meaning, or meanings does this symbol, image have for you? Whatever first comes into mind. What meaning, what answer, does this symbol have for you, closely now?

[pause four seconds]

Using your logical, conscious part of your adult mind. What do you most, like about this symbol? Look at it, examine it like a picture, a movie. What about this memory symbol do you like? You as an adult, what seems best or good? What is good or feels right about this symbol?

[pause six seconds]

Examining this symbol even more. What about it do you dislike? What about it seems not good or doesn't feel quite right, for you, the full-grown adult? What about this memory image, do you dislike? What about it seems not good or doesn't feel quite right about it, for you the full-grown adult?

[pause ten seconds]

As you think about these likes and dislikes. I want to give you the opportunity to treat this memory image, scene, symbol, or picture, even though it seems to be a memory of an actual event, treat it as a picture or drawing. Considering this memory symbol as a picture or movie. A picture or movie, which you as the director can modify, change, you can improve. So that the picture is more the way you would like it, so that it feels right, now.

[pause five seconds]

The picture is modified, changed, improved, edited, redrawn, so it feels right. The way you, the adult, wants it to be.

[pause two seconds between each question]

What changes? What modifications? What improvements? What editing? What redrawing did you make in this picture? Those changes that made it more to your liking. So that it feels the way the adult of you wants it to be, for you. So that the adult says it is more right for you. Making whatever and all the changes you choose to make, as you change, modify, upgrade, edit, redraw to improve this memory scene, image, picture, to whatever the adult in you says feels right for you.

Such changes, modifications, improvements, edits, or redraws are made rapidly or gradually. Which every way feels comfortable and all right for you, mentally, emotionally, and physically, consciously and unconsciously as you continue to upgrade, change, modify, edit, redraw, and improve this memory image, this symbol during the following hours, days, weeks, and these changes, upgrades, edits, improvements, redrawings, and modifications become an integral part of you, a new symbol in your unconscious of a more a healthful memory symbol.

Future Solution Pacing

Some solutions are more difficult to elicit by self-hypnosis. Generally the nearer the questioning comes to the core belief, the more difficult it is to elicit. The subconscious can share its information if it perceives no threat in doing so. The subconscious concept of time is circular. Therefore, yesterday is like today, which could just as well be tomorrow. All thoughts orient toward the present, which is always in change. This allows the psychotherapist to convince the subconscious to think something has already happened when it has not. The advantage is that it will give up a secret if it thinks it is no longer a secret. This is handy in getting the subconscious to reveal a solution to a problem that it is reluctant to change. Often it knows the solution but is afraid of the consequences of implementing it. Often children know what is good and correct but the situation will not permit it. The consequence of the right response is too severe.

The following script will future-pace the subconscious into thinking the solution has already been applied and is working. While in the future, it is safe to reveal the solution because the feared consequence is not occurring. Once we elicit the solution, we bring it back to the present. Similar to the previous scripts, first record on audio tape a light Induction Script of your choosing. Second, record the Future Pace Script and then the Awakening Script. Play back the entire tape while in a relaxed position and light trance.

Future Pace Script

Allow yourself, to become, more comfortably relaxed. Take three, slow, deep breaths. Pause between each breath. Everything working, more calmly, more efficiently, more relaxed.

[pause ten seconds]

If you wish, allow yourself to relax, even more relaxed, and wishing, allowing, yourself to feel, that state that you have felt in the past, but that you are experiencing, now. Allowing, yourself to feel, that state that you have felt in the past, but that you are experiencing, now. That you had felt, in the past, but are now experiencing.

[pause two seconds]

Relaxed state, that you experience now. To the past, now is future. To future, now is past. Your self now, can experience the future, for now is the future of past, and the future becomes now, at this moment, quickly, smoothly. Future is now, and now is past.

[pause three seconds]

Now is past and future is present, aware, that a day is past. Awareness focuses on the future, that is now. Now is past, a week has come and gone. You may now realize that weeks have come and gone, for that is what weeks do. You may now realize that months have come and gone, for that is what months do. And the month that was the future is here and past. You may now realize that six months have come and gone, for that is what six months do. You are aware that it has already been a year, for years and time has come and gone, for that is what time does.

[pause three seconds]

Find yourself now, thinking on this past year, that is now past. A year that has passed quickly, comfortably, easily. You reflect back how easily you were able to solve your problem, and to find your solution. Achieving the goals you desired to bring into your life, that are now a fact, an accomplished fact, how easy it was to eliminate doubts, fears, guilts, and all other concerns. How you dared to dream. Remembering how you changed. How comfortably you discovered. The past year's time. And you reflect back, now over this marvelous year. Recalling how you examined, and understood. As this past year progressed, you became healthier, happier, confident, successful. Recalling now the very first step you took. That very first act that signaled the change belief. The belief that accomplished this wonderful change.

[pause three seconds]

Here you are, a year later, the year has come and gone for that is what years do. All is accomplished, your achievement. Now a year later accomplishing all you desired and more than you ever dreamed it would be.

[pause two seconds]

Recollecting each step. Now a year. Recalling the thoughts, the dreams, the intuitive hunches, the spiritual guidance that gave you strength. Aware now of each step, which enabled you, to discover what was right for you. Recalling each major step, blockage overcame, eliminated. How you used your own special talents and abilities. To be the you that you are now. You now remember in detail every step, every thought, every step, every action, clear to you now, as you reflect. As you do, you find that you are using hindsight as insight, for now you can see steps that you could take, modify, change in some way. Resolving right now, if ever the need you would automatically use such knowledge.

[pause three seconds]

This accomplishment is fact, now, experienced, and accomplishment, now a part of you. Instantly available, to you at any time, in any time. Instantly, automatically available.

[pause two seconds]

So allowing the now that is future to return to the future, and returning now, to the past that is now. Now becoming the now. All this is automatically guiding you, so that in a year, a month, a week, or less, that future you, will be now. Returning to the present.

Awakening Script

As you take all this new and exciting information and insight well within, understanding, and absorbing, integrating, and knowing, processing, and changing, now with each moment. Bringing with you, what-every information or knowledge you feel comfortable to bring into your conscious awareness, bring ALL that you wish, and not more. Coming back to full awareness. Returning to the present, on the count of three. Counting up. One. Returning to present, now feeling just the way you wish to feel, with a smile and a deep chuckle of joy. Two. Coming on up, feeling rested and healthy, physically, mentally, emotionally, and spiritually. Counting up. Returning to present, now feeling just the way you wish to feel, with a smile and laugh. Two. Coming on up, feeling rested and healthy, physically, mentally, emotionally, and spiritually. And, THREE. Fully awake and aware.

[snapping the fingers on the count of three is helpful]

[allow a few minutes for processing and awakening]

Scripts Designed to Target the Fundamental Needs

The following five scripts are for those who wish to use trance to access belief systems with a target of a specific fundamental need. As before, record the scripts after recording your favorite Induction Script. Play your combined tape through a set of headphones. Then, while in trance, record your responses with a microphone and tape recorder or paper and pen. After awaking from trance, review your responses. Look for patterns. Decide how you want to change. Go back into the trance and reestablish your changed beliefs using the Modify Belief Script and then reinforce with the Future Pace Script.

As in the previous scripts, these are written for their subconscious and literal meanings. The goal is to elicit subconscious processes. **Use the wording exactly as written, even though it appears improperly written.** Repeated words and longer-than-usual pauses are necessary. Great care was taken to use the correct wording. Please do not substitute other words or phrases. Proper English usage is the least important objective in hypnotic scripts.

1. Safety and Security Script

[add Trance Induction Script of your choice here]

Think of some of the ways that a child goes through his or her life getting security and feeling safe in his or her life. And as you think of these, it will help you to go even deeper into the relaxed comfortable state of trance.

[pause two seconds]

Getting and having a way, to have the feeling of security, how he or she gets and feels safe and cared for in his or her life.

[pause two seconds]

Security and having the feeling or knowing, to have someone else, say or recognize that he or she has and receives care, safety, and security in his or her life. Is given security.

[pause five seconds]

For it is important that he or she gets feeling or way of knowing in his or her life, so that they have some assurance in his or her life's direction. Sometimes it's not a matter of doing what is important, or expected, or what is told, or what should or ought to be, of them, but rather getting the feelings or knowledge that they are cared for, safe, and secure in some way.

[long pause]

Becoming more comfortable, more relaxed with each word you hear. Understand and realize that we and you have examples, and feelings, and experiences of being secure, of being cared for, of safety, of protection and being protected. Even if only for the short time, a brief moment, and sometime in the first one to five years of life. We know, you know this has occurred sometime, in that time in your life. You are the proof, you have survived, you are alive. You have the memories that such events have occurred in your life. But for some reason, you may have chosen to inhibit, to ignore them, maybe even to deny such events and feelings, from being safe or secure.

[pause five seconds]

The only reason is that somewhere long ago, now in your learning, now in you present, you as that child, believe that there are greater benefits to be obtained in such denial, such not remembering. But for this moment let us, let you believe that such events did occur. Looking forward into the now, at that time, decisions are made of beliefs, for these beliefs may have seemed beneficial, looking into this time.

[pause three seconds]

In this time, in this now, the beliefs of childhood, they may seem unfair and unworkable. At times they work. We get some security. Maybe at some expense of negative attention or discipline. But, it works that they have some feelings of being safe, secure, and cared for in your life. That was fine for the child, fine, sometimes it works out fine.

[pause two seconds]

As the child grows into the adult, the acting out of these beliefs, begins to cost more and more. As that child thinks about the benefits you achieve by denying, times when you felt that you were unsafe, un-secure, or alienated. But, be fair, think back again into those times, and think about the times when you really were safe, secure, cared for, and protected. You may have been a child, a child that found the experience too strong, at that time, and decided, to believe, not to go back to that feeling again.

[pause three seconds]

But some children, somehow, don't learn that, when they grow into adult-hood. And so, they keep themselves stuck in the old patterns of the child. They just keep on believing and proving that they are in denial, that they are un-secure, and unprotected feelings that were not understood as that child. They react in childlike old patterns of attempting to get security by acting on the belief that "what," was not protection. They follow the old childhood beliefs. But these are childlike beliefs that no longer work to achieve having security, or safety, or cared for in the adult's world. What are some of the ways you show the world that you have security? Ways that make others see you as protected and secure?

[pause five seconds]

You can choose now to accept those feelings of security and feelings of being cared for and protected. Go back and re-live, recall those wonderful feelings you have as a child. Decide that you can have them now, and as an adult now.

[pause two seconds]

Going on down, deeper and deeper in trance. Thinking of ways that you have used to gain security. Thinking of ways that you have used to gain safety. Thinking of ways that you have used to gain security that you are protected and cared for by others. Thinking of ways that you have used to gain acknowledgment that you were secure.

[pause two seconds]

Going deeper and deeper into that comfortable familiar state of trance, deeper down, more relaxed, and comfortable. Thinking about security and safety, thinking about control of self and recognition of these qualities of self, and security. Does your behavior, your attitude, and actions, really go on demonstrating security to those around you? Does your behavior, your attitude, and actions, really go on demonstrating today that you still are protected by others and secure? Does your behavior, your attitude, and actions, really go on demonstrating security and what are the trade-offs to gaining that sense of being cared for and protected? What are the trade-offs to gaining that sense of being safe?

[pause three seconds]

Deeper and deeper now. More and more relaxed state of trance. Knowing that you have the power, knowing that you have the control, knowing that you are, you are the one, the one that really has the will to provide security, the one that has the say over your life. You don't have to wear a sign so that other people will be able to see that you feel secure. People will be able to see that you have security. You will know by your ability to be self-protecting. You will know by your ability to control your own security.

[pause three seconds]

Know to understand. Understand with knowing, that what looks to them as a lack of security. What looks to them as a lack of safety, is really your statement to the world about just how powerful you really are. Just how powerful you really are. Reexamine what you are doing to demonstrate your security. What you are doing to show others your security. Reexamine what you are doing to demonstrate your care of self and others. What you are doing to show others your ability to feel secure and cared for.

[pause five seconds]

Coming up a little lighter now. Using your full adult logic, your full adult mind, with all the knowledge you have accumulated there. Think about it, know the answer. It is really, today it is your choice. To choose today. What is it that you want? What is it that you want to use, to be, to demonstrate to others? What you want to use to show others that you have safety and security. Know that the adult demonstrates by using knowledge. Think of the ways that will work for you.

[pause two seconds]

At this time write them down or record them. Use them. They are yours. They are your security. After all isn't it the best way to show them you are secure and protected? Show that you care and protect yourself and others will follow. Live longer. Be healthier. Look happier. Act secure.

[add Awakening Script here]

2. Belonging and Acceptance Script

[add Trance Induction Script of your choice here]

Think of some of the ways that a child goes through his or her life getting acceptance and feeling belonging in his or her life. And as you think of these, it will help you to go even deeper into the relaxed comfortable state of trance.

[pause two seconds]

Getting and having a way, to have the feeling of acceptance, how he or she gets and feels belonging and love in his or her life.

[pause two seconds]

Accepted and having the feeling or knowing, to have someone else, say or recognize that he or she has and receives belonging and acceptance in his or her life. Is given acceptance.

[pause five seconds]

For it is important that he or she gets feeling or way of knowing in their life, so that they have some assurance in his or her life's direction. Sometimes it's not a matter of doing what is important, or expected, or what is told, or what should or ought to be, of them, but rather getting the feelings or knowledge that they are accepted, loved, and belong in some way.

[long pause]

Becoming more comfortable, more relaxed with each word you hear. Understand and realize that we and you have examples, and feelings, and experiences of being accepted, of being desired, of belonging, of loving and being loved. Even if only for the short time, a brief moment, and sometime in the first ten to sixteen years of life. We know, you know this has occurred sometime, in that time in your life. You are the proof, you have the memories that such events have occurred in your life. But for some reason, you may have chosen to inhibit them, to ignore them, maybe even to deny such events and feelings, from being recalled or remembered.

[pause five seconds]

The only reason is that somewhere long ago, now in your learning, now in your present, you may as that child, believe that there is greater benefits to be obtained in such denial, such not remembering. But for this moment let us, let you believe that such events did occur. Memories are like reading a magazine or a newspaper where you pick the section that you wish to read. Ignoring other sections. You may ignore certain sections while attending to others and then ignoring the other sections while attending this section. You attend to the section you believe is important, or think essential, and ignore those sections which you believe are not important. Attending to only those that are considered most important. Looking forward into the now, at that time, decisions are made of beliefs, for these beliefs may have seemed beneficial, looking into this time.

[pause three seconds]

In this time, in this now, the beliefs of childhood, they may seem unfair and unworkable. At times they work. We get some acceptance. Maybe at some expense of negative attention or discipline. But, it works that they have some feelings of belonging and acceptance in your life. That was fine for the child, fine, sometimes it works out fine.

[pause two seconds]

As the child grows to the adult, the acting out of these beliefs, begins to cost more and more. As that child thinks about the benefits you achieve by denying times when you felt that you were unloved, unwanted, or alienated. But, be fair, think back again into those times, and think about the times when you really were loved, wanted, accepted, and belonged. You may have been a child, a child that found the experience too strong, at that time, and decided, to believe, not to go back to that feeling again.

[pause three seconds]

But some children, somehow, don't learn that, when they grow into adulthood. And so, they keep themselves stuck in the old patterns of the child. They just keep on believing and proving that they are in denial, that they are unacceptable, and unloved feelings that were not understood as that child. They react in childlike old patterns of attempting to get acceptance by acting on the belief that "what," was not love. They follow the old childhood beliefs. But these are childlike beliefs that no longer work to achieve having acceptance, or love, or belonging in the adult's world. What are some of the ways you show the world that you have acceptance? Ways that make others see you as lovable and acceptable?

[pause five seconds]

You can choose now to accept those feelings of acceptance and feelings of loving and belonging. Go back and re-live, recall those wonderful feelings you have as a child. Decide that you can have them now, and as an adult now.

[pause two seconds]

Going on down, deeper and deeper in trance. Thinking of ways that you have used to gain acceptance. Thinking of ways that you have used to gain love. Thinking of ways that you have used to gain acceptance that you are lovable and belong to others. Thinking of ways that you have used to gain acknowledgment that you were accepted.

[pause two seconds]

Going deeper and deeper into that comfortable familiar state of trance, deeper down, more relaxed, and comfortable. Thinking about acceptance and belonging, thinking about control of self and recognition of these qualities of self, and acceptance. Does your behavior, your attitude, and actions, really go on demonstrating acceptability to those around you? Does your behavior, your attitude, and actions, really go on demonstrating today that you still are loved and accepted? Does your behavior, your attitude, and actions, really go on demonstrating acceptance and what are the trade-offs to gaining that sense of being loved and belonging? What are the trade-offs to gaining that sense of being accepted?

[pause three seconds]

Deeper and deeper now. More and more relaxed state of trance. Knowing that you have the power, knowing that you have the control, knowing that you are, you are the one, the one that really has the will to accept, the one that has the say over your life. You don't have to wear a sign so that other people will be able to see that you are lovable. People will be able to see that you have acceptance. You will know by your ability to be self-accepting. You will know by your ability to control your own belonging.

[pause three seconds]

Know to understand. Understand with knowing, that what looks to them as a lack of acceptance. What looks to them as a lack of lovableness, is really your statement to the world about just how powerful you really are. Just how powerful you really are. Reexamine what you are doing to demonstrate your acceptance. What you are doing to show others your acceptance. Reexamine what you are doing to demonstrate your love of self and others. What you are doing to show others your ability to love and accept.

[pause five seconds]

Coming up a little lighter now. Using your full adult logic, your full adult mind, with all the knowledge you have accumulated there. Think about it, know the answer. It is really, today it is your choice. To choose today. What is it that you want? What is it that you want to use, to be, to demonstrate to others? What you want to use to show others that you have love and acceptance? Know that the adult demonstrates by using knowledge. Think of the ways that will work for you.

[pause two seconds]

At this time write them down or record them. Use them. They are yours. They are your acceptance. After all isn't it the best way to show them you are lovable and acceptable? Show that you love and accept yourself and others will follow. Live longer. Be healthier. Look happier. Act loving.

[add Awakening Script here]

3. Love and Sexual Expression Script

[add Trance Induction Script of your choice here]

Think of some of the ways that a child goes through his or her life getting acceptance and feeling loved in his or her life. And as you think of these, it will help you to go even deeper into the relaxed comfortable state of trance.

[pause two seconds]

Getting and having a way, to have the feeling of love, how he or she gets and feels about sex and love in his or her life.

[pause two seconds]

Accepted and having the feeling or knowing, to have someone else, recognize that he or she has and receives love and sexual expression. Is given love.

[pause five seconds]

For it is important that he or she gets feeling or way of knowing in his or her life, so that they have some assurance in their life's direction. Sometimes it's not a matter of doing what is important, or expected, or what is told, or what should or ought to be, of them, but rather getting the feelings or knowledge that they are loved and have a healthy sexual way of expression.

[long pause]

Becoming more comfortable, more relaxed with each word you hear. Understand and realize that we and you have examples, and experiences of being loved, of being desired, of sexual expression, and being loved. Even if only for the short time, a brief moment, and sometime in the first ten to twenty years of life. We know, you know this has occurred sometime, in that time in your life.

[pause two seconds]

During your development you may have experienced differing stages of love. Stages of getting and giving love. Stages of love's development and associated emotions. Emotions connected to the giving and the receiving of love. Ways of giving love. What age level for giving or seeking the expression of love. Finding and defining the meaning of love. Finding and defining the meaning of sex. And how each is, and how each is separate or together in a maturing form. Knowing that it can always be upgraded.

[pause two seconds]

The first stage is the helpless baby stage of love. The stage when love is being taken care of. The stage of only expecting love to be given in the form of someone doing something for you.

[pause two seconds]

The next stage is when self-love transfers to another, feelings of another person begin to make you feel comfortable. You begin to show concern for others, but still demand to be taken care of. Do nothing to create love. Only receive, but is concerned that others are not upset.

[pause two seconds]

The third stage is when you begin to show love to other members of the family. Father or mother love, brother or sister love begins. We get satisfaction of showing love as well as receiving. We begin to learn that love can come from something you do or give. You learn that you can create love by doing something and asking. You no longer have to wait for love, but can be received by doing or asking, and giving of oneself. The old "take care of me" no longer works in this new stage.

[pause two seconds]

The fourth stage is the gang stage. Love is for people of the same sex, we like the same sex persons. The participation in groups and team sports are of this type. We are often critical of other sex in this stage. The others become funny and objects of "lesser than."

[pause two seconds]

The next stage of love's development is the adolescent stage. The adolescent stage is a period of transition for the object of love. This is where we learn to develop love for the other sex. We are easy to fall in love. Our affections are short-term, and temporary, and shallow. Sexual overtones become mixed with love, and love begins to overflow into the love and sex confusion. . . . The fairy tale stage.

[pause two seconds]

The lasting stage is the mature stage of love. Love grows as life's time passes. You learn to think of "we" instead of "us." Unconditional love becomes the undertone. Love, because of not what they are, but because of who they are, because they are. The mature love simply loves, and encourages the loved one to be the finest he or she can be. Love, even though they may not be functioning at this level.

[pause three seconds]

The only reason is that somewhere a long time ago, now in your learning, now in your present, you may as that child, believe that there are greater benefits to staying at one of these levels, or stages of love. But for this moment let us, let you believe that such events did occur. Looking forward into the now, at that time, decisions are made of beliefs, for these beliefs may have seemed beneficial, looking into this time.

[pause three seconds]

In this time, in this now, the beliefs of childhood, they may seem unfair and unworkable. At times they work. We get some love and sex. Maybe at some expense of negative attention or discipline. But, it works, that works to have some feelings of love in your life. That was fine for the child, fine, sometimes it works out fine.

[pause two seconds]

As the child grows to the adult, the acting out of these beliefs, begins to cost more and more. As that child, think about the benefits you achieve by denying times when you felt, that you were loved. But, be fair, think back again to those times, and think about the times when you really were loved. You may have been a child, a child that found the experience too strong, at that time, and decided, to believe, not to go back to that feeling again.

[pause three seconds]

But some children, somehow, don't learn that, when they grow into adulthood. And so, they keep themselves stuck in the old patterns of the child. They just keep on believing and proving that they are in denial, that they are unloved in the mature stage. They react in childlike old patterns of attempting to get love by acting on the belief that, "what" was an old stage of love. They follow the old childhood beliefs. But these are childlike beliefs that no longer work to achieve mature relations and love, and sex, in the adult's world. What are some of the ways you show the world that you have love? Ways that make others see you as lovable?

[pause five seconds]

You can choose now to accept those feelings of love and feelings of being able to request loving. Go back and relive, recall those wonderful feelings you have as a child. Decide that you can have them now, grow through the various stages of learning love, and as an adult with mature love now.

[pause two seconds]

Going on down, deeper and deeper in trance. Thinking of ways that you have used to gain love. Thinking of ways that you have used to gain sex. Thinking of ways that you have used to gain sexual expression that you are lovable and giving love to others. Thinking of ways that you have used to gain acknowledgment of your love.

[pause two seconds]

Going deeper and deeper into that comfortable familiar state of trance, deeper down, more relaxed, and comfortable. Thinking about love and giving love, thinking about control of self and recognition of these qualities of self, and loving. Does your behavior, your attitude, and actions, really go on demonstrating loving to those around you? Does your behavior, your attitude, and actions, really go on demonstrating today that you still are loved and being loved? Does your behavior, your attitude, and actions, really go on demonstrating love and what are the trade-offs to gaining that sense of being loved and sexual expression? What are the trade-offs to gaining that sense of being loved?

[pause three seconds]

Deeper and deeper now. More and more relaxed state of trance. Knowing that you have the power, knowing that you have the control, knowing that you are, you are the one, the one that really has the will to accept, the one that has the say over your life. You don't have to wear a sign so that other people will be able to see that you are lovable. People will be able to see that you are sexual. You will know by your ability to be self-accepting. You will know by your ability to control your own loving.

[pause three seconds]

Know to understand. Understand with knowing, that what looks to them as a lack of loving. What looks to them as a lack of lovableness, is really your statement to the world about just how loving you really are. Just how lovable you really are. Reexamine what you are doing to demonstrate your love. What you are doing to show others your lovableness. Reexamine what your are doing to demonstrate your love of self and others. What you are doing to show others your ability to love and accept.

[pause five seconds]

Coming up a little lighter now. Using your full adult logic, your full adult mind, with all the knowledge you have accumulated there. Think about it, know the answer. It is really, today it is your choice. To choose today. What is it that you want? What is it that you want to use, to be, to demonstrate to others? What you want to use to show others that you have love and are able to love. Know that the adult demonstrates by using knowledge. Think of the ways that will work for you.

[pause two seconds]

At this time write them down or record them. Use them. They are yours. They are your acceptance. After all isn't it the best way to show them you are lovable and loving? Show that you love and accept yourself and others will follow. Act loving.

[add Awakening Script here]

4. Autonomy Script

[add Trance Induction Script of your choice here]

Think of some of the ways that a child goes through his or her life getting autonomy and demonstrating control over his or her life. And as you think of these it will help you to go even deeper into the relaxed comfortable state of trance.

[pause two seconds]

Getting and having a way, to have a say about, how he or she gets and receives control over his or her life.

[pause two seconds]

Getting and having a way, to have someone else, say or recognize that he or she has and receives control over his or her life. Is given autonomy.

[pause five seconds]

For it is important that he or she gets some say in your life so that you have some say in your life's direction. Sometimes it's not a matter of doing what is important, or expected, or what is told, or what should or ought to be, but rather getting some way of getting a say in your life.

[long pause]

This may have been seen by the mother or father as misbehavior or rebellion. It may be seen as acting up or even bad by the parent. These are just a few of the ways children demonstrate to themselves that they have autonomy. Saying no just to have a say, not completing an assignment or directive, eating what they are ordered but then later throwing it up, going to bed when ordered but not going to sleep.

[pause two seconds]

At times they work. We get some control. Maybe at some expense of negative attention or discipline. But, it works that they have some say in their lives. That's fine, sometimes it works out fine.

[pause two seconds]

As the child grows to adult, the acting out will subside into other adult acceptable ideas and behaviors. Because the child learns that there are better ways to prove and demonstrate autonomy. Ways that don't work against you.

[pause three seconds]

But some children somehow don't learn that when they grow into adulthood. And so, they keep themselves stuck in the old patterns of the child. They just keep on rebelling and proving that they are in control, that they are in charge and rebels against all. They react in childlike old patterns of attempting to get autonomy by acting against what is expected of them. They follow the old childhood beliefs. Some may use drugs, alcohol, smoking, getting fat, getting skinny, acting up or acting out, disobeying the laws of society. And many other ways they learned as children. Ways that were to demonstrate autonomy. All these in a vain attempt in the adult world to gain autonomy, but are childlike beliefs that no longer work to achieve having a say in the adult's world. What are some of the ways you show the world that you have autonomy? Ways that make others see you as separate and in control?

[pause five seconds]

Going on down, deeper and deeper in trance. Thinking of ways that you have used to gain autonomy. Thinking of ways that you have used to gain control. Thinking of ways that you have used to gain recognition that you are separate from others. Thinking of ways that you have used to gain acknowledgment that you are special.

[pause two seconds]

Going deeper and deeper into that comfortable familiar state of trance, deeper down more relaxed and comfortable. Thinking about autonomy and self-directing, thinking about control of self and recognition of this control and autonomy. Does your behavior, your attitude, and actions, really go on demonstrating autonomy to those around you? Does your behavior, your attitude, and actions, really go on demonstrating today that you still have autonomy? Does your behavior, your attitude, and actions, really go on demonstrating autonomy and what are the trade-offs to gain that sense of having a say? What are the trade-offs to gaining that sense of having a say?

[pause three seconds]

Deeper and deeper now. More and more relaxed state of trance. Knowing that you have the power, knowing that you have the control, knowing that you are, you are the one, the one that really has the control, the one that has the say over your life. You don't have to wear a sign so that other people will be able to see that you have autonomy. People will be able to see that you have autonomy. You will know by your ability to control your own behaviors and emotional reaction and achievements that you will have autonomy. You will know by your ability to control your own behaviors.

[pause three seconds]

Know to understand. Understand with knowing, that what looks to them as a lack of control. What looks to them as a lack of power, is really your statement to the world about just how powerful you really are. Just how powerful you really are. Reexamine what you are doing to demonstrate your autonomy. What you are doing to show others your autonomy. Reexamine what you are doing to demonstrate your control. What you are doing to show others your ability to control. Is it really demonstrating power, control, and autonomy to the world around you?

[pause five seconds]

Coming up a little lighter now. Using your full adult logic, your full adult mind, with all the knowledge you have accumulated there. Think about it, know the answer. It is really, today it is your choice. To choose today. What is it that you want? What is it that you want to use, to be, to demonstrate to others? What you want to use to show others that you have control and autonomy. Know that the adult demonstrates by using knowledge. Think of the ways that will work for you.

[pause two seconds]

At this time write them down or record them. Use them. They are yours. They are your autonomy. After all isn't it the best way to show them you are autonomous and special, to beat them at their own game? Win the race. Make the most success. Be better than them. Live longer. Be healthier. Look better. Act better. Take care of yourself better. That's showing them!

[add Awakening Script here]

5. Spirituality Script

[add Trance Induction Script of your choice here]

Think of some of the ways that a person goes through his or her life getting a sense of greater purpose in his or her life. And as you think of these, it will help you to go even deeper into the relaxed, comfortable state of trance.

[pause two seconds]

Spirituality, this is the feeling we may have at some time, or the question we answer for ourselves, is this all there is? And this is in the answer, of how we answer this question. This is a part of all that is, and follows after our need to satisfy each of our other fundamental needs. Where at some point we may hear a voice. A voice that says, is this all there is? This may be heard at any time. It is meaningful. There is something else, an else that all and that each of us needs to know of a higher need.

[pause two seconds]

This is the need to have purpose and meaning one's life. This is the Truth and Beauty. This is the Wholeness and Completeness of Oneness. This is the Higher Power of all that is. For some this may be a God. [*Note*: If the word *God* is counter to your beliefs, leave out this last sentence.]

[pause three seconds]

This need and belief is the cement, the glue, the ground of being, for which we are interdependent with others and the world. As we are interdependent with each other, we are with all creation. This is the need for our spirituality.

[pause two seconds]

Think of the ways you get, and having a way, to have the feeling of spirituality, how you get and feel belonging to a purpose, to a higher power.

[pause two seconds]

Accepted and having the feeling or knowing, to have someone else, say or recognize that he or she has spirituality in life. Is belonging to spirituality.

[pause five seconds]

For it is important that he or she gets feeling or way of knowing in life, so that they have some assurance of life's direction. Sometimes it's not a matter of doing what is important, or expected, or what is told, or what should or ought to be, of them, but rather getting the feelings or knowledge that you are spiritual and belong in some way to a greater purpose of life.

[long pause]

Becoming more comfortable, more relaxed with each word you hear. Understand and realize that we and you have examples, and feelings, and experiences of spiritually belonging. Even if only for the short time, a brief moment, and some time in the first ten to twenty years of life. We know, you know this has occurred sometime, in that time in your life. You are the proof, you have the memories that such events have occurred in your life.

[pause five seconds]

The only reason is that somewhere long ago, now in your learning, now in your present, you may as that child, believe that there are greater benefits to be obtained in such denial, such not remembering. But for this moment let us, let you believe that such events did occur. Looking forward into the now, at that time, decisions are made of beliefs, for these beliefs may have seemed beneficial, looking into this time.

[pause three seconds]

In this time, in this now, the beliefs of childhood they may seem unfair and unworkable. At times they worked. We get some spirituality. Maybe at some expense of negative attention or discipline. But, it works that they have some feelings of belonging to a higher power and spirituality in your life.

[pause two seconds]

As the child grows to the adult, the acting out of these beliefs, begins to cost more and more. Think back again into those times, and think about the times when you really were spiritual, felt the touch of being part of a higher power, and had a greater purpose for your life. You may have been a child, a child that found the experience too strong, at that time, and decided, to believe, not to go back to that feeling again.

[pause three seconds]

But some children, somehow, don't learn to change that, when they grow into adulthood. And so, they keep themselves stuck in the old patterns of the child. They just keep on believing and proving that they are in denial, that they are unspiritual with feelings that were not understood as that child. They react in childlike old patterns of attempting to get spirituality by acting on the belief that "what," was not. They follow the old childhood beliefs. But these are childlike beliefs that no longer work to achieve spirituality in the adult's world. What are some of the ways you show the world that you have spirituality? Ways that make you feel, as part of a higher purpose?

[pause five seconds]

You can choose now to accept those feelings of spirituality and feelings of belonging to a greater purpose. Go back and re-live, recall those wonderful feelings you have as a child. Decide that you can have them now, and as an adult now.

[pause two seconds]

Going on down, deeper and deeper in trance. Thinking of ways that you have used to gain spirituality. Thinking of ways that you have used to gain the feeling of higher purpose. Thinking of ways that you have used to gain spirituality that you are purposeful. Thinking of ways that you have used to gain acknowledgment that you were spiritual.

[pause two seconds]

Going deeper and deeper into that comfortable familiar state of trance, deeper down, more relaxed, and comfortable. Thinking about spirituality and belonging, thinking about control of self and recognition of these qualities of self, and spirituality. Does your behavior, your attitude, and actions, really go on demonstrating spirituality? Does your behavior, your attitude, and actions, really go on demonstrating today that you still connected with a higher purpose in life? Does your behavior, your attitude, and actions, really go on demonstrating spirituality and what are the trade-offs to gaining that sense of being with a higher purpose? What are the trade-offs to gaining that sense being spiritual?

[pause three seconds]

Deeper and deeper now. More and more relaxed state of trance. Knowing that you have the power, knowing that you have the control, knowing that you are, you are the one, the one that really has the will to accept, the one that has the say over your life. You don't have to wear a sign so that other people will be able to see that you are spiritual. People will be able to see that you have spirituality. You will know by your ability to be self-determining. You will know by your ability to control your own spirituality.

[pause three seconds]

Know to understand. Understand with knowing, that what looks to them as a lack of spirituality. What looks to them as a lack of purpose, is really your statement to the world about just how spiritual you really are. Just how purposeful you really are. Reexamine what you are doing to demonstrate your spirituality. What you are doing to show others your spirituality. Reexamine what you are doing to demonstrate your sense of purpose to self and others. What you are doing to show others your ability to have a purpose to a higher power.

[pause five seconds]

Coming up a little lighter now. Using your full adult logic, your full adult mind, with all the knowledge you have accumulated there. Think about it, know the answer. It is really, today it is your choice. To choose today. What is it that you want? What is it that you want to use, to be, to demonstrate to others? What you want to use to show others that you have purpose and spirituality. Know that the adult demonstrates by using knowledge. Think of the ways that will work for you.

[pause two seconds]

At this time write them down or record them. Use them. They are yours. They are your spirituality. After all isn't it the best way to show them you are spiritual and purposeful? Show that you love and accept your spirituality and others will follow.

[add Awakening Script here]

Notes

1. Belief investigation is a technique modified from entelechial therapy's technique of belief busting developed by Joseph E. Spear, D. O., La Costa, CA.
2. A *symbol* is a representation of a concept, desire, or struggle by some mental image which manifests analogous attributes. Because of its repeated associations, it characterizes what it stands for.
3. The use of the word "script" means the written text used to prompt your voice for tape recording or for a client session.

Reference

Krippner, S. (1972). Altered states of consciousness. In J. White (Ed.) *The highest state of consciousness*. New York: Doubleday.

Appendix C

The Territoriality and Kinship of Psychodrama and Gestalt Therapy[1]

Most relationships contain aspects of cooperation and competition. Dependency and autonomy needs are well within the developmental relationship of psychodrama and Gestalt therapy. Eclectic psychotherapists and psychodramatists tend to consider both therapies as contributive, adjunctive approaches to a larger experiential set of therapeutic techniques. In addition to specific psychotherapies, both modalities are viewed primarily as healthy ways of being in the world

However, committed professionals of either therapeutic modality tend to disregard the other modality by inclusion or other respect through disagreement. Members of the former group, either state the *originality* of their preferred orientation or assume both are the same process. While reluctantly admitting to similarities, members of the latter group cite evidence supporting the ontological or epistemological correctness of their identified approach or admit personal preference.

In addition to the lay public, many professionals are confused, if not unaware, of the differences between and relationship of these two psychotherapies. There are few articles that clarify the relationship without obvious bias. The remaining literature tends to blend both modalities into a pseudomutual collective for the purpose of comparing these humanistic orientations to the analytic and behavioral trends.

Therapeutic competence is not insured by purification of process. By the nature of both systems, conformity is prescriptive and blocks spontaneity. Neither is competence enhanced by encouragement of an eclectic ethic. To use psychodrama and Gestalt therapy effectively demands the availability and knowledge of those respective skills. Congruence between the self as a person and the self as a therapist/director is imperative, but not in lieu of specific therapeutic principles that prevent countercathartic and counterproductive treatment.

As the differences become vague and similarities are assumed, alternative methods of treatment for diverse psychopathology are restricted. When differences are sanctioned to the exclusion of compatibility, competition fosters therapeutic territoriality protecting economic infringement.

Following is a comparison of the psychotherapeutic processes of psychodrama and Gestalt therapy among several variables. This comparison focuses on these two approaches as psychotherapies rather than philosophical worldviews.[2] The historical and political contexts of each system will not be discussed. Although there is no pure methodology of either therapy, what is presented is considered consistent with the intentions of each founder as well as reasonably consistent with the ways in which each system is most frequently practiced by their esteemed proponents. As the differences (territoriality) and similarities (kinship) are reviewed, each director/therapist may review his or her responsibility for personal divergence. Perhaps through role clarification and ownership of personal style, acceptance and cooperation will move to center stage as emergent Gestalt.

Following each presentation is a comparative critique, intended more as criticism of each approach by participants of the other than any current preference.[3] We hope these rather harsh myopic criticisms serve to caution us in our quest for integrity.

Territoriality

1. Theoretical Orientations

Psychodrama
Health is considered a person's ability for spontaneous role-flexibility and affective extension within any assumed role. The self as a construct of integrative identity emerges from role-clarification, expression, and movement. The protagonist is encouraged to extend a fixated role (catharsis) or to experiment with a new role with the intention of organismic (psychophysiological) awareness of constricted as well as more fluid styles/scripts of being. The resultant therapeutic process generates feelings of acceptance, endorsement for playfulness, and permission to try new behavior previously admonished under conventional norms.

Gestalt Therapy
A postulated "real self" underlies a more conditioned, phobic, defensive, or manipulative self. Psychological pain is unresolved conflict between two or more mutually manipulative aspects (sub-selves) of the self or between two

persons. A person remains stuck (at an impasse) when unwilling to yield to self-support and when there are insufficient environmental supports. The patient is typically defensive of and works to preserve the incompatibility out of fear of rejection or the risk of giving up known advantages.

As attempts at denial and avoidance are blocked, the person is required to become aware of her or his current, destructive manipulative existence. Focus is placed on the conflict as a personal choice, regardless of the person's manipulative efforts to externalize and deny responsibility. The goal is differentiation of the "I" into the conflicted sub-selves. Little, if any, emphasis is placed directly on change. Rather, the impasse is imploded, directing change to occur as a result of self-choice and not as another manipulative effort to please the therapist. A person is encouraged to be who he or she is, not someone else. The resultant therapeutic process allows feelings of genuine confrontation and promotes the growth from environmental support to self-support.

Critique
Both criticisms occur from divergent assumptions within each system. Fritz Perls saw psychodrama as multiple projections with the playing of roles by several people as a manipulative and distorted process. In Gestalt therapy, growth occurs as a result of being oneself and not playing a role. Roles are considered phony and manipulative. As J. Moreno has stated, ". . . many in the contemporary "encounter" movement understand "role-playing" in a pejorative sense: to play a role is considered to indicate "non-genuine behavior" in an interaction, while "being oneself" implies genuineness in human relations" (Moreno, 1975a). A common criticism of Gestalt therapy from a psychodramatic orientation is the conception of a postulated "real self" as over and against a manipulative self. More often, a "real self" is considered as underlying a phobic self. This assumption self-referentially justifies the values and behaviors of Gestalt therapy. Those persons that are then *healthy* or *real* are those who adopt a Gestalt therapy value system through an acceptance of the same process.

2. Therapeutic Orientations

Psychodrama
"Psychodrama is a form of the drama in which the plots, situations, and roles—whether real or symbolic—reflect the actual problems of the persons acting and are not the work of a playwright" (Moreno, 1975b). Healing results from the somatic and psychological catharsis of the persons who give the drama their projective script and by doing so, liberate themselves from it. Healing occurs through *tele*, an interpersonal-reciprocal-empathetic feeling. This concept includes transference but is not limited to the symbolic, disintegrative, and often unidirectional nature of that process.

Gestalt Therapy
Kempler (1973a) provides this definition:

Gestalt therapy is a model for psychotherapy that sees disturbed or disturbing behavior as the signal of a painful polarization between two elements in a psychological process. Such discordance can be found within one individual or it may manifest between two or more people. Regardless of location, treatment consists of bringing discordant elements into a mutual self-disclosing confrontation. This approach is ahistoric, focuses attention on immediate behavior, and calls for the personal participation of the therapist.

The patient-therapist relationship is central. Healing occurs as the therapist demands an expression of each discordant part of the person presently in conflict with another part. Previously Kempler (1967) stated that:

Symptoms are created and maintained by one part of the personality refusing to accept another part. Cure comes only when the two parts recognize and come to appreciate one another to the point that they have absolutely no conflict or dissatisfaction with each other. Only then do they lose their significance to each other, thereby ending their painful interactive process.

Critique
Both systems have been jointly criticized and have criticized each other's process in different ways for encouraging *acting-out* behavior when both emphasize *acting through* (Perls and Clements, 1975). Psychodrama has been accused of being a process that lends itself more to improvisational-theater acting rather than a primary psychotherapy dealing directly with etiology of conflict. Directors have been viewed as encouraging regressive playfulness or rage in lieu of establishing a therapeutic relationship. Patterson (1973) said:

Psychodrama and Gestalt therapy are in agreement about the value of role-playing to assist people to loosen their projections as a first step to reclaiming them. However, while Gestalt therapy considers such experience a reliable adjunct to the therapeutic process, psychodrama seems to equate it with the therapeutic process. Gestalt therapy considers the actual relationship of the therapist and patient as the core of the therapeutic process, and vigorously cautions against the use of tactics that might obscure the real identity of the therapist to the patient. A fine tactic like role-playing is a tempting place for therapists to hide their personal responses, and is recommended by Gestalt therapists as a sometimes valuable adjunct to the therapeutic process, but not to be considered the way of therapy.

Gestalt therapy has been accused of fostering a superficial intensity for emotional confrontation, which devalues intellectual understanding, and as a process that intensifies pain on the presumption of underlying/internal conflict in the face of obvious situational stress with reality as most people experience it. Gestalt therapists arbitrarily and impositionally demand exposure of feelings in lieu of an awareness continuum which is truly existential (that which arises from **this** situation) and which allows for cognitive understanding following experiential work. Gestalt therapy has been accused of being a style that attracts therapists who harbor needs of power and control, and who seek to fulfill these needs through a therapeutic modality consistent with endorsing them axiologically.

3. Group Dynamics: Roles and Rules

Psychodrama
Psychodrama is most frequently interpersonally oriented, allowing a maximum number of people to experience the various roles they play, particularly as other people experience them. A participant volunteers or is selected by group consensus to be the protagonist. All action is centered by the director around the protagonist. As the director continually seeks cues from the protagonist, other persons are selected to be *auxiliaries* and *doubles*. Although the director is ultimately responsible, as in theater or film, decisions are typically democratic, i.e., auxiliaries, doubles, psychodramatic setting, time orientation, and focused conflicts are chosen by the protagonist. The primary expectation is that directors must make therapeutic decisions regarding role-reversals, *asides*, and other techniques requiring a skilled and more holistic perspective.

Gestalt Therapy
Gestalt therapy is typically an interpersonal orientation, with primary action between the therapist and persons in a group context. The therapy is facilitated by rules that focus on taking personal responsibility for thoughts, feelings, and behavior. Such rules include:

1. The principle of the now—using the present tense.
2. I and Thou—addressing the other person directly rather than talking about him or her to the therapist.
3. *It* language and *I* language—substituting *I* for *it* in talking about the body, feelings, acts, and behaviors.
4. Use of the awareness continuum—focusing on the *how* and *what* of experience rather than the *why*.
5. No gossiping—addressing a person directly when she or he is present rather than making statements about him or her.
6. Self-assertion—asking the patient to convert questions into statements.

7. No *should, ought, have to, must*, and *can't* language—substituting *want to* for these words and changing *I can't* to "I don't want to."[4]

Other members participate through nonverbal identification and, when requested by the therapist, for support of the social reintegration of the patient. An exception is the theme-oriented Gestalt awareness workshop (Enright, 1970), or Gestalt experiential psychotherapy, both of which are more group centered. However, with the *hot-seat technique*, decisions are typically autocratic, with the understanding that whatever the therapist may demand, the patient is ultimately responsible for choosing to act on the request.

Critique
Improvisation and spontaneity are valued by both approaches, though they set different parameters within which this energy is to therapeutically explode/implode. The parameters of Gestalt therapy are the linguistic rules, and the demand of focusing on the *how* and *what* of experiences. The parameters of psychodrama are the specific characters or roles. Regarding the debate of the interpersonal versus intrapersonal orientations, Erving and Miriam Polster (1974) offer what I feel is a just appraisal.

> *Although both Perls and Moreno might disagree, we believe that this is primarily a difference in style rather than theory. Perls believed that since each of the roles was only a projection of parts of the individual, nobody else could play these parts. Nevertheless, projection or not, there is still a world out there—and it is capable of ever-changing configurations and susceptible to a variety of interpretations. Thus, if someone plays John's grandfather and John plays himself, the requirement for John to face the other guy's version of his grandfather could still be valid confrontation wherein John can investigate whatever possibilities for action John needs to recover in his life. This does not rule out the powerful experiences John might also have in playing himself and grandfather.*

My three exceptions to this paragraph are: (1) I believe there are some differences in theory, (2) I would change "could still be" to "is," and (3) I would delete "have to."

4. Group Opening

Psychodrama
The session begins with the director sitting on the second or lower stage to discover a common group concern, whether that be individual, communal, or sociometric in nature. A "warm-up," a specifically designed phase, is initiated

to mobilize energy for spontaneity and activity and to alleviate frozen affect, initial anxiety, isolation, withdrawal, and loneliness.

Gestalt Therapy
A group usually begins by a member making an affective statement, or by the therapist asking participants to get in touch with how they're feeling now. Frequently, a breathing exercise or a fantasy is offered to orient members to the present and reduce cognitive activity. Anxiety and discomforture are used to mobilize awareness of conflict.

Critique
Psychodramatic procedure is criticized by Gestaltists for offering relief of pain through techniques rather than demanding confrontation of the avoidance of pain itself. Gestalt therapy is criticized for setting affective requirements for appropriate therapeutic behavior.

5. Time Orientation

Psychodrama
Psychodrama may take place in the past, present, or future, depending on the protagonist's conflict and limited only by the director's imagination. Preferences for time orientation usually are chosen by the protagonist and are specific to the time of the conflict.

Gestalt Therapy
Gestalt therapy demands present orientation. Verbalization of yesterday's pain and tomorrow's fears are permitted only in the context of *now*. Any unresolved pain or future anxiety is included in the present being/experience.

Critique
Gestalt therapy views past orientation as mind-manipulating rumination and repetition-avoidance through storytelling. Focus on the future is either a rehearsal or pure fantasy. While possibly delightful, it is counterproductive to organismic awareness and release of painful energy. *Aboutism* is the enemy of awareness. Centering awareness demands taking responsibility for the internal conflict rather than displacing it onto something or someone in the environment. Psychodrama views Gestalt therapy as requiring an unrealistic demand for present orientation. Restrictions on language limit behavior to one role—a *now*-oriented person with the appropriate language, which fosters self-righteousness in the name of optimal health. As some believers are reinforced and some are rejected, a philosophical legalism surfaces. *Walden Two* comes in the back door of techniques designed for universal health. Intended to promote a lifestyle of freedom and joy, such value judgments perform an opposite function (Orcutt and Williams, 1974).

6. Space and Setting Orientations

Psychodrama
Psychodrama may be conducted in any space without props. Preferable is a quasi-theater setting with a three-tiered concentric stage, all levels of which are used for various forms of action. Lighting is used for specific scenes to elicit or suppress various affects. Chairs, tables, boxes, and pillows are used for set design. Human-size and smaller foam cushions are used for catharsis of anger. A semicircular or traditional audience seating arrangement is common. Rear-stage balconies, wings, and side-stage columns, although part of original theater design, are uncommon in most theaters today.

Gestalt Therapy
Gestalt therapy is conducted in a closed circle, the therapist in the circle. Demonstrations have been given with three chairs on a standard stage with traditional audience seating arrangement, although this is infrequent. More commonly, when the hot-seat technique is employed, chairs are placed in a circle. Foam cushions have been used for release of aggression.

Critique
Although Moreno's intention was to *spot-light* the patient through elevation of the stage design, and through the traditional-reciprocal-participatory relationship between actors and audience, psychodrama has been criticized for using a theatrical setting that spatially separates audience from actors. The criticism of Gestalt therapy's spatial setting is consistent with the criticism waged against its group dynamics. The group is a *group* by virtue of participants adhering to predetermined rules and circular seating, not by spontaneous and shared physical movement and expression by a maximum number of members.

7. Group Closure

Psychodrama
Psychodrama's third segment, after the warm-up and the psychodrama, is the *sharing*. The protagonist is seated next to the director on middle stage. The director, auxiliaries, doubles, and all other members of the audience are encouraged to share personal distressing events similar to that of the protagonist. *Sharing* is entirely supportive of the protagonist. There are no criticisms or compliments, no confrontation or psychodramatic analysis.[5] This process encourages humility through a common expression of human fallibility, grief, and pain. Open tension systems are closed, as other participants join in a time-honored storytelling process that allows the protagonist to see his or her problem as not unique and to feel that he or she is not alone. Moreno (1967) said:

> It is there that therapy begins. One after the other, the members of the group
> now express their feelings, adding to these by revealing personal experiences of

a similar kind. In this way, the patients now undergo a new type of cathar-sis—a "group catharsis." One of their group made them a gift of love, and now they return his love. The members of the group share their problems with him, just as he shared his with them. Each bears the other's burden, and gradually the catharsis purges all those present.

Gestalt Therapy

A closure is engaged following the main session. Participants are encouraged to complete any unfinished business, i.e., to express to any member of the group any feelings that previously have been suppressed for reasons of time, fear, or lack of awareness. Closing Gestalts is often facilitated by encouraging partici-pants to express resentments and appreciations directly to the other members.

Critique

Common practice has indicated that insufficient time has been allocated to sharing and closure in both processes.

Kinship

1. Organismic–Dynamic Nature

Both systems theoretically are based on a similar premise of dynamic fluidity. Both theories assume that when an emotion is organismically reexperienced, the process allows natural growth of the organism. Growth is *processing*, not a product. Growth is not something one must activate; it is something one prevents to avoid pain. *Impasse* may be equated to role-fixation and role-restriction.

Psychodramatically, no role is so disadvantaged that any person can afford to abandon it completely. Focus is on deemphasizing one role and extending or adding another that is more suitable per occasion. In both systems, there are no negative feelings. Those feelings that remain suppressed from fear or risk of verbal expression inhibit growth.

2. Experiential–Affective Nature

Both process are oriented in cathartic release and expression of feelings, as contrasted to didactically/discursively oriented therapies. Both therapies are action oriented.

3. Responsibility for Conflict

Both systems demand the patient/participant assume responsibility for her/his complaints, disease, organic discomforture, interpersonal conflict, sympto-mology, or psychopathology.

4. Linguistic Preferences

Neither psychodrama nor Gestalt therapy use psychiatric diagnostic labels. Although each therapy employs concepts consistent with its own process (e.g., top-dog, under-dog, awareness continuum, surplus reality, tele, sociogram, and aside), no therapy uses language incorporating the terms *conscious* or *unconscious, id, ego, superego, oral, anal,* or *genital.*

5. Organismic–Responsiveness Focus

In choosing singular concepts that would most accurately represent the thrust of each approach, *spontaneity* (psychodrama) and *responsibility* (Gestalt therapy) are fundamental. *Responsibility* is essentially the ability to respond, or rather the freedom to initiate and accept consequences. *Spontaneity* is defined as the "readiness of the subject to respond as required" (Moreno, Z. 1975), or rather the freedom to act and be responsive to that which is required next. Regardless of some theoretical discrepancies, it appears that the vision of a *healthy* organism is quite similar in the spectrum of role differentiation and human variance.

6. Group Emphasis

Although Gestalt and psychodramatic orientations can be used in individual therapy, both psychotherapies were designed for and are most effective in a group context. The theoretical assumptions of both therapies support the social/self-environmental nature of disease, disharmony, disequilibrium, and disintegration by requiring embodied dialogue in a social matrix.

7. Group Affect

Participants of both orientations often report communal feelings of acceptance and intimacy. In psychodrama, feelings of commonality emerge as participants psychodramatically share each other's roles as well as become aware of the roles they present to others. The burden of pain is relived at least temporarily through a cathartic modality that views pain as a common human denominator and its expression as imperative for growth. Circumstances are changed as old roles become fluid and new roles are created.

In Gestalt therapy, a feeling of group cohesion and solidarity emerges. This affective Gestalt makes the whole of the group more than the sum of its individual members. Participants most often describe this group Gestalt as a pervading feeling of intimacy occurring from identification of intrapsychic conflict. The similarity exists between the *affective Gestalt* of a group and the *tele* of a group.

8. Creative Nature

Both modalities require spontaneous invention of techniques per therapeutic patient/context, and by their very natures lend themselves to the extrapolation of techniques by eclectic practitioners.

Notes

1. This paper was originally published by T. L. Orcutt in 1977 under the title "Roles and Rules: The Kinship and Territoriality of Psychodrama and Gestalt Therapy," in *Group Psychotherapy, Psychodrama and Gestalt Therapy, 30*, 97–107. Permission to reprint from The Horsham Foundation, Ambler, Pennsylvania, is gratefully acknowledged.
2. A comparison is made of the emergent "upfront" aspects of the psychotherapeutic processes of these two orientations. This comparative approach is limited by an abstraction from the whole healing context, which although primary, is more subtle. Both psychodrama and Gestalt therapy are more ways of being/living in this world than professional psychotherapies. "To be a psychodramatist means to see the world and deal with it in psychodramatic and sociometric terms—that is, man's interconnectedness with others and their interdependence with one another as well as with the universe" (Moreno, 1975). Gestalt therapy "is something that you do *with* others, not *to* them. Hopefully, the Gestalt therapist is identified more by who he is than by what he is or does" (Kempler, 1973).
3. Whether or not in literature, all of the criticisms here have been voiced in my presence as either participant or psychotherapist. Although these criticisms are sometimes a source of amusement, proponents of each modality tend to focus on the seriousness of differences rather than on the sincerity of personal preference.
4. I have added this "rule" to those widely cited by Levitsky and Perls (1970).
5. There is typically a post-session analysis by the director and other selected participants.

References

Enright, J. (1970). Awareness training in the mental health professions. In J. Fagan & I. L. Shepherd (Eds.), *Gestalt therapy now* (pp. 263–273). Palo Alto, CA: Science & Behavior Books.

Kempler, W. (1973a/b). Gestalt therapy. In R. Corsini (Ed.), *Current psychotherapies* (pp. 251–286). Itasca, IL: F. E. Peacock Publishers.

Kempler, W. (1967). The experiential therapeutic encounter. *Psychotherapy, 4*, 166–72.

Levitsky, A., & Perls, F. S. (1970). The rules and games of Gestalt therapy. In J. Fagan & I. L. Shepherd (Eds.), *Gestalt therapy now* (pp. 140–149). Palo Alto, CA: Science & Behavior Books.

Moreno, J. D. (1975). Notes on the concept of role-playing. *Group Psychotherapy and Psychodrama, 28.*

Moreno, J. L. (1975). Mental catharsis and psychodrama. *Group Psychotherapy and Psychodrama, 28,* 5–31.

Moreno, J. L. (1967). Reflections on my method of group psychotherapy and psychodrama. In H. Greenwald (Ed.), *Active psychotherapy* (pp. 130–143). New York: Atherton Press.

Moreno, Z. (1975). Dedication. *Group Psychotherapy and Psychodrama, 28,* 1.

Orcutt, T., & Williams, G. (1974). Toward a facilitative ethic in the human potential movement. *Interpersonal Development, 4,* 77–84.

Patterson, C. (1973). *Theories of counseling and psychotherapy* (pp. 344–376). New York: Harper & Row.

Perls, F. & Clements, C. (1975). Acting out vs. acting through. In J. O. Stevens (Ed.), *Gestalt Is.* Maob, UT: Real People Press.

Polster, E., & Polster, M. (1974). *Gestalt therapy integrated.* New York: Random House.

Glossary

The following definitions apply to the structure and function of integrative psychotherapy.

accommodate to modify mental processes to make room for a new concept or idea; to adapt one's mind; to alter the larger for the smaller to fit

advice verbal directions given to fix a problem for a client, or directly telling someone to do something

affective methodology a procedure that (1) encourages or requires awareness and expression of feelings and emotions; (2) assumes that logical thoughts and effective behavior will follow increased awareness and expression of feelings

altered state of consciousness (ASC) defined phenomenologically as a qualitative shift in mental patterns of functioning

assimilate to alter and thoroughly comprehend; to make similar; to alter the smaller to fit into the greater

associative causality an assumption that the cause of some event or state of being occurred immediately before that event or state of being

attitude a predetermined position or belief originated for a specific purpose, whether conscious or unconscious

autonomy state of being separate from everything and everyone else; to be self-determining and self-governing

behavioral methodology a procedure that (1) encourages or requires modification of action; (2) assumes that effective behavior will elicit logical thoughts and appropriate emotional responses

belief, life-enhancing a belief that causes increases in the possibilities of optimal organismic health, emotional and psychological fulfillment

belief, life-limiting a belief that causes a reduction of the possibilities of optimal organismic health, emotional and psychological fulfillment *belief, supporting* a belief formed from events similar to the original event, which is then interpreted in support of the original belief

belief system a combination of core beliefs and supporting beliefs that form patterns

catharsis a technique to liberate emotionally charged memories and suppressed feelings that cause conflict, stress, and undesired symptoms

cognitive dissonance a theory of Leon Festinger that explains human conflict as a result of incongruence between beliefs and behavior

cognitive methodology a procedure that (1) encourages or requires understanding of thoughts, beliefs, values, reasons, and meanings; (2) a procedure that assumes that logical thoughts increase awareness, expression of feelings, and effective behavior

core belief conditionings, programs, or patterns learned to fulfill core needs

core need fundamental and universal striving of the human organism for physical and emotional survival

creative theoretical structure (1) an imaginative mastery, arising from a shift in consciousness, and resulting in the power to grant new form in thought, action, or behavior; creative theoretical structures describe the focus of expanding awareness and self-definition beyond self to include others and the world; (2) a metaphor for describing a quantitatively inclusive and qualitatively expansive paradigm from productive and innovative theoretical structures; (3) an organized structure of principles oriented to enhance personal development through living as if a desired result had already occurred

dependent completely reliant on someone else to fulfill needs and wants

dynamic the functional approach of our subconscious drives, processes, and their interactions

explorative a technique of applying psychotherapeutic observations that lets clients know that alternatives exist and then provides methods and directions by which to search for them

expressive a technique of applying psychotherapeutic observations that involves either the client releasing emotional energies or the psychotherapist demonstrating feelings about a situation

hole theory a theoretical presupposition of the etiology of human conflict and pain based on Newtonian physics and conventional science

imposition the act of establishing or applying something, usually values, as compulsory

independent completely free of reliance on anyone's help or support

informed opinions attitudes made on the basis of either scientific fact or carefully evaluated personal experiences

innovative theoretical structure (1) an organized structure of principles based on values of health for personal and social development; (2) the introduction of a novel idea, thought, method or device; as applied to psychotherapy, innovation occurs when psychotherapists effectively employ a theoretical structure that results in a definitively novel implementation that is meaningful to both the client and the psychotherapist

intentional consciously directed to an object or person

intercession an act for the purpose of reconciliation between people

interpersonal perceptual attitude an interpretation of harmony or conflict originating from socially compatible or incompatible aspects of relationships

intradependent acceptance of dependency on others while retaining control and responsibility to delegate satisfaction of desired needs

intrapsychic perceptual attitude an interpretation of harmony or conflict originating from various hypothetical internal dynamics of personal development

intuitive feeling spontaneous insight or revelation; global perception of answers, purpose, and direction in one's life, including spiritual experiences of immediate cognition without evident rational thought and *psi* phenomena

judging ascribing positive or negative opinion outward

metaphoric a technique of applying psychotherapeutic observations by combining two ideas or elements, one familiar and the other not, to form a new perspective for the client

methodology see *Psychotherapeutic methodology*

model a system of psychotherapy identified by title and founder

narrative a technique of applying psychotherapeutic observations by telling a story that is as similar as possible to the client's situation, that contains the results of the solution but excludes the steps leading to the solution

ontological evolutionary focus (1) the spatial and temporal context of the developmental origination of human harmony and conflict—the locus of attention within the evolution of self-development; (2) the encouragement or requirement for clients to attend to past experiences, present awareness, or future desires

organizational perceptual attitude an interpretation of human conflict or harmony originating from the entire family or organization of which a person is a member

paradoxical a technique of applying psychotherapeutic observations by indirectly encouraging or motivating the client to do the very things that are feared or avoided

parataxic the ability to differentiate experiences without logical connection

parental role the presentation of the socially expected behaviors of mother and father that are adopted in implementing psychotherapy

perception the cognitive process by which people interpret information through the five organismic senses and *psi* phenomena

perceptual attitude the way people receive and interpret information based on prearranged interpretations of their experiences

personality the interrelationship of the self with its outside world and society by the dynamics of its belief systems

prejudice attitudes developed on the basis of stereotypes

productive theoretical structure a conceptual framework based on the principles of originating and furnishing desired results in which the consequences of an act determine, not influence, the value of the act; (2) an organized structure of psychological principles that equate psychological conflict, dysfunction, and pain with physical disorders

protaxic a child's developmental time frame before being able to logically distinguish between time and place

psychotherapeutic methodology (1) the operational functions and workability of specifically applied psychological, theoretical structures, as defined by language, to inquire and obtain desired results; (2) a process inclusive of psychological strategies and techniques

psychotherapeutic orientation (1) the global structure and function of psychotherapy, including the perceptual attitude, theoretical structure, methodology, model, techniques, strategies, and boundaries of imposition; (2) the global therapeutic direction or inclination of interest

relationship the state or character of being related, showing or having established a logical or causal connection between, or to have meaningful social relation with, as in the state of being mutually or reciprocally interested

secretive a technique of applying psychotherapeutic observations by suggesting that there exists a solution to the client's situation, but it is best that the client find it for him- or herself

sensate feeling a sensory experience of the external environment outside of and including the skin of the organism

sequential logic an assumption that the cause of some event or state of being occurred immediately before that event or state of being. *See also* associative causality

somatic feeling an organismic experience of and inside the body

strategy a sequence of techniques determined prior to implementation

symbiosis (1) the living together in more or less intimate association or close union of two dissimilar organisms, and (2) the intimate living together of two dissimilar organisms in a mutually beneficial relationship

symbolic feeling an emotional attachment or charge about a personal value or belief

syntax the ability to use society's verbal symbols and perceive logical relationships between and among experiences

technique a detailed implementation for achieving a goal

theoretical structure (1) the underlying beliefs by which we personally and professionally interpret human behavior; (2) the supportive rationale of our psychotherapeutic beliefs and applications; (3) the foundational structure of principles that define the nature of human behavior and substantiate perceptual attitude and methodology *trance* an altered state of consciousness in which an individual has increased suggestibility, alertness, awareness, and concentration

transcend to go beyond, exceed, or extend the usual or conventional limits of ordinary experience and knowledge

treatment plan a sequence of methodologies determined prior to use in dealing with a specific client

universal perceptual attitude an interpretation of human conflict or harmony indicative of metaphysical lessons and tests that are opportunities to enhance personal and spiritual development

valuing ascribing positive or negative opinion inward

whole theory a theoretical presupposition of the etiology of human conflict

Author Index

Subject Index